*"Fascinating and
Disturbing Book!"*

"In his new book Vance Packard explores the viselike grip in which each of us is held by his place in the national pecking order.

"He takes issue with those who claim that postwar prosperity has rendered us virtually a one-class people. On the contrary, he claims, the very prosperity which was supposed to free us from class differences has frozen the social classes and made it increasingly difficult to move upward.

"He is an excellent and painstaking reporter and his book is journalism of the highest rank. A fascinating and disturbing book."
—*The New York Times Book Review*

THE STATUS SEEKERS was originally published by David McKay Co., Inc., at $4.50.

Other books by Vance Packard

*The Hidden Persuaders

†The Human Side of Animals

The Waste Makers

*Published in a CARDINAL edition.

†Published in a POCKET BOOK edition.

VANCE PACKARD

THE
STATUS
SEEKERS

CARDINAL
EDITION

POCKET BOOKS, INC. • NEW YORK

The Status Seekers

David McKay edition published April, 1959

GIANT CARDINAL edition published November, 1961
1st printing...September, 1961

This GIANT CARDINAL edition includes every word contained in the original, higher-priced edition. It is printed from brand-new plates made from completely reset, clear, easy-to-read type.

•

GIANT CARDINAL editions are distributed in the U.S. by Affiliated Publishers, Inc., 630 Fifth Avenue, New York 20, N.Y.

•

Notice: GIANT CARDINAL editions are published by Pocket Books, Inc. Trademark registered in the United States and other countries.

L

For Randall, Cynthia, and Vance
who will live in this world we are creating

contents

vii

PART THREE
strains of status

PART FOUR
trends

PART FIVE
implications for the future

the status seekers

"You!" said the Caterpillar contemptuously. "WHO ARE *you?*"
—LEWIS CARROLL, *Alice in Wonderland*

1

a classless society?

WHAT HAPPENS TO CLASS DISTINCTIONS AMONG PEOPLE WHEN most of them are enjoying a long period of material abundance?

Suppose for example, that most of the people are able to travel about in their own gleaming, sculptured coaches longer than the average living room and powered by the equivalent of several hundred horses. Suppose that they are able to wear a variety of gay-colored apparel made of miraculous fibers. Suppose they can dine on mass-merchandised vichyssoise and watch the wonders of the world through electronic eyes in their own air-conditioned living rooms.

In such a climate, do the barriers and humiliating distinctions of social class evaporate? Do anxieties about status—and strivings for evidences of superior status—ease up notably? And do opportunities for leadership roles become more available to all who have natural talent?

The recent experience of the people of the United States is instructive. In the early 1940's an era of abundance began which by 1959 had reached proportions fantastic by any past standards. Nearly a half-trillion dollars' worth of goods and services—including television, miracle fibers, and vichyssoise— were being produced.

Before this era of fabled plenty began, it was widely assumed that prosperity would eliminate, or greatly reduce, class differences. If everybody could enjoy the good things of

1

life—as defined by mass merchandisers—the meanness of class distinctions would disappear.

Such a view seemed reasonable to most of us in those pinched pre-plenty days of the thirties because, then, differences in status were all too plainly visible. You could tell who was who—except for a few genteel poor—by the way people dressed, ate, traveled, and—if they were lucky—by the way they worked. The phrase "poor people" then had an intensely vivid meaning. A banker would never be mistaken for one of his clerks even at one hundred feet.

What, actually, has happened to social class in the United States during the recent era of abundance?

A number of influential voices have been advising us that whatever social classes we ever had are now indeed withering away. We are being told that the people of our country have achieved unparalleled equality. Listen to some of the voices.

Some months ago, a national periodical proclaimed the fact that the United States had recently achieved the "most truly classless society in history." A few weeks later, a publisher hailed the disappearance of the class system in America as "the biggest news of our era." Still later, the director of a market-research organization announced his discovery that America was becoming "one vast middle class." Meanwhile, a corporation in paid advertisements was assuring us that "there are more opportunities in this country than ever before." Whatever else we are, we certainly are the world's most self-proclaimed equalitarian people.

The rank-and-file citizens of the nation have generally accepted this view of progress toward equality because it fits with what we would like to believe about ourselves. It coincides with the American Creed and the American Dream, and is deeply imbedded in our folklore.

Such a notion unfortunately rests upon a notable lack of perception of the true situation that is developing. Class lines in several areas of our national life appear to be hardening. And status straining has intensified.

This prevailing lack of perception of the developing situation might in itself justify a book that attempted to set things straight. I did not, however, undertake this exploration of the present-day American class system—and its status seekers—merely for the delight of poking into an aspect of life we like to pretend does not exist. My purpose was not to hoot at our self-deception—which is too easy to document to be challenging—but rather to try to offer a fresh perspective on our society and on certain disquieting changes which, it seems to me, are taking place within it.

The approach of class analysis—looking at Americans through their class behavior, their status striving, their barriers—offers the possibility of seeing our unique and fast-changing society in a new light. Even our institutions, such as schools, clubs, churches, political parties, and, yes, matrimony, take on new meaning.

We shall see that the people of the United States have, and are refining, a national class structure with a fascinating variety of status systems within it. These status systems affect a number of intimate areas of our daily lives and have some surprising and preposterous ramifications. At points it will be noted how our class structure now differs from that of other countries. And finally we shall examine several growing areas of cleavage in the American class structure that seem to demand recognition. In particular, I think we should be disturbed by the stratifying tendencies appearing in the places where millions of us work, live, relax, vote, and worship.

Since class boundaries are contrary to the American Dream, Americans generally are uncomfortable when the subject of their existence arises. Sociologist August B. Hollingshead of Yale University found that psychiartists—supposedly uninhibited, open-minded individuals—"tend to react with embarrassment when the question of social class is raised." One responded to a direct question about the social classes in his town of New Haven, Connecticut, by saying, "I don't like to think too much about this."[1]

Until recent years, even sociologists had shrunk away from a candid exploration of social class in America. Social classes, they realized, were not supposed to exist. Furthermore, Karl Marx had made class a dirty word. As a result the social scientists, until a few years ago, knew more about the social classes of New Guinea than they did of those in the United States of America.

Webster defines status as the "position; rank; standing" of a person. (The word can be pronounced either "stay-tus" or "stat-us.") Although present-day Americans in this era of material abundance are not supposed to put differential labels of social status on fellow citizens, many millions of them do it every day. And their search for appropriate evidences of status for themselves appears to be mounting each year. There is some evidence that wives, generally speaking, tend to be more status conscious than their husbands.

The majority of Americans rate acquaintances and are themselves being rated in return. They believe that some people rate somewhere above them, that some others rate somewhere below them, and that still others seem to rate close enough to their own level to permit them to explore the possibility of getting to know them socially without fear of being snubbed or appearing to downgrade themselves.

When any of us moves into a new neighborhood—and 33,000,000 Americans now do this every year—we are quickly and critically appraised by our new neighbors and business acquaintances before being accepted or rejected for their group. We, in turn, are appraising them and in many cases attempt not to commit what some regard as the horrid error of getting in with the wrong crowd.

Furthermore, most of us surround ourselves, wittingly or unwittingly, with status symbols we hope will influence the raters appraising us, and which we hope will help establish some social distance between ourselves and those we consider below us. The vigorous merchandising of goods as status symbols by advertisers is playing a major role in intensifying status consciousness. Emotionally insecure people are most vulnerable.

Others of us, less expert in the nuances of status symbols or more indifferent to them, persist in modes of behavior and in displays of taste that themselves serve as barriers in separating us from the group to which we may secretly aspire. They can keep us in our place. If we aspire to rise in the world but fail to take on the coloration of the group we aspire to—by failing to discard our old status symbols, friends, club memberships, values, behavior patterns, and acquiring new ones esteemed by the higher group—our chances of success are diminished. Sociologists have found that our home addresses, our friends, our clubs, our values, and even our church affiliations can prove to be "barriers" if we fail to change them with every attempted move up the ladder. This is a most disheartening situation to find in the nation that poses as the model for the democratic world.

Many people are badly distressed, and scared, by the anxieties, inferiority feelings, and straining generated by this unending process of rating and status striving. The status seekers, as I use the term, are people who are continually straining to surround themselves with visible evidence of the superior rank they are claiming. The preoccupation of millions of Americans with status is intensifying social stratification in the United States. Those who need to worry least about how they are going to come out in the ratings are those who, in the words of Louis Kronenberger, are "Protestant, well-fixed, college-bred."[2]

Even our children soon become aware of the class labels that are on their families and are aware of the boundaries that circumscribe their own daily movement. If even children know the facts of class, you may inquire, why is it that so many opinion molders have been announcing their conclusion that classes are disappearing?

The discrepancy arises partly as a result of a generalized desire on the part of United States adults—particularly businessmen—to support the American Dream. Also it arises from the widespread assumption that the recent general rise in available spending money in this country is making everybody equal. Class, in fact, has several faces and income is just one of them. With the general diffusion of wealth, there has been a crumbling of visible class lines now that such one-time upperclass symbols as limousines, power boats, and mink coats are available to a variety of people. Coincidentally, there has been a scrambling to find new ways to draw lines that will separate the elect from the non-elect.

A working-class man, however, does not move up into another social class just by being able to buy a limousine, either by cash or installment, and he knows it. In terms of his productive role in our society—in contrast to his consuming role—class lines in America are becoming more rigid, rather than withering away.

In truth, America, under its gloss of prosperity, is undergoing a significant hardening of the arteries of its social system at some critical points.

As I perceive it, two quite sharply divided major groupings of social classes are emerging, with the old middle class being split into two distinct classes in the process. At the places where most Americans work, as I will try to show, we are seeing a new emphasis on class lines and a closing-in of the opportunities available to make more than a minor advance. In modern big business, it is becoming more and more difficult to start at the bottom and reach the top. Any leaping aspiration a non-college person has after beginning his career in big business in a modest capacity is becoming less and less realistic.

Furthermore, stratification (formalized inequality of rank) is becoming built-in as our increasingly bureaucratized society moves at almost every hand toward bigness: Big Business, Big Government, Big Labor, Big Education. Bigness is one of the really major factors altering our class system. As an executive of a $250,000,000 corporation explained it to me, this bigness is made necessary in our technological age by the high cost of launching new products (research, development, advertising). He said, "You have to be big today, or else be able to run awfully fast." He complained that even his $250,000,000 company was not big enough.

In the hierarchy of the big corporation, stratification is being carried to exquisite extremes. Employees are usually expected to comport themselves in conformity with their rank, and generally do so. Industrialists are noting that the military experience millions of our younger generation have had has made them more accepting of rank. (With all this growth of bigness and rank, the best opportunities for the enterprising non-college man today are found not with the large producing company but rather on Main Street, where it is still often possible to start small and grow, or with a small or pioneering producing firm.)

Employees in big offices, as well as big plants, are finding their work roles fragmentized and impersonalized. There has been, perhaps unwittingly, a sealing-off of contact between big and little people on the job. And there has been a startling rise in the number of people who are bored with their work and feel no pride of initiative or creativity. They must find their satisfactions outside their work. Many do it by using their paychecks to consume flamboyantly, much as the restless Roman masses found diversion in circuses thoughtfully provided by the emperors.

Although we still tend to think of equality as being peculiarly American, and of class barriers as being peculiarly foreign, the evidence indicates that several European nations (such as Holland, England, and Denmark) have gone further than America in developing an open-class system, where the poor but talented young can rise on their merits. And they have done this while preserving some of the outer forms of class, such as titled families.

In brief, the American Dream is losing some of its luster for a good many citizens who would like to believe in it. If, and when, the patina of prosperity over our land is ever rubbed off by a prolonged recession, to use the polite word, the new stratifications will become uncomfortably apparent and embarrassing, unless action is taken to broaden the channels for upward mobility.

It is my impression that status lines are more carefully observed in the East and South than in most of the other parts of the country. Californians, with their yeasty social climate, seem the least status-conscious people I've encountered in the nation. This might be explained by the fact that—with their violently expanding economy and their multitude of relatively small new enterprises—they are close to the free-and-easy frontier spirit. In the San Joaquin Valley, some of the most widely and highly esteemed families are of Armenian or Korean background. They have prospered, and their forebears were Early Settlers.

Perhaps I should say a few words about how I came by the material and concepts supporting the views I will develop. First, I have drawn upon eight investigations I have made in the past three years into specific situations bearing on class. These were informal studies, but quite intensive. I have, in addition, discussed aspects of class with knowledgeable local people in eighteen United States states and five European countries; and I have conferred with several dozen sociologists and market-research specialists who have interested themselves in aspects of class behavior.

Most important, in terms of the impact of this book, I have brought together the findings of more than 150 United States sociologists and other students of the social scene who have been investigating phases of our social stratification, and I have tried to assess their findings.

Since the World War II era began, United States scholars, particularly sociologists, have by the scores been appraising our class behavior. Some have focused their gaze on specific communities. Examples: Statesboro, Georgia; Decatur, Illinois; San Jose, California; Wasco, California; Indianapolis, Indiana; Morris, Illinois; Oakland, California; Danielson, Connecticut; Burlington, Vermont; Philadelphia, Pennsylvania; Park Forest, Illinois; New Haven, Connecticut; Lansing, Michigan; Franklin, Indiana; Kansas City, Missouri; Sandusky, Ohio. And then there are, of course, the earlier classic studies of Newburyport, Massachusetts, by the W. Lloyd Warner group and the study of Muncie, Indiana, by the Lynds.

Other sociologists have focused their fascinated attention upon specific groups. Ely Chinoy worked in an automobile plant; August B. Hollingshead lived among 735 adolescents for eighteen months, and later studied psychiatric patients from various social classes; William Foote Whyte lived for three and a half years among street-corner gangs of a New

England city slum. Still other sociologists have studied differences in behavior by classes in jury deliberations, in patronage of taverns and cocktail lounges, in verbal accounts offered of an Arkansas tornado. Some of the sociologists have attempted nationwide studies, and have taken national samples of class attitudes.

Business groups, I should add, have shown a lively interest in sponsoring studies of class behavior. They have sought to know their customers better. Home developers have been studying the stratification patterns—and status-striving motives —of home buyers. Madison Avenue has been busily trying to understand our tastes and buying behavior by social class. To understand the Chicago market better, the *Chicago Tribune*'s Research Division has spent approximately $100,000 on a comparative study of three homogeneous communities in the Chicago area representing three different class levels. The director, Pierre Martineau, long an enthusiast of the sociological approach to marketing, has concluded from his many years of studying our class behavior that "the vast majority of people live and die within the boundaries and tastes of their own class."

Finally, Social Research, Inc., of Chicago, has done a number of revealing studies of our class behavior. In a recent one for Macfadden Publications, it analyzed the contrast in emotional make-up of women in the working classes and women in the white-collar classes. The study indicated that, though these women might live in the same neighborhood, there was an "invisible wall" between them in the way they think, live, and even make love. Social Research concluded that social distinctions today are "none the less sharp because they are subtle."

Taken together, all of these studies—requiring several hundred thousand man-hours of research—represent a lode of fascinating and valuable information about how Americans really behave. These investigators often disagree among themselves on the precise nature of the American class structure, and I assume many will disagree with some details of the conception of it that I have arrived at. However, they are virtually unanimous in agreeing that mid-century America very definitely does have a system of social stratification.

My debt to all these investigators is very large. In terms of insights, I owe the greatest debt, perhaps, to E. Digby Baltzell, Bernard Barber, Richard Centers, Milton M. Gordon, Arnold W. Green, August B. Hollingshead, Herbert H. Hyman, Joseph A. Kahl, Russell Lynes, Raymond W. Mack, Bevode C. McCall, Pierre Martineau, C. Wright Mills, Liston Pope, and W. Lloyd Warner.

The chapters that follow will in large part take the form of a roving over the social landscape of America. This exploration may give some readers a better insight into their own behavior and that of their neighbors. Also, it may give them a better understanding of people in their locality who seem uncomfortably different from themselves. For those readers who must, in the performance of their duties (as educators, business managers, public officials, etc.), deal regularly with people of different class levels, this exploration may shed, also, some useful insights on coping with their problems realistically and sympathetically. Finally, I hope that for all readers the exploration will make more apparent some noteworthy points about the current drift of our society.

PART ONE

changes of status

2

an upsetting era

*"The transformation we're now seeing will make
the Industrial Revolution of the 18th Century
look like a pink tea."*—LOUIS LEVINE, Chief
Analyst in Employment Security, United States
Department of Labor.

←→o→←→o→←→o→←→o→←→o→←→o→←→o→

I SUPPOSE I FIRST BECAME INTERESTED IN SOCIAL STRATIFICA-
tion as a farm boy in northern Pennsylvania when my father
pointed out to me that one of our cows, I believe her name was
Gertrude, always came through the gate first at feeding time.
We had about eighteen cows and all the others deferred to her.
Later I observed that another, rather runty cow almost always
came through the gate last. In fact, each cow seemed to know
its appointed place in the lineup. When we bought a new cow
who butted and bluffed her way to the top spot within an hour
after entering the barnyard, our dethroned Gertrude developed neurotic symptoms and became our meanest kicker at
milking time.

This, I've since learned, was not surprising. Psychologists
investigating sub-human behavior have frequently encountered variations of butt orders or pecking orders (i.e., chick-
ens).

A few years ago, while I was chatting with the man who
teaches the world-famous performing chimpanzees at the St.
Louis Zoo, I inquired how he managed to keep eight rambunc-

tious chimps under control during the arduous training and during the intricate performances. He said, "First, I stand back and watch a new group for a while to see who is going to be boss. Once that is settled I have little difficulty. The boss chimp, when I get him on my side, keeps the rest of them in line. They are more scared of him than they are of me."

To come down—or up—to the human level, every society of any complexity examined by social scientists has revealed a pattern of stratification. There has always been a group that ran things at the top and, at the bottom of the scale, a group assigned to do the dirty work. Aristotle was one of the earliest to observe this tendency. A vivid example of the way people tend to accept a rank or order is seen in the study William Foote Whyte made of the young men in the New England Italian slum who spent almost all their non-working hours, even if married, loitering at their favorite street corner. Whyte observed:[1] "Each member of the corner gang has his own position in the gang structure. . . . The leadership is changed not through an uprising of the bottom men, but by a shift in the relations between men at the top of the structure."

These men, under the leader of the gang, were voluntarily accepting a type of human pecking order. In some human societies, assignment of rank order is pretty much settled at birth. The populace of pre-Revolutionary France was divided by regulation into specific estates or degrees. India even today has its thousands of castes. Individual progress is pretty much confined to what is permissible within caste lines, though caste lines have recently been crumbling under the impact of urbanization and industrialization.

Despite the fact that some very ambitious efforts have been made to set up truly classless societies, such societies have never been achieved on any large sustained basis. The most publicized attempt, of course, is that of the Soviet Union. The goal of the class struggle as conceived by Karl Marx was the elimination of the bourgeois class and—after a brief, benign dictatorship of the proletariat—the emergence of a truly class-less society. Four decades have passed since the Russian Revolution. The Soviet Union, despite its professions of achieving a society of true equality, is becoming more precisely stratified each year. The need of the expanding industrial machine for a hierarchy of managers and specialists as well as workers of varying skills provided, and in fact perhaps demanded, a social structure to match.

Alex Inkeles, who spent several years studying the new Soviet society for the Russian Research Center at Harvard University, concluded that Russia, under the Communists, had evolved a ten-class social system.[2] The classes ranged from the ruling elite (officials, scientists, top artists and writers) down through managers, bureaucrats, and three classes of workers and two classes of peasants to the slave laborers. To formalize its classes—and emphasize lines of authority—Russia has been requiring more and more millions of its civilian citizens to wear uniforms so designed as to indicate their exact status in the system. In 1958, a group of Russian managers and technicians billed by the Soviets as "ordinary" Russians visited America. Inquiry revealed that their average income was about five times that of the typical Soviet worker.

A more sincere and genuinely persistent recent effort to establish a classless society is that attempted by the farm collectives in Israel. They were begun nearly a half-century ago and number in the hundreds. Today, the original ideals— complete democracy and complete equality in the sharing of material goods—are still carried out. But social strata have emerged.[3] Originally, "productive" workers (manual workers and farmers) were the ones glorified because their talents were greatly needed to settle the arid land and few of the immigrant Jews had any experience at that sort of work. They were mostly intellectuals and white-collar people. "Brain" or "clean" work was scorned as non-productive. In the early days, they elected managers more or less on a rotation basis. Over the years, however, it developed that highly regarded, capable men were elected as managers again and again. They tended to return less and less to "productive work," and the higher prestige began shifting from "productive" to "brain" work. Further, an aristocracy of old-timers emerged, and has become the main source for managerial talent.

The experience of early American efforts to create communistic societies was much the same, with an elite consisting of the most talented or capable ultimately emerging.

America as a whole, since the Revolutionary War, has struggled to preserve ideals of equality in the face of persistent tendencies for elites to develop and consolidate their power, prestige, and wealth. Long after the Revolution, a few families continued to dominate the affairs of many New England towns. Some observers have suggested America came closest to a genuine system of equality of opportunity (as contrasted to the more utopian equality of status) around 1870. The industrial era was just getting started and vast areas of frontier were being opened for settlement and development.

Liston Pope, Dean of the Yale Divinity School and a student of stratification, found that by 1940 the process of social stratification in the United States had been "proceeding rapidly for several decades." The Lynds discovered in their revisit to "Middletown," well known to be Muncie, Indiana, during the thirties, a decade after their first study there, that the class lines had hardened during the interval. Another of the pioneer groups to investigate the social life of an American community, led by W. Lloyd Warner in "Yankee City" (Newburyport, Massachusetts) during the thirties, found there not only an elaborate social structure but a general awareness of its details.

Still, lest we forget it, America by the beginning of the present era (around 1940) had opportunities for upward mobility and social contact that are much less present today. For example:

—Most Americans still lived in communities representing all walks of life.

—Many men of little education still had reasonable grounds for hoping they could rise to the heights.

—Most companies were still small enough so that most employees knew top officials of the companies at least on a nodding basis, and often on a first-name basis.

—There were many lodges and social clubs where men from many social and income levels could and did meet.

—People in most neighborhoods still knew one another well enough personally so that people could be judged for their personal worth rather than by the trappings of status they exhibited.

Beginning with World War II, and still continuing today, an upheaval in the American way of life occurred that has profoundly affected the class structure of America, and caused many to conclude (I say over-optimistically) that we are on the verge of a truly classless society.

Some observers in the field of social science have even asserted that our system of values has changed more in this period since 1940 than in the entire remainder of the history of the United States. Louis Levine, Chief Analyst in Employment Security for the United States Department of Labor, informed me that more money is being spent for industrial research now in a single year than was spent in the first 150 years of the nation's history. We are feeling the impact of the unleashing of not one but two mighty forces, electronics and atomics.

For just a moment, let us look at ten changes in our national economy that have affected the class structure (and status striving) in the United States. Taken together they represent a transformation in a nation's way of life.

1. Perhaps most obvious is the truly spectacular increase in individual wealth since 1940, and particularly during the past decade. Even allowing for inflation, our individual buying power has increased by more than half. Some groups have prospered much more than others (as I will show later), but most families have seen paychecks doubling or tripling. As they say along the New England coast, "The rising tide lifts all the boats." The number of families earning more than $4,000 a year after taxes more than doubled from 1950 to 1956. Americans consequently have been living higher off the hog than ever before in their lives. A mass merchandiser of packaged foods is now offering such items as crepes suzette and hearts of palm. And in 1957 more than 50,000 Americans

installed swimming pools in their back yards. The greatest rises in income, on a percentage basis, have been among those who had below-average incomes. A higher standard of living for working-class people, however, doesn't necessarily change their class status. The rich, meanwhile, have not been suffering. In one recent year, the number of Americans with annual incomes of more than $100,000 increased by a fifth.

2. This brings us to the second big economic change affecting class: the graduated federal income tax. Some have described it as the great leveler. The federal-government income taxes began rising in the thirties to fight the Depression, and soared even more steeply in the forties to finance World War II. They still remain near the wartime levels. As a result, it has become virtually impossible for a man to become a multimillionaire by salary alone. He needs to have capital gains, only one quarter of which he loses in taxes, or be an oilman and get a "depletion allowance." Still, in 1958, I was able to find, without too much difficulty, several dozen Americans who have established fortunes of at least $10,000,000 in the twenty years since income taxes have become so high.[4]

Despite the laments about high taxes, the number of American families with a net worth of a half-million dollars has doubled since 1945. Most of the very rich manage, one way or another, to hold onto the bulk of their new incomes each year. Meanwhile, corporate lawyers have applied their ingenuity to find non-taxable benefits for key executives. These range from deferred payments in the form of high incomes for declining years and free medical checkups at mountain spas, to hidden hunting lodges, corporate yachts, payment of country-club dues (according to one survey, three quarters of all companies sampled did this), and lush expense accounts. One sales manager declined a $10,000 raise and took instead a $10,000 expense account which, it was specified, he didn't have to account for.

Travel for tax-deductible business reasons became popular. In the summer of 1957, several thousand United States lawyers and their wives attended the American Bar Association convention in New York and then boarded boats to complete their conferring in England with brothers-in-law across the sea. One item of business they accomplished in England was to appoint a committee on protocol to decide what their wives should wear to the Queen's garden party.

Some time ago, a plane owned by a United States corporation and loaded with the company's top executives, as well as two pilots and a mechanic, turned up at a landing strip in the wildest reaches of northern Saskatchewan. The group dallied for several days fishing for graylings at nearby lakes. Some of the executives had read an article in *The Saturday Evening Post* about the delights of grayling fishing in this area. The official imperative business reason why all these executives, simultaneously, were in Canada was to inspect a mining camp the company happened to own several hundred miles away.

3. The lessening contrast in the material way of life of rich and poor. The ostentatious turn-of-the-century behavior of millionaires who staged $100,000 parties and smoked cigars wrapped in $100 bills is being soft-pedaled. One probable reason is that the Depression threw a scare into the really rich, and they have learned to be discreet, almost reticent, in exhibiting their wealth. They have learned that in modern America you can exert power only by denying you have it. Another reason for the lessening contrast is the mass selling of standardized goods and services once available only to the better-off. Most American women, regardless of class, for example, now wear nylons, have permanent waves, buy frozen steaks, and wear clothes that are copies (or copies of copies) of Paris designs.

The increasing difficulty in obtaining servants, because of the availability of higher-prestige jobs, has also diminished the contrast. In fact, the word "servant" is disappearing from the language. A disgruntled reader of the *Wall Street Journal* complained that in order to keep a cook he had to call her a housekeeper, and address her as "Mrs." Even cleaning women are hard to hold. A sociologist in Pennsylvania told me that his cleaning woman not only drives a better car than he does, but has remarked on the fact. She says she just doesn't care for cars more than two or three years old. "She expects my wife to prepare her lunch," he added.

4. The massive shift in vocational skills needed by our economy. We have been seeing demand for skills changing with lightning rapidity. Some occupations are becoming largely or entirely outmoded, and hundreds of new occupations are emerging. The man at the United States Labor Department in charge of the Dictionary of Occupational Titles advised me he had to add 375 brand-new occupations in 1956. (Examples: video recording engineer, automation "programmer," radiation detector, and "port steward" for overseas airliners.) Other observers at the Department offered these examples of occupations then expanding or becoming overcrowded enough to cite to young people planning careers. For example:

Expanding	*Crowded or declining*
airplane mechanics	bakers
electronic craftsmen	shoemakers
draftsmen	type compositors
technical writers	railroad mechanics
physicists	telegraphers
medical technicians	actors
computing-machine operators	navigators
typists, stenographers, secretaries	rural mail carriers
plumbers	general clerks
college professors	entertainers

Looking at the changes in demand in terms of the larger trends, the following two seem most significant in their effect on class structure. One is the really spectacular rise in industries that furnish services (in contrast with those such as mining, manufacturing, and farming that produce goods). As our mechanized farms, mines, and factories have become able to produce ever-increasing amounts of goods with fewer people, the service-field industries (the selling and servicing of goods, and providing insurance, banking, amusement, education, medicine, travel) have been taking up much of the slack.

The other long-range trend of note, and it is really a by-product of the first, is the recent great gain of white-collared workers over blue-collared ones. The service fields are primarily staffed by white-collared people. In 1940, only a third of our employed people were in white-collared occupations. Today nearly half are.

Some observers have enthusiastically seen this growth of white-collars as evidence of a great upthrust of "working"-class people into the "middle" class. There has unquestionably been some social upgrading, but two cautions should be noted. First, a large percentage of the people recruited into white-collared ranks are women who previously didn't work. Second, many of the new white-collar jobs are essentially manual or require little skill, and so represent no real advance in prestige. One happy consequence to the economy of these trends to white-collar, service jobs, however, is that more people now work on a salaried basis rather than an hourly-wage basis and so are less likely to be discharged quickly in case of an economic downturn. This represents a gain for stability.

5. The great increase in moving about of the population. Some people still live in the houses they lived in twenty years ago, but they are rarities. The average American picks up roots about every five years. I know of one corporate executive who moved his family sixteen times in the course of moving up through the ranks of two companies to his present job. Of the 1,280 families who moved into one Long Island development a decade ago, 805 have moved elsewhere. The result of this geographical mobility is that social status is established less and less by family background, which may be unknown to the judges, and more and more by such currently visible factors as job, consumption standards, behavior, school, club membership, and so on. Furthermore, as we shall see in Chapter 21, all this moving about produces an upsurge in status striving.

6. The great growth in leisure time that has accompanied increased productivity. In the days of Thorstein Veblen, a display of oneself enjoying leisure was one of the better ways to prove one's superior class rating. Then the average man had to work fifty to sixty hours a week. Today the average man works about thirty-eight hours a week, and it is the harassed

business executive who is likely to put in the fifty-sixty hours. As a result, leisure has lost most of its potency as a status symbol.

7. The trend toward large, bureaucratic organizations. Everywhere—in both government and private industry—the trend is to bigness. Every spring sees a new burst of corporate mergers. The number of civil servants in the federal government has multiplied ten times in five decades. In industry today, 2 per cent of the companies employ a majority of all workers. As Peter M. Blau of the University of Chicago put it after making his study of bureaucratic trends: "A large and increasing proportion of the American people spend their working lives as small cogs in the complex mechanisms of bureaucratic organizations."[5] The hierarchies of these growing bureaucracies carry over into the prestige markup of social status. Furthermore, the men handling job placement for these large organizations feel more secure if they place men on the basis of objective criteria since they are usually dealing with strangers. Thus they are obsessed by the idea that anyone considered as potential executive timber should be a college man or woman.

8. The shrinkage in the number of small entrepreneurs and self-employed people. Such independent entrepreneurs originally constituted a true middle class in the United States. They found economic security by commanding their own destinies, however small. In Jefferson's day, nearly four fifths of all Americans were self-employed enterprisers. By 1940 only about one fifth remained.[6] And today the number has shrunk to approximately 13 per cent. The other 87 per cent— or the overwhelming majority of our working populace—are now employed by others. We have become an employee society.

This lack of entrepreneurial experience is most vivid in the ranks of our industrial executives. More than three fifths are the sons of men who, at one time, ran their own businesses. Yet, according to one survey,[7] only one executive in six today has ever had such experience.

9. The trend to breaking jobs down into narrow, and if

possible, simple specialties. The growth of bureaucratic thinking—with its passion for job definition—is partly responsible for this. More responsible, however, is the emergence of efficiency engineers who know that money can be saved for a company by reducing a job to a simple repetitive level so that any alert twelve-year-old with a capacity for withstanding boredom could handle it. This practice, while saving money for management, reduces the social prestige attached to the job and reduces the employee's job satisfaction and self-esteem.

10. The mass production of homes, with the attendant growth of homogeneous suburban communities. In earlier days, an American community was usually a scale model of all society, with a fair share of butchers, bakers, candlestick makers, creamery owners, manufacturers, laborers. Such towns are relentlessly being replaced by one-layer towns, which encourage birds-of-a-feather flocking. Many of the new suburban towns, built around shopping centers born full grown, not only attract buyers of specific income level (almost everyone's income will fall, say, between $5,000 and $6,250) but also people of specific ethnic backgrounds. Further, they are rather narrowly age-graded. A town built by a home marketer specializing in houses ranging in price from $27,500 to $32,500, for example, will attract families of middle-management men and other successful couples capable of paying that price. Typically, only couples over forty years of age qualify. In such developments you will see few small children—and few grandmothers.

3

emerging: a diploma elite

"This whole town's . . . made up of tight little circles of people who have the same community of interest, about the same amount of money and act the same. They're all on different levels just like a stairway. . . . You'll find little circles and crowds picking and clawing at each other."—A LOCAL INFORMANT in August B. Hollingshead's "Elmtown."

◄─o─►·◄─o─►·◄─o─►·◄─o─►·◄─o─►·◄─o─►·◄─o─►

AGAINST THE BACKGROUND OF ECONOMIC UPHEAVAL JUST described, what in broad outline is the class system that seems to be unfolding in America?

Several hundred United States sociologists have been applying themselves to this puzzle. Their task is complicated by the fact that class boundaries not only are invisible but often are not acknowledged. According to our creed, they are not supposed to be there. While the investigators still disagree on some points there is, as Hollingshead puts it, "general agreement" that mid-century American society is stratified. Any investigation of status striving should properly begin with an understanding of the current class structure—and its barriers—within which the striving typically takes place. One of the better definitions of class still appears to be the classic one of sociologist T. H. Marshall: "It is the way a man is treated by his fellows and reciprocally, the way he treats them."[1]

As I see it, the boundaries of class are best perceived not as

24

fixed lines or ceilings but rather as sieves or bottlenecks. Few investigators now believe that everyone falls neatly into one of four or six or fourteen classes. We are probably closer to the truth when we view the American populace as being arranged along a continuum with an infinite number of possible divisions.

While there is a continuum, it is also true that people will tend to cluster so that the continuum is actually a series of bulges and contractions. The major bulges might be called the major class groupings. Sociologist Richard Centers tried to describe the division between any two classes by saying there is "no sharp, neat point where day changes to night." Instead, he said, the situation is "like the pictures one sees in a biological textbook of a cell that is beginning to divide, there being masses of material concentrated at two ends of a continuum with a gradient of stuff between."[2]

One way to picture the situation graphically is to imagine a host of people strung along a trail up a mountainside. Some have given up the idea of climbing higher and have pitched their tents. But many would like to climb still higher. At several points the trail becomes precipitously steep, and so narrow that only a few people can pass at a time. Between these difficult passages are broad, gentle inclines where large numbers of people can spread out as they climb or rest. Some few will be finding the climbing beyond their capacity and will be retreating down the mountainside. Going downward can be even more painfully difficult than going upward.

While caution must be used in generalizing from studies of individual communities, class structures do seem to show many consistent resemblances from town to town. Bevode McCall of Indiana University found that, in the Georgia town he studied, the social classes resembled those found in community studies in New England, the Midwest, and in Mississippi. One of the pioneers in community studies is W. Lloyd Warner of the University of Chicago, who spent a great deal of time with associates not only in "Yankee City" but also in the corn-belt town of "Jonesville." (This last town was also studied by Hollingshead and called "Elmtown." In the course of this book you will encounter several communities which have been given fictitious names by investigators in order to assure informants they could speak with confidence. Examples: "Elmtown," "Jonesville," "Plainville," "Vansburg," "Northeast City," "Prairieton," and "Georgia Town.") Warner, after assessing his findings and comparing them with other findings, concluded that there is at least something of Jonesville in all American communities.

While different communities have revealed a different number of major class groupings or clusters, the number that appears more persistently than any other is five. Warner found five major classes in Jonesville and in his three-year study of communities in the Chicago area. This was a modification of his earlier finding of six classes in his old New England Yankee City, where he had divided the upper class into the old and new uppers because antiquity in New England was such an important factor. Bevode McCall found five main classes in his Georgia Town. August B. Hollingshead, in his study of New Haven, Connecticut, found a "rather rigid five-tier class structure."

To me, most impressive is Hollingshead's discovery of five classes in Elmtown, because of the technique he used to arrive at that number. Hollingshead, then of Indiana University and now of Yale University, went to Elmtown to study adolescent behavior as it might relate to social class.[3] His first problem was to decide if the town did have a recognized class structure. To do this, he selected twenty-five different residents as raters. To each he handed a pack of thirty cards. On each card was printed the name of a husband and wife well known in the community. There were thirty couples, thirty cards. He simply asked each rater to place each couple in the "class" or "station" to which the couple belonged. He gave no further instructions. Yet more than three quarters of the raters divided the cards into five piles or "classes." Furthermore, the raters were in agreement on more than three quarters of their placements of specific couples. Later, Hollingshead took twenty of the cards and presented them to twelve brand-new raters. This time an even higher proportion (10 out of 12) isolated five piles or "classes."

Sociologist Joseph A. Kahl of Washington University, in surveying the various community studies, commented that while there were differences as to the number of classes the differences "are not really contradictory, for the basic outlines are agreed upon."[4] He then gave what he thought was the best way to describe the situation with a "minimum of distortion" by arbitrarily presenting five classes. He called them "ideal types." The five classes these various sociologists have found are, of course, not identical in all respects but they do have fundamental resemblances. The five classes I will describe later on in this chapter are also roughly comparable to them.

This number "five" seems to carry over even into West European class structures. The British branch of the Institute for Motivational Research accepts a five-class system. And, in Denmark, three sociologists from the University of Copenhagen have found a five-class system operating in that country.

There have been exceptions, but most sociologists have tended to see the primary break in the class structure as between the blue-collar, or working-class, world and the white-collar world. This was seen as the barrier most difficult to pass. Other class lines could be more easily crossed. The Lynds pointed to this boundary as the crucial one in their famed Middletown studies in the twenties and thirties; and many sociologists have continued to stress it.

Here I would disagree. In the past decade, the most fundamental split in our social structure has moved upward a notch. It is now between the so-called lower middle class and the upper middle class (or between Class 2 and Class 3 on most five-class scales).

This new, more formidable boundary results from the growing insistence on college diplomas as a minimum entry requirement for most of the higher-prestige occupations.

Meanwhile, we have been seeing a revolutionary blurring of the boundary line between white- and blue-collared people. The recent upheaval of our economic system has brought about this blurring. Let us pause for a moment to note what has been happening.

In the past, many investigators have arbitrarily assigned all white-collar workers to a class above *any* blue-collar worker. Thus store clerks and stenographers have been rated above skilled craftsmen. The reasoning apparently was that the white-collared person worked in a world carrying more prestige. The white-collar working world was clean rather than dirty, and it seemed more dignified, more brainy. There was close proximity to management, and people in white collars sought to live in the style of their superiors. The pay not only was better than blue-collar pay typically but usually came in the form of a weekly salary rather than the less dignified hourly-wage form.

Just about every basis on which white-collared clerical people have claimed superior status to blue-collared workers, however, has been undermined in recent years. This applies not only in America but in other advanced industrial nations.

The change may have started during World War II when many people quit office jobs for the more glorified jobs of riveters in shipyards. The spectacular growth in the number of people finishing high school likewise had an undermining effect. In the past, the high-school diploma was a ticket of admission to a white-collar job. Now, many millions of American youngsters have the ticket, so there is less prestige attached to putting on a white collar. Actually, the color of the collar is losing much of its significance as a label. Many steelworkers don't wear blue collars any more on the job, they wear sports shirts. And so do supposedly white-collared missile engineers.

Furthermore, in hundreds of companies, there has been a sharp downgrading in the amount of skill and dignity associated with the average clerical job. Scientific management procedures and the introduction of office machinery have been creating working conditions very similar to those out in the plant, which simultaneously has been cleaned up and made to look more like an office. Many white-collared office workers —billing clerks, key-punch operators—are actually machine attendants, manual workers in any honest nomenclature. The work of some clerical people is so routinized, dull, and easily learned that people are often chosen for their special capacity to endure boredom.

Even the layout of the large office is coming more and more to resemble that of the factory, with straight-line flow of work and in some cases assembly belts for moving paper work from point to point. Each worker does a fragment of the complete operation. The repetitive task of a comptometer operator, for example, depends upon the repetitive tasks of file clerks, stenographers, accountants, and messengers before and after her task is performed.[5]

Finally, in many of the larger plants, the white-collared functionary is isolated from his or her bosses so that even the psychological satisfaction of closeness to management is being denied. C. Wright Mills, Columbia University sociologist, points out that the skill of shorthand is becoming obsolete with the growing use of dictaphones. He writes: "Dictation was once a private meeting of executive and secretary. Now the executive phones a pool of dictaphone transcribers whom he never sees and who know him merely as a voice."[6]

From the male's standpoint, another factor bringing a decline in prestige to clerical work is the fact that many of the jobs in this growing field are being filled by women, who typically command somewhat less money for the same job than men. In the occupations of bank teller, bookkeeper, and cashier, long dominated by men, women are taking over.

The change in status of white-collar jobs is most sharply reflected, however, in the comparative financial rewards of white- and blue-collar employees. At the turn of the century, a white-collar job commanded twice as much money as a factory job. Today, the unionized blue-collar worker has overtaken and moved ahead of the white-collar worker. Sales workers earn less than craftsmen and foremen who typically have three years less schooling. (The 1950 Census was the first in history to show blue-collar workers surpassing in income a category of white-collar workers.)

The extent of the shift shows up vividly in figures released by the United States Labor Department on wages in seventeen labor markets as of 1956. Male office clerical workers earned a third less than men in "maintenance and powerplant."

A sign of the change is the kind of jobs that blue-collar factory workers were accepting as stopgaps when they lost their jobs temporarily during the 1957–58 recession. Some found themselves in "clean" white- or semi-white-collared-type jobs. *Life* magazine, in an article describing the impact on Peoria, Illinois, of a layoff at a local tractor-manufacturing plant, featured a machine-shop worker who had been earning $80 a week. Out of a job, he put on a white collar and tie and began working mornings at a local supermarket as an attendant. In the afternoons and early evenings, wearing a white jersey, he worked as an apprentice masseur. Although he worked twelve and one half hours a day, six days a week, at these non-blue-collar jobs, he still earned about $10 a week less than he had at the factory.

Perhaps the most spectacular falling off in money and prestige has occurred with retail salesclerks. In ten Northeastern and Southern cities, I sought to find why customers were grumbling so much about service they were receiving at the hands of clerks. The answer was best summed up by a New Yorker in the merchandising field. He stated: "Retail stores are trying to compete in the labor market by offering the most undesirable hours, the lowest wages, and working conditions that can't compare with those of office workers."

A variety-store manager in Nashville, Tennessee, told me, concerning the hours: "It's the six-day week that beats us— and the lack of Saturday off, especially if the girl's husband has Saturday off." As for the pay, the manager of a variety store outside Paterson, New Jersey, said: "Moneywise, we don't pretend to compete with factories and offices." The average young man entering retailing is likely to make considerably less than his brother going to work in a factory. While factory workers average around $80 a week, clerks in general-merchandise stores on an average earn less than $50.

Still, I found women, as in Greenville, South Carolina, working as low-paid salesclerks rather than taking higher-paying factory jobs because of pride of class. Some felt their family's status in the community could not survive the assumed comedown.

The unions have sought, with only modest success, to exploit the growing frustration of clerical and other white-collar workers with such sneering slogans as "You Can't Eat Air Conditioning." Unions feel an urgent need for white-collar recruits because the supply of blue-collar workers, who constitute the great bulk of union membership, is shrinking. John L. Lewis's mine workers' union is one third the size it was in his pre-World War II days of glory and power. Most white-collar people still aspire to rise, and this makes them poor prospects for the unions. Many are caught up in a panic about their status and strain to demonstrate that they are different from the working class. Meanwhile, many lead lives of quiet conformity trying to live like—and to please—their superiors. The most eloquent summation of this feeling of frustration that afflicts many such people was offered some years ago, when times were harder, by George Orwell's salesman, Mr. Bowling, in *Coming Up for Air*. He states: "There's a lot of rot talked about the sufferings of the working class. I'm not so sorry for the proles myself. . . . The prole suffers physically, but he's a free man when he isn't working. But in every one of those little stucco boxes there's some poor bastard who's never free except when he's fast asleep and dreaming that he's got the boss down the bottom of a well and is bunging lumps of coal at him."

While the boundary between white and blue collar is blurring, the boundary between lower and upper white-collar groups is becoming sharp and formidable. (By upper white collar I mean the managers, professional people, etc.) It has become the great dividing line in our society. And it is becoming more formidable every year.

The boundary is formidable because the ticket of admission is steep: a college diploma of some sort. About one in eight youths today has the ticket. More and more, opportunity at the higher levels begins and ends with the choice of education. After one is educated the mold is usually set. Only rarely will a person who begins in a lower white-collar job without a college degree be able to move across the line into the upper group.

Our so-called great "middle class" actually is being split down the middle by this requirement. One of America's leading social theorists, Harvard's Talcott Parsons, states: "Probably the best single index of the line between 'upper middle' class and the rest of the middle class is the *expectation* that children will have a college education as a matter that is a status right, not because of the exceptional ability of the individual."

In smaller communities, there are still many upper-middle-class males who never went to college; but they represent the opportunity situation of more than a decade ago. (A number of college graduates, on the other hand, have never succeeded in winning acceptance as upper middle class.) The number of today's youths, however, who will achieve an upper-middle-class status without the benefit of a college degree will be far more limited.

Our class system is starting to bear a resemblance to that which prevails in the military services. In the services there are, of course, status differences between a private and a corporal and between a lieutenant and a captain. The great division, however, is between officers and enlisted men, with only quite limited opportunities for acquiring, while in service, the training necessary to pass from one division to the other.

The system of horizontal social strata which I perceive emerging in America is in two great divisions. Within each division there are classes or major bulges. Here appears to be the most graphic way to suggest by generalization the situation that is developing:

THE DIPLOMA ELITE
I. The Real Upper Class
II. The Semi-Upper Class

THE SUPPORTING CLASSES
III. The Limited-Success Class
IV. The Working Class
V. The Real Lower Class

The diploma elite consists of the big, active, successful people who pretty much run things. The supporting classes contain the passive non-big people who wear both white and blue collars: the small shopkeepers, workers, functionaries, technical aides. Here briefly is a description of the five classes, as I see them, that comprise these two main divisions.

I. THE REAL UPPER CLASS. These are the people who are likely to be on the board of directors of local industries, banks, universities, and community chests; who send their daughters to finishing schools and their sons, probably, to a boarding school and, certainly, to a "good" college. They have heavy investments in local land, industry, banks—they probably inherited much of it—and they can swing a great deal of weight around town when they wish. These also include the high-prestige professionals such as the more fashionable doctors, lawyers, and architects who come from well-connected families or have an upper-class clientele. The Episcopal minister also would normally be included here.

These people of the real upper class would have you believe that wealth has little bearing on their social pre-eminence. Rather, it is the gracious, leisurely way of life they have achieved as a result of their innate good taste and high breeding. In smaller communities, "old" family background is especially important.

The real-upper-class people tend to view the new rich as uncouth and will accept them only when the self-made newcomers become so powerful that they must be consulted on the important decisions involving the community and only if they have the right kind of money. (Wealthy undertakers are not typically accepted.)

It is true that only the rarest of the new rich can take on the genteel, austere airs of the old rich without a good deal of practice and observation. But although manners are important, money is more so. One of the most articulate local informants in Hollingshead's Elmtown, a Mr. Henry Dotson, explained what it takes to stay in the top class in Elmtown:[7]

"First, I'd say money is the most important. In fact nobody's in this class if he doesn't have money; but it just isn't money alone. You've got to have the right family connections, and you have got to behave yourself or you get popped out. And if you lose your money, you're dropped. If you don't have money, you're just out."

In Northeast City, where I spent several weeks exploring the elite structure of a representative middle-sized metropolis, an old-family social matron talked nostalgically of social relations in the old days. Then, she said, "family" really counted. Many of the best families would never have received the people they do today. But, she sighed, "money is money."

Most communities with a population of more than 10,000 have a fairly well-defined upper class. At the higher reaches of the upper class are what might be called the "upper uppers." They live in the most exclusive sections of large metropolitan areas and are still very rich or very powerful even when viewed on a national basis.

II. THE SEMI-UPPER CLASS. This is the class that sociologists still usually call the "upper middle class." My only objection to that phrase is that it implies "upper middle" is part of a larger body called the "middle class" and so is intimately related to what the sociologists call the "lower middle class," also assumed to be a part of the larger "middle class" body. My contention is that they are becoming two quite distinct clusters and shouldn't be confused. However, I concede that it is convenient to refer to whatever is between upper and lower as "middle." When, subsequently, I cite findings of sociologists who use "upper middle" I will accept their terminology.

At any rate, members of the semi-upper class—to revert to my terminology—are mostly confident, energetic, ambitious people who went away to college, then began a career somewhere away from their home town or neighborhood. Most of them are with fairly large organizations where they are decision makers serving as managers, technologists, or persuaders. The remainder are professional men or successful local businessmen.

Members of this semi-upper class are the hyperactive civic boosters who devote themselves actively to their roles in service clubs and country clubs, and their wives power the local charity drives.

Below the two classes cited, which comprise the diploma elite, is a gulf; and beyond the gulf are the supporting classes. Its members are the people who are, in the words of sociologist Joseph A. Kahl, "the anonymous or little people—the vast masses who can be hired interchangeably to do the routine jobs in factory or office."[8] His judgment may seem a bit harsh in its sweep. I know that my garbage man—one of the most fascinating conversationalists of my acquaintance—would resent being called either little or anonymous. Perhaps it is only people who serve as functionaries or cogs for big organizations who feel little and anonymous. In any case, Kahl's statement does suggest that the work role of most of these people is in the lower division. They are outside the area of decision and play essentially supporting roles as workers, functionaries, or aides.

III. THE LIMITED-SUCCESS CLASS. This group is the one still characteristically referred to by sociologists as the "lower middle class." Its members place great store in demonstrating that they are respectable, proper, cultured, and socially above the working masses. They are more conforming, more morally proper, and more active in the churches than any other group. To pursue the military parallel, they are the non-commissioned officers of our society.

Virtually all its members have high-school diplomas, and many of them have a year or two of post-high-school training in technical schools, two-year colleges, or secretarial schools.

In offices they are the clerks, excepting the routine machine attendants, and secretaries. On Main Street they are clerks in the quality store or the small shopkeepers or the smaller contractors. In industry they are the foremen, technical aides—a spectacularly expanding group—and skilled craftsmen. They also are the smaller farmers.

In short, they include the lower ranks of the genuinely white-collar world and the higher ranks of the blue-collar world, the aristocrats of labor. Both groups are success minded, but in a different way. The blue-collared elite are at the top of their ladder and so don't worry too much about trying to upgrade themselves socially by their choice of status symbols. The white-collared people do worry, and do strive. They feel that they haven't arrived, and wonder if they ever will. As Kahl puts it, they are "constantly striving to get ahead: *yet most will never get very far, and after they have outlived the romantic dreams of youth, they know it.*"⁹

Both the blue- and white-collar members, then, are of roughly equal prestige although their ways of life differ. And they both can be called "limited successes," but for different reasons.

IV. The Working Class. The heads of families of this class frequently have not finished high school. They work steadily, in good times, at jobs that require little training and can be mastered in a few days or, at most, a few weeks. They constitute the backbone of the industrial unions and numerically are the largest class (nearly 40 per cent of the total).

Most are semi-skilled factory operatives. Others wear white shirts and man machines in offices or work as deliverymen. Still others are truck drivers, miners, filling-station attendants, supermarket clerks and attendants. As Elmtown's Henry Dotson put it: "They are the good solid people who live right but never get any place."

Their work often bores them, especially if it is a repetitive job, and they live for the pleasures their paychecks can buy. If you ask them what they do for a living they say, "Oh, I work for Standard." It wouldn't occur to them to explain what they do there. It is too boring, and not a source of pride. While they resent the airs put on by white-collared folks, they like to feel they are good citizens.

V. The Real Lower Class. These are the people everyone else looks down upon. They live in the decrepit slum areas that just about every American town has. (Slums are much less apparent in Europe's towns and cities.) They usually leave school as soon as legally allowed, if not before. They work erratically at unskilled or semi-skilled tasks, and try to find their pleasures where they can. Henry Dotson said of the Elmtown lower class: "There is a really low class here that is a lulu. It is made up of families who are not worth a . . . damn, and they don't give a damn. They're not immoral; they're not unmoral; they're plain amoral. . . . They have animal urges and respond to them. They're like a bunch of . . . rabbits."

Allison Davis, University of Chicago sociologist, found in a study of the motives of the underprivileged that people in this class are so used to living on the edge of hunger and disaster that they have never learned "ambition" or a drive for higher skills or education. "In a sense," he reported, "ambition and the drive to attain the higher skills are a kind of luxury. They require a minimum *physical* security; only when one knows where his next week's or next month's food and shelter will come from can he and his children afford to go in for long-term education and training. . . ."

These people are not as frightened of losing a job as the rest of us because they fatalistically expect they will lose it anyhow; and unlike the rest of us they know that even when everything is lost friends and relatives will take them in without any loss of respectability. There is little to lose. "The harder the economic noose is drawn, the tighter the protective circle," Davis reports.

Meanwhile, the unmarried male spends his nights in sexual exploration. He lives in a world, according to Davis, "where visceral, genital and emotional gratification is far more available" than it is to most of us.

These people know that most of us look down on them and despise them. There are two natural reactions to this contempt: either kick back, which youths do and then are arrested for juvenile delinquency, or retreat into apathy, which is what the older lowers do. What these people need more than charity or prosperity is recognition.

Quite a few people, it should be noted, do not fit neatly into any of these horizontal identifications. They are in between the major bulges of class, or their characteristics make them hard to place. This is particularly true of many intellectuals, who tend to have high-class tastes and educations with incomes that often do not match. Further, they value nonconformity and so develop their own ways of snooting.

Perhaps they get a hideaway on Fire Island or Majorca. And inevitably the less imaginative well-to-do begin copying them by going there.

The peculiar behavior of intellectuals, or eggheads, will be examined in subsequent chapters. Anyone who considers himself well read, of course, can set himself up as an intellectual, or as a bohemian or an upper bohemian, to use Russell Lynes's term. Bohemia is a state of mind inhabited by those who, whether or not they are creative or particularly intellectual, like to stand on the margins and scoff at the babbitts. They cherish, within limits, differentness of behavior.

Genuine eggheads are the working intellectuals who create culture (i.e., scholars, artists, editors, philosophers, novelists, composers, etc.) or who disseminate and interpret culture (i.e., academic people, critics, actors, etc.).

These people tend to develop their own quite tight stratification systems outside the main body of the class system. Most would be very ill at ease trying to converse with a genuine proletarian. They share the diploma elite's ideals about higher education and higher income. And often they are quite avid status seekers within the marginal group they wish to impress. If, as is likely, they live in a "contemporary" home, they will, while visiting other "contemporary" homes, carefully note the kind of eating utensils considered most appropriate for such a house.

Union leaders likewise are among those hard to classify. A study of the power structure in the steelmaking city of Lorain, Ohio, revealed that in recent years union leaders have come to exert a dominant influence in political and school affairs. Furthermore, they are persons of great influence in many civic activities. The influence of upper-class business and professional families in these areas has at the same time been greatly curtailed. Socially, however, the position of the union leaders and their families is ambiguous. They were found to be rated less highly in terms of social status than many business and professional men who had far less influence in the community than they did. This, of course, may be a transitional situation.

obstacle course for outsiders

*"The commuting villages of Connecticut's Fairfield
County . . . show three distinct social categories,
vertically divided. First, there are the Yankees,
descendants of the original settlers and still the
wielders of power. Second, there are the Italians . . .
who initially came . . . as track layers . . . and
remained to become the storekeepers, artisans
(etc.). . . . Third, there are the New York commuters, also called the lambs, or the pigeons, or
the patsies."*—MAX SHULMAN.

◄─○─►·◄─○─►·◄─○─►·◄─○─►·◄─○─►·◄─○─►·◄─○─►

NOW WE TURN TO THE OTHER HALF OF THE STORY ABOUT OUR
social-class structure. Max Shulman in his novel, *Rally Round
the Flag, Boys!*, showed that a novelist can sometimes be
more perceptive than a sociologist in spotting cleavages.[1]
Until recently, most sociologists in talking of our class structure have concerned themselves only with the *horizontal* layers
(such as we discussed in the last chapter). People are identified
with a layer primarily in terms of *prestige*.

It now seems clear, however, that the American populace
is also organized into *vertical* strata, on the basis of *differentness*.

A class, as I perceive it, is any group of people within a
population who have a common status or origin that tends
to set them apart—and who develop a style of life that em-
phasizes the apartness. If I say that a man is a wealthy Boston

39

banker, automatically in your mind you assign him a high-prestige rating. But if I add that his name is Lazienki, a new dimension has been added, even though you may still agree he deserves a high-prestige rating.

Sociologist Raymond W. Mack told me of an interesting exercise he sometimes gives his students in stratification. He asks them to "place" in the class structure a man with these characteristics: "He is a graduate of Indiana University and has a law degree from Ohio State. His father, a small businessman, was a high-school graduate. His mother had two years of college. He drives a 1958 Buick . . . he has his own law office . . . he is a Methodist . . . he has a $12,000 income . . . his two children are university students." At this point Mack asks the students if they now have the man pretty well pegged as to status. Usually they nod that they have. Then he adds: "Oh, yes, and one other thing. He is a Negro." That last bit of information forces them to readjust the whole concept they have been building in their minds. Mack says the students look at him as though he had cheated because he held back the most important fact.

We tend to think of "minorities" as a minor part of our society. Actually, they constitute more than 50,000,000 of the United States population.

Sociologist Milton M. Gordon, now of Wellesley College, was one sociologist who began wondering uneasily, in the early fifties, if a series of horizontal strata told the whole story of the American class system.[2] The position of the millions of Americans who belonged to various ethnic groups bothered him. Their ethnic status seemed to set them apart with invisible boundaries—and limit their area of "intimate social contact in the adult world"—just as thoroughly as the social-class system (horizontal) based on the prestige of occupation, education, etc. In the past, sociologists had tended to consider Negroes as a caste apart but to assign all other people with ethnic backgrounds to whatever horizontal social stratum best fit them in terms of prestige. Gordon disagreed that Negroes should be considered apart. As he saw it, their situation differed in degree rather than in kind from that of other ethnic groups.

He proposed that American society is "crisscrossed" by two sets of stratification structures (social class and ethnic class) and that while they should be kept conceptually apart they should both be considered a part of the "full outlines of the social class system."

Meanwhile, August B. Hollingshead had shifted his community investigations from the largely Protestant, old-American Elmtown in the Midwest to New Haven, Connecticut, a city with a heavy ethnic population. He found, as in Elmtown, five main horizontal classes. But as far as socializing was concerned, each ethnic group in New Haven appeared to have its own social structure of five classes. He concluded that New Haven had "parallel class structures."[3] His findings indicated that the community's current structure is "differentiated vertically along racial, ethnic and religious lines, and each of these vertical cleavages in turn is differentiated horizontally by a series of strata or classes that are encompassed within it." The horizontal classes are based on such prestige factors as occupation, schooling, address. The result, he said, was a social structure that is "highly compartmentalized."

Hollingshead offered a vivid example to illustrate the parallel class structures, each having its elite. He found that New Haven had not one but seven different Junior Leagues for its elite white young women. The top-ranking organization, he reported, "is the New Haven Junior League which draws its membership from the 'Old Yankee' Protestant families whose daughters have been educated in private schools. The Catholic Charity League is next in rank and age—its membership is drawn from Irish-American families. In addition to this organization there are Italian and Polish Junior Leagues within the Catholic division of the society. The Swedish and Danish Junior Leagues are for properly connected young women in these ethnic groups, but they are Protestant. Then too the upper class Jewish families have their Junior League.

"This principle of parallel structures for a given class level by religious, ethnic and racial groups," Hollingshead said, "proliferates throughout the community." The cultural characteristics typical of each horizontal level carry through all the parallel (or vertical) structures. And the cultural pattern or "master mold" for each horizontal class running through the entire structure is set by the "Old Yankee" core group.

Other observers, in chewing on this puzzle of how to describe the class structure, proposed the concept of a series of free-standing pyramids, each with its own layers. *Harper's* Russell Lynes found, in exploring the behavior of the aristocracy of the business world, that the leaders in the communications industry, for example, were more flamboyant and adventurous in their behavior patterns than men in the older, more conservative industries. He would put the higher echelons of the industries, at least, in different pyramids.

The vertical structures based on the differentness of groups overlay—to revert to the grid concept—the horizontal classes based on prestige. They vary, of course, from community to community both in composition and in the proportion of their total membership in the higher-prestige classes.

Here, however, are the four criteria most commonly used by Americans in determining that certain fellow citizens are sufficiently *different* from themselves to justify a wall. The people are differentiated:

1. *By recency of arrival in the locality.* Old-timers in almost any community like to feel they have a monopoly on local prestige, and tend to view all newcomers as upstarts. A motivational study of home buyers in the Philadelphia area disclosed that people would rather move into a brand-new development-type community than go through the torment of becoming accepted in an older, established neighborhood. The wealthier women of Elmtown had two clubs: one for the older, more exclusive families and one for the newer rich.

Interesting collisions have been developing in many United States communities as a result of the growing industrial practice of dispersing plants into smaller cities and towns. Once the plants are built, managerial personnel in large numbers move in and in some cases feel superior to the town's existing upper class. Gregory P. Stone and William H. Form of Michigan State College followed the progress of one of these massive clashes in a Michigan town of 10,000, which they call Vansburg.[4] It had attracted national manufacturers because of its low-cost labor. Managerial personnel moved in who did not accept either the "conventional symbols or the conventional norms of status" prevailing in Vansburg.

These invading newcomers or "cosmopolites" were oriented in their life style to the sophisticated, blasé, and busy life style of the metropolis. Immediately they "joined together and made status claims that called into question the status of the 'old families' of the community. Rather than attempting to achieve social honor by emulating the life style of the entrenched 'upper classes' the members of this group imposed their own symbols upon the social life of Vansburg and established themselves as a separate status group. They appeared publicly in casual sports clothes, exploited images of 'bigness' in their conversations with established local businessmen, retired late and slept late. With all the aspects of a coup they 'took over' the clubs and associations of the 'old families.'"

At the country club, which they came to dominate, most of the old families resigned in protest. The old families at last report had chosen one club in town as a "last bastion of defense against the 'upstart invasion.'" Resentment of newcomers seemed even more intense at lower social levels than at the highest levels.

Such wholesale invasions have caused the old guards in many communities to react by emphasizing the importance of ancestry. Throughout the Midwest, many of the towns staging centennial celebrations have been manipulating the occasions to exalt the families still in town whose ancestors happened to get there first. Elmtown was celebrating such a centennial during Hollingshead's visit and he noticed that all the pageantry centered on old prominent families with Anglo-Saxon names. "Eventually," he says, "it became clear that the backers of the centennial were primarily interested in glorifying their own ancestry." People who had helped build the town after the pioneer era were not included.

In Northeast City, which I visited, the old families were very much on the defensive socially because of the recent influx of talented, prosperous, charming people. One night I was chatting in a restaurant with a woman widely regarded as one of the city's social arbiters. Her great-grandfather was an Early Settler. She had with her an elderly companion. At one point, while the companion was away from the table, she whispered to me confidentially, "You know, he's not really accepted here by some of the best families. His family was from Poughkeepsie and brought him here when he was six."

2. *By national background.* Hollingshead made an analysis of the ethnic origins of the people of New Haven and found a third were of Italian origin. Other groups in descending order of size were Irish; Russian, Polish, Austrian Jews; British-Americans; Germans; Poles; Scandinavians; Negroes.

"Although all of these groups," Hollingshead states, "have been in the community for at least a half century, they are keenly aware that their ancestors were English, Irish, Italian, Russian, German, Polish or Negro." Each group when it arrived kept to itself and developed its own occupational specialties.

He noted that as each newly arriving group has entered the occupational system the groups that have arrived earlier moved up a notch. This same phenomenon—where immigration is massive—has been observed in Hawaii, where planters have imported in succession a half-dozen nationality groups as plantation hands. The Chinese were the first to arrive. Today, few Chinese can be found on the plantations. Most of the men are in the cities in professional, proprietary, clerical, or skilled classes of employment. In New Haven, the Italians, although now numerically the largest group, were among the latest to arrive and, with immigration drying up, still have made relatively little headway in moving into the highest occupations. The great majority are still manual workers.

3. *By religion.* While the large majority of Americans are Protestant, 36,000,000 are Roman Catholic and 5,500,000 are Jewish. The social philosopher, Will Herberg, has stated that, as the melting pot gradually dissolves other differences

of newcomers such as language and dress, America will coalesce into three great sub-cultures—Protestant, Catholic, and Jewish.

There are arguments against calling Jews a race, an ethnic group, or a religious group. (For example, as a race African Jews are black, and Chinese Jews look much like other Chinese.) While many Jews who have taken up other religious faiths are still regarded as Jewish, the fact remains that religion is the primary binder that holds together the Jewish community in America. For whatever reason—whether Gentile barriers, Jewish cohesiveness, or both—Jews do tend, as we shall see in a later chapter, to lead a segregated social life. And in many communities they maintain a division among themselves. The quiet, conservative German Jews, the first large Jewish group to reach America, often turn their backs on the more flamboyant and lively Polish and Russian Jews who began arriving several decades later. In some cities, the two groups have their separate elite social clubs.

Catholics, too, tend to split up by national origin. The Irish, in some cities, remain aloof from the Italians; and the Italians do not intermingle much with the Poles.

And Protestants, especially at the elite level, frequently try to draw a line that excludes both Catholics and Jews. Some years ago, one listing of several thousand socially select New Englanders contained only about a dozen Catholics and still fewer Jews.[5]

4. *By pigmentation.* For the one American in ten who is a Negro, the boundaries of status are hardly invisible. To a somewhat lesser extent the same applies to Americans of Chinese, Mexican, or Indian origin. Among Negroes, the color of their skin is almost universally recognized as a barrier to full dignity of treatment from their fellow citizens. Consequently, many of them strain to "marry light" and tend to grant high status to fellow Negroes who have the lighter complexions. While perhaps 10,000 light-skinned Negroes "pass" the boundary each year and are accepted as white, these constitute but a tiny fraction of their race. Most of the rest must live with the grim fact that, while a white person

can sometimes work up from a low social status to a high one, a colored man can never work up to being a white man. Many restaurants in the United States which serve the most uncouth white trash would refuse to serve such a distinguished Negro as Dr. Ralph Bunche. And as Kimball Young and Raymond W. Mack have pointed out: "A Negro may be a college graduate and an experienced pilot in the U.S. Air Force and yet be rejected as a job applicant by a commercial airline needing pilots."[6]

What some can do, however, is seek to separate themselves as far as possible from the general run of lower-class Negroes through achievement and style of life. Across their caste line they have set up a horizontal social structure based on the white model. And many Negroes have been able to move up from the bottom (Class V) to Classes IV, III and in a few cases to Classes II and I. They have been moving into skilled, clerical, managerial, and professional jobs. Some have built fortunes. *Ebony* magazine estimates that several hundred Negroes now have assets of more than $100,000. They have built their fortunes in real estate, the beauty business, owning restaurants, insurance, baseball, boxing, medicine, and so on. Some of these new-rich Negro businessmen with an all-Negro clientele feel something of a vested interest in segregation.

These higher-status Negroes pattern their behavior after what they perceive to be the white model. They speak softly and precisely to show they are not like noisy, low-class Negroes; they shun emotional religions; they have small families; they encourage their children to study Latin as a mark of culture; and they prefer to shop at higher-class white stores. One of Chicago's department stores was considering building a branch in an upper-middle-class Negro neighborhood. The management was advised by local informants in effect: "Don't come. You'll become a Negro store. The people here would rather go in town to your white store."

Their behavior, in short, has become more like that of their opposite class numbers among the whites than like that of the main body of their own people.

The strain of this striving for differentness and superiority is beginning to show, according to Negro sociologist E. Franklin Frazier of Howard University. They are more stiff in their behavior and more desperately absorbed in surrounding themselves with status symbols such as limousines and mink coats than their white counterparts. In fact, Frazier accuses the "black bourgeoisie" of being engaged in such a "wild flight from reality" that it is failing to provide responsible leadership for Negroes as a whole.[7]

Meanwhile, there is evidence that Negroes are no longer the lowest-prestige group among the nation's ethnics. Occupationally at least, many of the Puerto Ricans migrating to the United States—especially the darker-skinned ones—are taking over the most menial jobs. Today, in New York, it is not uncommon to see a Negro bus driver cussing out a Puerto Rican pushing a hand truck in the garment district. A decade ago it might have been an Irish bus driver cussing out a Negro.

In New York City's principal detention house for juvenile delinquents, the Negro and white boys combine to snub Puerto Ricans; and in housing developments Negro tenants often fuss in superior fashion about their new Puetro Rican neighbors.[8]

The barriers put up by other ethnics to the Puerto Ricans also are interesting. A few weeks ago, I talked with an Italian-born barbershop proprietor in a section of New York that only recently became predominantly Puerto Rican. How did the change affect his business? He said that "of course" he personally would not consider cutting a Puerto Rican's hair. However, he had solved the problem, he said, by hiring a Puerto Rican barber named Francisco. When a Puerto Rican customer comes in the door, the Italian proprietor, even if he is not busy and Francisco is busy, will call, "Hey, Francisco, here's a customer for you." He added to me, "I explain nicely to the customer that I am not accustomed to cutting his kind of hair." A few, he conceded, are offended and leave. Most stay and wait. Francisco, incidentally, is not visibly offended. The system provides him with more commissions.

We have, then, a two-dimensional class system. The horizontal levels are based on prestige deriving principally from such social-class factors as wealth, job, education, style of life. The vertical divisions are based on the seeming differentness of people caused by their ethnic background, their religion, etc. For most of us, the horizontal rankings have by far the larger impact on our lives, perhaps because they have a hard economic base and because they affect everybody. During the Depression, for example, many working-class people began to realize for the first time that their common social-class interests as workingmen were far more important to them than the religious, racial, and ethnic rivalries that had separated them. When in the remainder of the book I speak of classes I will be referring to the horizontal ones unless I qualify the reference.

If I were to try to sum up the emerging picture with another figure of speech, I would say that the class structure of the United States is more like a jungle gym than a ladder. Or to be more precise, in view of the gulf developing between the diploma elite and the supporting classes, it is like *two* jungle gyms. One jungle gym is on the ground floor of a building. The other, directly above it, is on the second floor. To move from the lower jungle gym to the higher one, you must go outside and climb up the fire escape of higher education.

We are now ready to examine, in some detail, the indicators of status that are most commonly recognized, and most commonly sought. These marks of status establish the prestige rating we receive in the class structure.

We become assigned to a certain prestige classification on the basis of not one factor but rather the combined influence of a number of factors: occupation, education, residence, family background, behavior, beliefs, income, and so on.

Consumption patterns, too, are extremely revealing. After years of studying them, Pierre Martineau, Research Director of the *Chicago Tribune*, states that our consuming and spending habits equal our position in the social-class structure.

Ideally, we should be judged on our individual skill, responsibility, and personal worth. These factors, however, in our age of movement and complex organizational structures, are often difficult to judge. We may know that the man who lives three houses down the street has something to do with the fertilizer business. What his responsibilities and income are, however, are not within our area of reliable observation, as they were in former days. Thus we tend to "place" people on the basis of what is visible: such as type of home, automobile, clothing, home furnishings. These are all visible.

In the following section we shall examine a number of these factors that, whether we like it or not, have come to be generally accepted as indicators of status. They include one's home and neighborhood, occupational rank, patterns of spending, patterns of behavior, patterns of mating, patterns of socializing, patterns of beliefs and attitudes, and patterns of indoctrinating the young.

PART TWO

marks of status

5

snob appeal = today's home sweet home

"An unbelievably lavish, hand-crafted manorial estate for a very limited number of affluent families of good taste . . . $47,900."—FROM AN ADVERTISEMENT of a Roslyn, Long Island, developer.

◄─o─►·◄─o─►·◄─o─►·◄─o─►·◄─o─►·◄─o─►·◄─o─►

THE HOME DURING THE LATE FIFTIES BEGAN SHOWING SIGNS of supplanting the automobile as the status symbol most favored by Americans for staking their status claims. There are a number of explanations for this change (see Chapter 21), but the most important one, undoubtedly, is that with the general rise of incomes and installment buying a luxuriously sculptured chariot has become too easily obtainable for the great multitudes of status strivers. A home costs more money, a lot more. Another explanation is the appearance in profusion of mass merchandisers in the home-selling field, who have become skilled—partly by copying mass-selling strategies developed in the automobile field—in surrounding their product with status meanings. Example: "Early American Luxurious Ranch . . . $27,900 & Up." That's in Long Island, not the Texas Panhandle.

While observing the 1958 convention of the nation's home builders in Chicago, I heard one of the featured speakers, a home-marketing consultant, report that he and his aides had conducted 411 "depth interviews" in eight cities to find what people are seeking when they buy a home. In many cases, he reported, mid-century home buyers are buying themselves a symbol of success; and he discussed at length strategies for giving a house being offered for sale "snob appeal."

Many other experts in home selling have recently cited "snob appeal" as one of the great secret weapons. One strategy, he said, is to drop some French phrases in your advertisements. French, he explained, is the language of the snob. Later in the year, we began seeing newspaper advertisements of housing developers drenched in French. One, penned by a developer in Manetto Hills, Long Island, exclaimed: *"C'est Magnifique! Une maison Ranch très originale avec 8 rooms, 2½ baths . . . 2-Cadillac garage . . . $21,990 . . . No cash for veterans."* And a builder in Bel Air, Florida, unveiled his $42,000 chateaus by proclaiming his prototype *"une autre maison contemporaine de Floride."* His entire ad, except for the price, was in French. Some builders began referring to their 15' x 18' living room as "The Living Forum" or the "Reception Galleria," and to their 9' x 14' bedroom as "The Sleeping Chamber." A split-level house on Long Island became "a Georgian split, with a bi-level brunch bar in a maître d' kitchen." And tiny parcels of ground became "Huge ⅗ acre Estate Sites." According to one rule-of-thumb, cited by a building consultant, any lot larger than one-fourth acre can reasonably be described as an "estate," and anything larger than half an acre can be labeled as a "farm."

American families in the past few years have been giving more and more thought to the problem of establishing a home that adequately reinforces the status image they wish to project of themselves. And home builders have happily helped the trend along by emphasizing status appeals. William Molster, who directs the merchandising activities of the National Association of Home Builders, confirms this new trend in home selling. He points out that postwar builders who erected minimum-shelter mass communities to answer the war-stimulated demand are being replaced by the builders who are carefully sizing up the desires and needs of their market.

Today, he states, the status symbol in home selling has become a key to large-volume business.

A Pittsburgh home-selling consultant, in telling builders how to sell to the "snob," advised salesmen in their selling pitches to stress such phrases as "upper brackets," "exclusive neighborhood," and "executive-type buyers."

One developer outside Chicago, in describing to me the buyers of his $20,000–$30,000 houses, called them "striving, frightened people." He plays upon both those traits, he happily explained, in promoting the sale of his houses. This man, another enthusiast of the motivational approach to home selling, helps the buyers feel that buying a home in his higher-priced development "means they have arrived." He plays the role of the lofty, temperamental designing genius. His aides are instructed not to permit a prospective couple to consult with him about possible distinctive, made-to-order touches and accessories for their prospective home, such as a chandelier, until they have placed a token deposit to demonstrate genuine interest. His approach, in talking with the wife of the prospective buyer, is to help her see the $40,000 home as a "love symbol." He has noticed that most of his buyers are newly prosperous people—not the kind who inherit wealth—and the husband has struggled so long and arduously at his pajama factory that he has had little time to demonstrate his love to his wife. Thus, the builder shrewdly offers his house to the neglected lady as something she "deserves." (A Kansas City builder has drawn many prospects by advertising a "love couch" in the master bedroom for marital courting.)

In moving to a higher-income level, we find the same striving, but in a somewhat more discreet form. Researchers for the *Chicago Tribune*, exploring the attitudes of people in the semi-elite suburb they studied, summed up the prevailing attitude toward homes in this way: "You have to *look* successful. A house is a very tangible symbol of success . . . and the residents regard it as a goal and a symbol, as well as something to live in."

A man promoted to the vice-presidency of a machinery company, with headquarters in New York City, explained that he had bought a better house and finer furniture because he felt obliged to live on a higher scale. He felt that expectation was a part of the promotion.

One of the most spectacularly successful men who set himself up as a builder in an Eastern Seaboard town in the postwar era saw what he thought was a way to make a strike. He perceived this opportunity while trying to analyze why so many businessmen with New York offices sought homes in this town, which had a reputation as an upper-class settlement. Its natural beauties were surpassed by a number of others within commuting range of New York. He deduced, I'm told, that most of the prospects were "status-climbing phonies."

Armed with that insight, he set out to offer them for about $50,000 what they really wanted, a big show of genteelness. This builder constructed the biggest-looking house he could. He bore down heavily on the old New England look. Every house had a pair of coach lanterns outside. Inside, he skimped, used the cheapest materials he could. Instead of using hardwood floors, he installed soft wood covered with plastic tile. He used steel bathtubs, plastic bathroom tile, did little insulating, and installed the lowest-cost heating system available. His homes became enormously popular. I'm told he plans soon to take his profits and settle down far from the Eastern Seaboard. Meanwhile, another builder in the same town famed among experts for the quality of his houses was having a desperate time staying in business.

The really successful corporate executives do not, especially in the East, favor the gaudy palaces common at the turn of the century. Servants are usually kept discreetly in the background—shadows (but still visible)—at dinner parties, instead of paraded as showpieces. The master himself may cook the steaks over the wide, and often elevated, living-room fireplace. He must do this carefully, and without the benefit of too many Scotches, or grease may drip on the wall-to-wall carpeting.

In the Northeast, at least, the top executive is likely to have a gem of an estate, beautifully manicured on the outside, highly polished on the inside. The house will be Georgian, Colonial, Federal, old English, or old French, with clipped hedge or rustic fence, and, inside, a central hallway and period furniture. There will be old portraits or family portraits on the walls of the living room, and, if there is wallpaper—there probably won't be—it will be used just to add decorative touches. Most of the walls will be painted a solid color, usually with dark trim. The rugs will be either a solid-color wall-to-wall type or Oriental. The built-in bookcases will contain mostly leather-bound volumes. The gleaming, mahogany dining-room table will be enhanced with silver candlesticks. The walnut-paneled den, with its green- or red-leather chairs, will have old hunting and sailing prints. The decor probably was supervised by an interior decorator specializing in the executive look.

As you move a block or two away to the vice-presidential-level home, you find much the same but on a less sedate and authentic scale. The vice-presidents' wives, as Russell Lynes has pointed out, seem "a little quicker to point out the really good pieces of furniture, and to tell you something about the artist who painted the picture over the mantel."

In Texas, of course, you find a little more flamboyance, even in executives. The houses are likely to be the rambling-ranch type, but with expensive details. A Dallas builder, specializing in catering to businessmen who feel a need for homes in the $100,000 to $250,000 bracket, has built one section that he calls "President's Row" because so many heads of companies live there. The houses he builds have such distinctive touches as His and Her bathrooms, color television in the bedroom ceiling, push-button drapes, air-conditioned dog houses, authentic soda fountains, and hallway fountains. "Our clients," he says, "like these little touches of plushiness." And he added, "We try to create a desire to keep up with the Rockefellers. Then, you've got to have snob appeal."

A great deal of thought, on the part of builders, has gone into finding symbols of higher status that will provoke gasps of pleasure from prospective buyers. And the higher-status people themselves have obviously given a good deal of thought to symbols that will produce the same results with guests in their homes.

The favored way to do this, in many areas in America, is by the use of symbols indicating the owner has ties that go back into American history. One of the wealthiest suburban areas in America, the Green Bay Road of Lake Forest, Illinois, still uses gas lights. In fact, the residents have resisted proposals for modernization to the extent of setting up a society for the prevention of improvement of their road. A builder in Charlotte, North Carolina, now is putting flickering gas lamps on the outside of his most expensive models.

A Midwestern man who had made many millions of dollars moved to the North Shore area of Boston, built himself a tremendous Italian-style villa. His wealthy neighbors shunned him. After brooding about his ostracism for a few years, he diagnosed the trouble, tore down his villa, and replaced it with an Early American type estate. The hostility eased, and now his family is well accepted.

A large development firm in the Detroit area promotes its new "estates" with expensive brochures illustrated with a host of Early American symbols: hitching posts, spinning wheels, muskets, town-crier bells, horseshoes, old lanterns, wooden eagles. This firm converted an ancient stable on one of its tracts into a historical museum, as a crowd drawer. It placed gray-haired hostesses in period costumes in its model homes, and it transported prospects about the project in horse-drawn carriages.

In San Jose, California, a builder tries to make each prospective buyer feel like a bona fide frontiersman or woman. His promotions are heavily flavored with historical allusions. They exhort: "TRADE IN YOUR LOG CABIN FOR A BEAUTIFUL NEW FIRESIDE HOME." They offer prospects of "warmth" and the "good things in life for which the pioneers came to this fertile valley in the West." Instead of talking about two-Cadillac garages, they advise prospects that they can park "two Conestogas" in their "extra large wagon shed." The talk about financial terms, however, is strictly twentieth century: "$16,-950–$18,450. . . . No Down to Vets."

Illumination on what this is all about came to me from Richard Doan of Newtown, Connecticut, who, until recently, was a highly respected dealer in antiques, and is now a radio executive. Mr. Doan said that most of the persistent buyers of antiques "definitely are trying to give themselves an Early American background. They buy a pair of ancestor portraits and, after a few years, they find themselves telling people that those ancient people in the portraits are their own great-grandparents. That is fairly common." Concerning the problem of selling antiques, he said, "It is my impression that class appeal is involved, snob appeal. Only one buyer in fifty has any real interest in antiques. The rest are giving themselves family backgrounds." The same motivation is involved, he felt, in much of the purchasing of pre-Revolutionary homes. Before long, he said, the buyers "try to make it seem to be the old family homestead." He told me of a vice-president of an advertising agency, living in Westchester County, who bought a tri-cornered hat. He puts it on when he comes home at night and "steps down into the eighteenth century."

Mr. Doan related that one night he and his wife were watching Edward R. Murrow's television program, "Person-to-Person," while Mr. Murrow was "visiting" the New York apartment of a theatrical celebrity. The camera came to rest on a pair of eighteenth-century portraits. The Doans gasped in excitement. The portraits had, a few years before, hung in their own living room until they had found a buyer. The theatrical celebrity modestly explained to Mr. Murrow, "Ed, those aren't my folks. . . . They're my wife's ancestors."

Support for the Doan thesis on the purchase of antiques comes from the suburban study conducted by the *Chicago Tribune*. It was found that, if a suburbanite aspires to move up into the "lower-upper class, he will buy antiques—symbols of old social position bought with new money."

Antiques, in some cases, become so important for their symbolic value that they are cherished even when their functional value is dubious. If you walk along Beacon Street, Boston, you may note that certain windows have defective panes. The glass is purplish. The defectiveness of those panes is highly cherished. The panes were part of a shipment of inferior glass foisted off on Americans by English glassmakers more than three centuries ago.

In Wichita, Kansas, too, you will find many homes with symbolic features of uncertain utilitarian value. In one development of picturesque houses ($35,000), which look like something out of *Grimm's Fairy Tales,* you may see false holes near the gables. Those false holes have symbolic importance. French aristocrats used to have these holes in their homes as roosts for hunting birds. The symbolic importance of the holes is that only aristocrats in early France were permitted to own guns, and so only they had holes in their gables. The holes were, in an earlier era at least, an important status symbol.

The man who alerted me to this false-hole situation was James Mills, researcher and publisher of *Home Facts* (for home builders). He and his staff have spent two years making a nationwide study of the new trends in home selling. Mr. Mills finds that, in merchandising homes to present-day Americans, "you get a very layered situation." Foremen, he explains, don't want to buy in the same development with workmen. They want to buy a house in another development well known to offer homes at a higher price.

Another common device people employ to enhance their class status through their homes is to add casual but obviously costly touches. One touch coming into increasing popularity is the gold-plated bathroom fixture. Gene Dreyfus, vice-president of Cooperative Homebuilders (northwest of Chicago), showed me a gold-plated faucet, and said he has found it has such tremendous appeal that he is starting to introduce it, as an optional accessory, in some of the houses in his higher-priced ($30,000 to $50,000) development. The gold faucet, he has found, is a little $500 extra that provides the buyer with an excellent conversation piece, and adds substantially to the resale value of the house.

The air conditioner is similarly cherished in many areas as an obviously costly, status-enhancing touch. It has two features of special interest, whatever its utilitarian value, from the standpoint of status enhancement. First, it is still uncommon enough in homes in most areas to provoke conversation. And, second, evidence of its presence can be seen by outsiders passing the home. This visibility factor was a potent force in selling television to the three lower classes in TV's early days. Within a city or development, TV aerials did not begin appearing at random. Instead, they began sprouting in clusters. When one pioneering family put up its aerial for all to see, nearby neighbors felt impelled to emulate the pioneer.

Even today, the TV aerial has symbolic significance in some areas of the nation. In the southwest corner of Michigan, for example, the most conspicuous feature of the landscape is the proliferation of tremendously high TV aerials. Some, on tripod towers, are fifty-five feet in height. Many two-room shacks have thirty-foot towers above them, which might, one would imagine, topple the homesteads if a really strong wind struck. In many cases, installation of the tower costs as much as the TV set inside the home. What is more puzzling is the fact that houses on high ground are likely to have towers just as high as nearby houses on low-lying ground. A native informant, with electronic training, informed me that many of the houses could get perfectly good reception with a ten-foot aerial, but that their owners bought the towers "in order to stay even with their neighbors. . . . Around here there has been prestige in having a high aerial."

The status strivers also seek out goods for home decoration that can be pointed to as hand wrought. As Veblen pointed out some decades ago, hand labor is a more wasteful way to produce goods than machine labor; and so the handmade product, with its crudeness and its imperfections which can be pointed to, and its obvious costliness, is cherished as a status symbol for the well-bred and the well-heeled. The display given, in upper-class homes, to man-blown glassware is a case in point.

The owner of a linen shop in Stamford, Connecticut, reports that she is enjoying a substantial boom in the sale of initialed towels, which are bought almost exclusively for guest-room bathrooms or downstairs powder rooms. It is her impression, she says, that most of her sales are to women who are in a hurry. They are rushing to get their houses ready for the arrival of important guests.

Finally, visible signs of culture have their value in conveying the impression of high status. James Mills, the home-marketing expert, argues that one reason the home is replacing the automobile as a favored way for demonstrating status is that a home can be a showcase for "culture." In a home you can display antiques, old glassware, leather-bound books, classical records, paintings. These are things a car can't do. And the American home-buying public currently is on what some building experts call a "Kultural kick." In the mass home market, the room that used to be the "game room" became first the "recreation room" and is now the "den" or "study." Soon, Mills predicts, it will be the "library." Whatever the name of the space, Mills acknowledges sadly, people shove a television set into it and sit around it at night in semi-darkness.

The family with a large, well-read library usually is indeed a family of high intellectual attainment, and at least some affluence. Some, however, seek shortcuts. A high administrative officer of one of the largest universities in the East bought a large house befitting his eminence. Since he wanted his new home to convey to visitors a sense of high intellectuality, he went to a local bookstore and placed a large order for used books by "good" authors. He proposed to pay for them by the yard.

Aside from all the status striving, some features of the home do afford quite reliable clues as to the social class of the owner. One is the infatuation found among the higher classes for well-aged objects. An Englishman pointed out to me that, in his country, the upper classes cherish their old grates in stoves, whereas people in the lower classes take pride in new ones. The lower classes have never grasped the subtlety of honoring the long-used object. Perhaps they have had too much forced experience with hand-me-downs. If the upper-class person does have to endure newness, as in a home or piece of furniture, he would like it to be ultra-modern. People in the lower classes are frightened by modernity. One very large maker of prefabricated houses found itself in trouble because it took the word of a leading architect that "contemporary" one-pitch roof and openness of interior design were what everyone wanted these days. Today, this mass-marketing firm has gone back to the traditional house with the interior clearly divided into separate rooms as its mainstay.

In the matter of color preferences, there is also a parting of the ways along class lines. The Color Research Institute of Chicago has found, from sampling the responses of many thousands of people, that people in the higher classes (higher income and higher education) favor muted and delicate colors, whereas the lower classes like their colors in brilliant hues and large doses. They particularly like the warm, bold reds and orange reds. And, I might add, their preference for paintings (reproductions) for their walls run to orange or pink sunsets, which an upper-class person professes to find revolti.1g, or to highly sentimental scenes, which are equally objectionable to the upper-class person. (Greeting cards preferred by the three supporting classes likewise tend to run to flowers and to what the diploma elite considers to be excessive sentimentality.)

You find much the same sort of separation regarding preference for design as you go down the class scale. The upper class favors the primly severe, the lower class the frankly garish. Pierre Martineau relates that his investigators asked people of all classes to choose, from pictures, their favorite homes and home furnishings. They found people completely different in taste as they move up the scale. The lower class likes more "frills on everything," whereas the upper class wants things to be "more austere, plain." This showed up, for example, in the preference for sofas. The lower-class people preferred a sofa with tassels hanging from the arms and fringe around the bottom. The high-status people preferred a sofa with simple, severe, right-angled lines. People in the working class, I could add, are prone to attaching an imitation-brick wing onto an aluminum trailer and calling it home.

Social Research, Inc., of Chicago, in its study of the tastes of the Wage Town, or workingman's, wife for Macfadden Publications, found: "The Wage-Town wife thinks in terms of 'decoration' rather than 'decor.' She uses bright colors and bold pattern, and side-by-side mixtures of both. Muted tones and severe lines are apt to be too 'cold' for her taste. What might seem garish to the white-collar wife is 'warm' or 'cheerful' to the Wage Earner wife." In another study, Social Research, Inc., found that the upper classes in most cases prefer solid-color rugs, whereas patterned rugs become more popular as you go down the scale.

Furthermore, as W. Lloyd Warner has pointed out, the cost of home furnishings is not necessarily the determining factor in what is bought. The woman whom he calls Mrs. Middle Majority (from what he calls the upper-lower and lower-middle classes) fills her kitchen with more appliances than the upper-class woman does. Perhaps it is because the kitchen looms larger in the life of Mrs. Middle Majority, and is often the center of her world. The upper-class wife would rather put the money into a little Braque for her living-room wall, or into riding school for her daughter.

One interesting further distinction between the horizontal social classes is the uneasiness that people in the lower classes feel about socializing with neighbors in developments. Craig Smith, Vice-President of Detroit's Sullivan-Smith, feels that the main difference between blue- and white-collar working people who are thrown together in a development is that the blue-collar people are not gregarious. They feel insecure, and are more likely to become lonely. To illustrate, Mr. Smith said, "We find these blue-collar people resist the idea of sharing a driveway with a neighbor. They are afraid of an argument with the neighbors, or an invasion of their privacy. The white-collared people wouldn't mind."

Privacy is tremendously important, James Mills pointed out, to people of working-class background who may have had to sleep three or four to a room sometime in their lives. They want walls around every room, and they want doors to the rooms, not entry ways. The open layout characteristic of "contemporary" houses, with rooms often divided only by furnishings, frightens them. On the other hand, a West Coast builder of "contemporary" houses has become famous in home-selling circles for his success as a mass builder for eggheads. His open houses, severely "contemporary" and terribly *avant-garde,* have been tremendously popular in an area near the Stanford University campus favored by local intelligentsia. Eggheads have enough self-assurance so that they can defy convention, and they often cherish the simplicity of open layout.

As we move from the horizontal social-class groupings to the vertical ethnic-class groupings, we find even more clear-cut differentiations in preference for homes and home furnishing. As Mr. Smith, who has had a great deal of experience analyzing the preference of the many nationality groups of the Detroit area, stated: "Each of the ethnic groups has its particular tastes in housing. It is enough to drive one crazy."

Detroiters who trace their ancestry to Great Britain are most likely to favor what some builders jovially call "Early American gestunk." They want a white fence and the white clapboard house. Mr. Smith pointed out that they like the "snob appeal" (there's that phrase again) of a rustic-looking lantern. They typically want their house to be made of wood. Any brick used should be the reclaimed, ancient-looking kind.

Americans of Italian background insist, more than any other group, on having a dining room even if it means sacrificing a bedroom or chopping up the living room. They have a strong family spirit, and like to sit around the table after a good meal, chatting. They also like what builder Gene Dreyfus calls "lots of goop" in their houses—shadow boxes, splashes of marble, stucco, and rococo furnishings.

As for the Polish-Americans, they like their homes to be "very garish, with loud, screaming colors," according to one builder. (Among Polish-Americans of Buffalo, pink and turquoise are preferred in decorative touches.) Polish-Americans want their houses to be of brick, and they want it to be hard "face" brick. They also demand a large kitchen. Mr. Smith pointed out that they will not accept the supposedly chic, open-beams, or studio-type, construction. It reminds them of the barns they knew back in Poland. Furthermore, they resist the idea of the rear-view living room, so popular with many builders. They want their living room to look out on the street, Mr. Smith explained, and they want a big picture window in that living room, and in that window they want to be able to place an enormous lamp. I thought perhaps Mr. Smith was generalizing, but some months ago I passed through a large Polish section of Chicago and I noticed that fully 80 per cent of the homes did indeed have picture windows facing out on the street with huge, often old-fashioned, lamps in the middle of them.

Jewish people (who sometimes are categorized, loosely, as an ethnic group) are, perhaps, most interesting of all in their preference for homes and home furnishings. As Gene Dreyfus put it, Jewish people "don't care about having a back yard." While a prosperous Gentile will want his grounds to be as large as possible (and with a winding driveway), the Jew is a little horrified at the thought of owning a place with large grounds. First of all, he and his wife like to be close enough to neighbors so that they can talk back and forth. Furthermore, frequently the Jewish man has neither the temperament nor the know-how to putter around trimming hedges or repairing screen doors, or other delights of the do-it-yourself. Relatively few Jews ever earn their livelihood at manual work, and so are not handy at such things; and, in fact, are often appalled by the prospect of them.

Jewish people prefer stone or face-brick construction to wood. And, more than any other group, Jews are receptive to "contemporary" architecture, with its openness and modernity. They don't try to prove through their houses that they had ancestors in pre-Revolutionary Vermont, as one builder put it, because no one would believe them if they did try to. In one high-cost area northwest of Detroit, there are more than seven hundred upper-class homes, from which Jews are excluded. Virtually all the houses are copies of Early American. Bordering this settlement is a predominantly Jewish community where the houses also are high cost. Seventy-five per cent of these houses are modern or "contemporary." Although many of these houses are beautifully designed, one Jewish builder deplored this juxtaposition. He felt it gave the already prejudiced Gentiles a physical evidence of Jewish "differentness" to point to.

Jews, as this would indicate, have their own upper class, and their own way of achieving high status within their group. Near Chicago there is a new development of "one-maid" split-level houses occupied primarily by young married Jews, many under thirty years of age. I'll call it Grandview. Most of the houses of Grandview are close together on plots of less than one-third acre. Houses nearby, just across the boundary from Grandview, which look very much like the houses inside Grandview, sell for around $45,000. The houses inside the Grandview border sell at prices ranging from $55,000 to $100,000. The land on which this high-priced development is built is flat and unwooded. Some of it is reclaimed swampland. Grandview has neither water view nor commanding view nor fine old trees to recommend it to the elite, yet some of the land, when broken up into lots, has been sold for as much as $50,000 an acre.

I have tried to indicate that, based on objective factors alone, these houses, while tastefully and carefully built, are no great prize at the price charged. Yet they are in tremendous demand, and the developer of Grandview does virtually no advertising. An envious Jewish builder, showing me this colony, explained why these houses were in such demand, "If you are a Jewish person, you have arrived if you get one of these homes."

He explained that those Jewish parents who, in recent years, have succeeded in an outstanding way financially, want their sons and daughters starting out in marriage to have the "best," and Grandview is believed by them to be the best. It has had an aura of social selectness around it from the beginning. My guide pointed out that residents of Grandview do not own Cadillacs, and do not send their children to private school. "They don't need to," he explained. "They've managed to get one of these houses." Later, he introduced me to Grandview's developer, who cheerfully acknowledged that Grandview homes were unsurpassed status symbols for a young Jew. The developer said, "There is a snob appeal in getting in here in the first place. The buyers like the idea of living in this general area because it has one of the highest per capita incomes in the country . . . and it is well known that I have an expensive house."

The role of the neighborhood in helping fix one's status with the status-conscious will be explored more fully in the following chapter.

6

choosing a proper address

"We had to eliminate a few places that were pretty good simply because I knew they were poor addresses for a management man in our company."—Wall Street Journal, quoting a young personnel official of a food company who was relating some "basic decisions" he had to make.

◄─◎─►·◄─◎─►·◄─◎─►·◄─◎─►·◄─◎─►·◄─◎─►

A PERSON WHO HAS LIVED TWENTY YEARS IN THE SAME HOUSE, as many pre-1950 Americans did, usually will not bother to tear up his roots and move simply because the house no longer accurately reflects his status in the community. He has learned to love the place. Joe Chapin, of John O'Hara's *Ten North Frederick,* didn't leave his stately homestead on North Frederick Street simply because that street over the years had been supplanted by the newer Lantenengo Street as the place where people who begin "to amount to something" go. However, with our greatly increased geographic mobility—more than 25,000 United States families move and face new neighbors every day—millions of Americans judge not only homes but neighborhoods much more carefully than before, if only at the subconscious level, in terms of status attached to them. And they strive, in their home hopping, to upgrade themselves with each hop as far as they dare. A housewife in Glenview, Illinois, when asked by sociologists what her goal was ten years hence, said, "I would like a bigger home in the adjacent village of Golf, which is much more exclusive."[1]

The importance people attach to address can be seen in two items involving Long Island. A builder in Manhasset, in promoting his houses, began stressing that: "Most important—your address is Munsey Park; and Munsey Park in Manhasset is more than an address, it is a symbol of tradition and prestige—a supreme achievement in luxurious, suburban living." Meanwhile, a group of residents living a few miles away in the northern part of Wantagh, which is adjacent to Levittown, sued the United States government in an effort to get their mailing address changed. The Post Office Department had ruled that their area, for convenience, be served by the nearby Levittown Post Office. Levittown is nationally known as the site of one of the nation's most famous housing developments. The group bringing the suit wanted their mailing address changed to "North Wantagh."

People at the management level working for a large company who move—or are moved—to a new community frequently find there is a design at work that dictates (or tries to dictate) where they will nest. It is just as dangerous to move into an area above their level as one that is below. They might, in fact, find themselves on the receiving end of some quiet organized discipline if they try to move into a neighborhood dominated by people from a clearly higher level than themselves in the hierarchy at the company.

Even when we go down the scale to the limited-success level, there still is a great deal of anxious concern about the status meaning of the particular home the family will have in a new neighborhood. People see themselves establishing a social beachhead, and the big question in their minds is whether they are going to be accepted. The builder of a development of split-level houses, Lawrence Park, in Delaware County, Pennsylvania, conducted a motivational study, directed by a University of Pennsylvania professor, among his home buyers to find their subconscious motives in making the move to his development. Many of the buyers were moving out from Philadelphia row houses or multiple dwellings. The developer, Ralph Bodek, reports: "Moving to Lawrence Park represented an improvement in social status for many buyers. They like this idea of improvement, but they also fear it. They hope they will be accepted by the new neighbors. At the same time, they hope that they are not taking on too much new status. . . ." He quotes one buyer as saying, "I sure hope there are people like me who will not look down their nose at me." Fear was expressed that owners of the big "custom" homes in the neighborhood would "look down" on the people in the development. At the same time, many new buyers were impressed by these expensive, "custom" homes near the development. "They deduced," Mr. Bodek reports, "that such a neighborhood would bring their children into contact with people of better culture."[2]

The W. Lloyd Warner group, studying Yankee City, found that the social meaning of neighborhoods was so important that people there used street names to designate social classes. The investigators found, for example, that people referred to as "Hill Streeters" often actually didn't live on Hill Street (upper class); and they found that people designated as "Riverbrook" people often didn't actually live in Riverbrook (lowest class). They concluded that these terms were oblique, "democratic" ways to indicate social-class designations without crudely specifying them.

The importance of neighborhood, as an indication of class status, is also seen in a sociological study of wedding announcements of sons and daughters of socially prominent people in a New York newspaper. For one third of the families covered, two addresses were given, both fashionable.[3] Thus, the announcement might identify the proud parents, to use a fictional case, by saying: "Mr. and Mrs. John Coyle Tarryton III, of 783 Park Avenue, New York, and 'Hideaway,' Fisher's Island, N.Y. . . ."

Every city has its one area where there is an especially heavy concentration of upper-class people. Although New York City covers 315 square miles, most of the rich and fashionable live in just one of these square miles: the area between Sixty-fifth Street and Seventy-eighth Street on the east side of Central Park, from Fifth Avenue to Third Avenue.[4] (Others argue that the north-south boundaries should be extended to Eighty-sixth and Sixtieth Streets with added tiny clusters along the East River.) In Houston, River Oaks, with its costly castles, is as fashionable an address as you can have. In Atlanta, it is the Buckhead section; in New Orleans, it is Bayou Liberty; and in Charleston, South Carolina, it is the wedge formed by South Battery and East Battery. While Philadelphia and Boston have several islands for the elite, the name Chestnut Hill, by coincidence, is unsurpassed for prestige in both.

And each community has its own way of deciding where the elite can be found. With many, elevation is the principal factor. As you wind your way up Lookout Mountain outside Chattanooga, Tennessee, the homes become more and more costly. A hillside in Waterbury, Connecticut, has mostly working people at the bottom and mostly elite at the top. Hundreds of people in the Hollywood movie colony live in the area of Beverly Hills, north of Santa Monica Boulevard. As you go up the very gradual rise from the boulevard, the yards become wider and the houses larger. By the time you reach the homes of Jack Benny and Desi Arnaz, they are very wide and very large indeed. Recently, an acquaintance of mine took me on a tour of the most elite section of Erie, Pennsylvania. We seemed to keep rising as we drove, and when he came to the most spectacular houses of all, he said, "This is the highest point in town." Even within homogeneous developments (which, for economy reasons, are most often built in potato fields or areas bulldozed flat), prospects compete for the houses on high ground, and hold back (even when bargain prices are quoted) from buying low-lying homes others can look down upon.

In some communities, nearness to water is the prime determinant of elite residential location. Sociologist Ernest R. Mowrer of Northwestern University has been making a long-term study of the residential patterns of the Chicago suburbs. He points out that along the North Shore the towns, such as Winnetka and Wilmette, overwhelmingly are settled by executives and professionals. As you go back from the water, you find occasional islands of wealth, but in general you start encountering the lower levels of business people (small merchants and salesmen). By the time you reach Des Plaines, you find whole neighborhoods of skilled trades. Much the same pattern exists along Boston's North Shore.

Nearness to the golf course becomes the measure of eliteness of address in many other towns. In communities such as Lancaster, Pennsylvania, Wichita Falls, Texas, and Bel Air, California, many of the most-prized home sites face the golf course. A realtor who was showing an executive's wife possible homes in Darien, Connecticut, received pretty explicit instructions on where to look. The wife said, "My husband recently became vice-president of his company. . . . We want to be in the club area."

A friend of mine in suburban Connecticut recently had a neighbor, a thirty-six-year-old vice-president, whose social-climbing tendencies were notorious in the neighborhood. He sought aggressively to get onto every status-giving community project. Although he had bought a new $60,000 house, he had blundered into a relaxed, non-socially-conscious neighborhood that was not regarded by the elite of the town as a particularly good address. Within fourteen months he sold his house and moved to a more expensive and less well-built house that was a quarter of a mile from the golf course.

In this same town the most successful real-estate salesman is an astute woman. She earns $20,000 to $25,000 a year in fees because she is fully aware she is selling an address as much as a home. She sells the community and its upper-class citizens. Regardless of the particular house she plans to show a prospect, she manages to get there by a route that passes the country club. She waves to members and chats in familiar terms about its more notable members.

To continue with the factors that make a neighborhood highly fashionable, in many towns an area becomes the most elite in town simply because the area's leading citizen decided to build or buy there. Sam G. Russell, Denver realtor, points out that all the houses in an area rise tremendously in value when that happens. The houses are "still the same houses" but "immediately there is a demand" for homes and home sites near the noted personage. For many years, realtors in mid-Fairfield County usually mentioned that Lily Pons, the celebrated singer, lived "just around the corner" if they were showing a house within a four-square-mile area centering on her home in Norwalk, Connecticut. Actually, she "lived" there only in a legal sense. It was a rare year that she visited her property even once. She has since disposed of the property to a builder who promptly split up most of it into a dozen building sites.

Still other towns use the railroad track as the dividing line for separating the select from the non-select.

And in many cities the desirability of an address can be determined by its distance from the downtown business district. Most of the prize fighters are recruited from the lower, most hard-pressed segments of our society; and a sociological study of their origins has revealed that virtually all of those investigated came from the run-down, blighted areas next to the downtown business districts. In Chicago, for example, the fighters came from the Near South and Near West Sides.

Cities, like trees, grow by adding rings at their perimeters. As you move outward from the center, the houses tend to become progressively less aged, and (other things being equal) more desirable for those who can pay the higher prices. A few old high-prestige neighborhoods manage, by investing in paint and polish, to maintain their status; but most areas lose their elite status within thirty to fifty years. Their middle-aged mansions become funeral parlors or Moose lodges. Even

Boston's long-elite Beacon Hill and New York's Riverside Drive are far past their prime.

The pressure is always outward. Members of minority groups who have managed to succeed financially as businessmen or professionals seek to move out from the blighted, overcrowded central area where their people have been confined. They hope to set themslves apart from their still-depressed lower-class neighbors and live in the better houses that they now can afford. Their new neighbors note only their East European-sounding names or their tan skins, and recoil in panic. They make no distinction between these successful, well-educated people, who by all objective socio-economic standards are their own kind of people, and the masses who have the same foreign-sounding names or dark skins. (Some of the most beautiful modern buildings in America, for example, are being designed by Negro architects.) As the residents hasten to sell, before the inundation they have been led to fear sets in, real-estate values sometimes fall. This permits the poorer members of these minority groups to afford to move into the area, and soon the character of the neighborhood is transformed. Realtors have been known to encourage the panic by calling property owners and asking them if they want to sell before it is too late. The people who profit most from a fast turnover of a neighborhood, of course, are the realtors. They work on commission. A panic sale of 10,000 houses within a year can bring them $5,000,000 in fees. In one area of New York City, a public school within one year underwent a complete turnover from light-skinned to dark-skinned students. A large area of Chicago has undergone four virtually complete turnovers of population since 1940: from white-collar white to poor Southern white to Japanese to Negro.

White homeowners in the Springfield Garden section of Queens, New York City, have been conducting a fascinating battle to maintain a racially balanced community. For many years, individual Negro families have lived amicably in this community of one- and two-family houses; and in the past five there has been some increase in spots. The trend has been aggravated by real-estate dealers from outside the area. Almost every spring and fall they have attempted "block-busting" tactics on the residents. As soon as one house was sold to Negroes, there would be a swarm of real-estate agents excitedly going up and down the street, telephoning, and passing circulars. They would report that the entire block was going Negro and tell people they had cash offers for their houses.

In 1958, many of the residents, weary of these block-busting tactics, began holding block meetings to check the rumors and hold the line. At one meeting, a homeowner said realtors had told his neighbors he had already sold his house (a report without basis). In the fall of 1958, many dozens of residents began putting up "Not For Sale" signs to keep real-estate men away and to check rumors.

In Detroit, many whites along Chicago Boulevard who panicked and sold their homes to Negroes have, on second thought, been moving back and getting fine values on their underpriced former homes.

One of the firmly held articles of faith among realtors and homeowners is that property values go down when a Negro family moves into a white neighborhood. This permits people to put discrimination on a we're-tolerant-but-you-gotta-be-realistic basis. The Commission on Race and Housing, which, with the help of social scientists from a dozen universities, spent three years investigating the residential problems of non-whites in mid-century America, looked into this assumption of a deterioration of values.[5]

It found that sometimes values go down, sometimes they remain stable, and sometimes they go up. The values usually go down only where the neighborhood is run down anyway, and the entry of non-whites simply provides "evidence" of the deterioration, or where the neighbors panic and glut the market with houses for sale. In such cases, the expectation of a drop in value thus becomes a "self-fulfilling prophecy." The report said: "On the other hand, if white residents of an area are in no hurry to leave, but non-whites are eager to come in, the pressure of non-white demand may bid up the price of houses. Several situations of this type have been observed. . . ." It added: "In general, the conclusion seems warranted that non-white entry into residential areas does not necessarily depress real estate market values. . . . Among neighborhoods actually investigated for this Commission . . . the entry of non-whites was found to have had either no effect or a favorable effect on property-selling prices in the majority of cases." "Inundation" is particularly unlikely if the area in question is some distance removed from the nearest large settlement of non-whites; if the area has not physically deteriorated; and if the prices asked would appeal only to middle- or higher-income non-whites.

When waves of settlers move out of the run-down residential area surrounding the business district, the void nowadays is typically filled not by immigrants from Europe, as in earlier decades, but by migrants from American soil: Southern Negroes and Puerto Ricans. In Buffalo, New York, for example, as medium-income whites moved to the suburbs, the white population of the city dropped approximately 13,000. This loss was more than made up by an influx of 14,000 Negroes. One Negro official has complained, "Before long most of the city will be Negro, the suburbs white. That's segregation all over again."[6] Undoubtedly, he was being overly pessimistic. Negroes constitute only 10 per cent of Buffalo's population today, and the city planners are struggling valiantly to reverse the flow of whites across the city lines.

Planners in other cities are grappling with this same problem. Philadelphia is now one-fifth Negro. Many of the Negroes live in the low-income "blighted" central area, and can make only a relatively small tax contribution to the city's exciting billion-dollar program for urban renewal. Mayor Richardson P. Dilworth, in 1958, blamed the city's growing ratio of Negroes on what he called the "white noose" around Philadelphia. Tens of thousands of whites have moved to the suburbs, and a number of suburbs do not welcome Negroes. People in at least one fought violently to repel them. Mayor Dilworth hopes to correct the situation by abolishing slums, wooing back whites, and breaking the noose.[7]

Meanwhile, the Commission on Race and Housing predicts

that by 1970 "many cities" will find non-whites and Puerto Ricans constituting at least a third of their total population if their present city limits remain and if current trends in the circulation of people are not altered.

We have recently been seeing the outpouring of tens of millions of people who can afford it (and who are acceptable) to suburbs mass-produced to house them. Many of these new communities are geared to specific economic levels and, in some instances, to people of specific religious and ethnic groups. And thousands of these development "communities" are—by dictate of the builders—100 per cent white. Racial segregation is much more sweeping in new development-type towns than in established, old-fashioned-type communities. The Commission on Race and Housing charges that the mass builders have done much to intensify racial segregation in America.

The result of all this clustering by kind is the creation of many hundreds of one-class communities unparalleled in the history of America. Each mass-produced community has its own shopping center and community center. There is no need to rub elbows with fellow Americans who are of a different class. The more expensive of these one-layer communities, where homes cost $50,000, import their teachers, policemen, and store clerks from nearby communities in a lower price range.

Some of this homogeneous layering was dictated by the problem of mass production of houses. It is more economical to put up 620 houses that sell for precisely $12,750 than it is to offer in a development the full range of houses found in the old-type American community. If the development is big enough, it may have one section of a few thousand houses in the economy class (say, $11,500), and another large area filled with more expensive (say, $17,500) houses. In both cases, trim can be alternated so that only every fifth house is *exactly* alike. The trend is toward a wider variety of choice in façade and accessories.

One large development I visited, in southeastern Pennsylvania, was primarily promoting two sections: one of $12,000 houses and the other of $19,000 houses. The $12,000 house was bought primarily by the limited-success type. Here, from one block, are the occupations and salaries of six buyers: instrument salesman ($5,800); machinist ($4,400); mechanic ($6,000); life-insurance agent ($4,680); brakeman ($4,680); office manager ($6,500). And here, from a street a mile away in the $19,000 section, are seven occupants, primarily semi-upper class: cost accountant ($10,500); assistant brokerage manager ($10,000); engineering salesman ($13,000); construction engineer ($9,700); Navy officer ($8,200); salaried doctor ($9,000); housing sales manager ($12,000).

There is, however, another factor behind the growth of one-layer towns, which at least abets the developer's vested interest in homogeneity. That is our own habit of seeking out our own kind. The fact that we have recently become, in effect, a nation of strangers and near-strangers has aggravated this birds-of-a-feather tendency. In our insecurity we search for our own kind of people. Ralph Bodek, the builder, concluded from his motivational study of buyers that "people prefer to live near others as much like themselves as possible." Then he added what to me is a disheartening thought:

"They do not seem interested in the possibility of new stimulating associations with people different from themselves."

Even in the development, however, we do not have one big happy class of intermingling people. Northwestern's Ernest R. Mowrer, in his study of suburban life, has found that democratic intermingling is characteristic only of the early stages of a big development. At first, everybody is interested in the same things. But soon small clusters begin forming, based on specialized interest. Doctors start running with doctors, and so forth. Thus, within the relatively homogeneous economic layer of residents, symbols of status reassert themselves and class distinctions begin to reappear. These are, of course, based not on the usual classes found in a total society, which would be impossible, but in terms of different levels of status possible within the development's particular slice of society.

What happens to the personalities of people who live in communities where the houses for miles around are virtually identical, and the people seen are all from the same socio-economic slice? It is too early to tell. From outward appearances, most people seem to find the atmosphere congenial rather than oppressive, although changes, as we'll see in Chapter 21, are appearing.

One developer, selling 1,200 houses in the $10,000 to $15,000 range near Philadelphia, states that his customers do not object to the fact that their houses are basically the same, though appearances vary somewhat. One woman shrugged, "After twelve hundred houses, how individual would you be?" For the most part, he has concluded, reaction against uniformity simply is not a factor in selling his houses. And he reasons, "People are probably so conditioned from childhood up to uniformity of consumption patterns in their class that they are not aware of any desire to be particularly distinctive in housing. . . ."

The impact of these developments apparently is far greater on the personalities of children than on their parents. I share the apprehension of David Boroff, who made a lengthy study of life in New York City's new suburbs. Commenting on his findings at one large Long Island development, he concluded that children are feeling the effect vastly more than their parents, "for they don't have their parents' experience with the wide, wide world beyond. The lone and level plains of this development are all they know. Who can tell how inexorably packaged their personalities will prove to be?"[8]

Even more oppressive than the uniformity of these new one-layer town developments is the synthetic, manipulated quality of the community life found in many of them. A top executive of a development in southwestern New Jersey proudly related to me how his firm had helped generate a "tremendous community spirit." Employees of the firm "started" sewing groups, musicales, Girl Scouts, Boy Scouts, Brownies, and a Little League. He explained that these activities "interweave a fabric . . . tie a community together." Within seven or eight months, he said, his home buyers formed a civic association. "We helped guide it," he said. "We wanted the right people in charge, people oriented to our problems. You get a rabble rouser in and you have a very genuine problem."

This official mentioned he was currently trying to "sell" the Catholic diocese on the idea of building a Catholic school in the development. The aim, evidently, is to make the development more attractive to Catholics. He said his firm aims to keep a 50–50 balance between Jews and non-Jews, and turns down sales that threaten to upset the balance.

In general, residential barriers against Jews, long excluded in many areas by covenants and "gentleman's agreements," have been slowly melting. Polls have regularly been taken on the question: "Suppose a Jewish family moves in next door, how would you feel?" In 1950, 69 per cent said it would "make no difference." By 1954, the "make no difference" figure was up to 88 per cent. It should be noted, however, that amiability on the Jewish question declines as you go up the class scale. Whereas only 8 per cent of the people in the working class say they "wouldn't like it" if a Jew moved in next door, that figure climbs to 35 per cent by the time you reach the upper class.

Some of the elite residential communities near Detroit, favored by automobile-industry executives and other upper-class people, have very few or no Jews. I happened to show a Jewish Detroit builder a population breakdown of one of these towns. It stated: "Jewish —— .8%." He was astonished and exclaimed, "That must be a janitor."

The twin trends toward the manipulated one-layer community and toward more straining for a fashionable address, taken together, offer a depressing commentary on our success as a civilized people. The home, I should think, should properly be a private and very individual haven. Progress would seem to lie in the direction of turning inward rather than outward for inspiration in the creation of one's homestead.

totem poles of job prestige

*"In this town I'm snubbed socially because I only
get $1,000 a week. That hurts."*—LAMENT of a
Hollywood writer to Leo G. Rosten.

━◆─○─►·◄─○─►·◄─○─►·◄─○─►·◄─○─►·◄─○─►·◄─○─►╸

THE DIRECTOR OF A FORTY PLUS CLUB WAS TRYING TO EXPLAIN
to me where it drew the line in accepting applicants. The club
is an association of unemployed older businessmen seeking
new "positions." Its appeal, to some extent, is in its exclusiveness. He said, to illustrate the dividing line, "We take accountants, but not bookkeepers."

In the prestige structure of a college campus, physicists
typically look down on biologists, who look down on ballet
teachers, who look down on home economists, who look down
on professors of physical education. This assumes their title
rankings are equal.

Our occupational rank looms as a powerful factor in fixing
our status in the public's mind. What is it that establishes the
prestige or status rating for each of our thousands of occupations? Certainly some of the discrepancies in valuation we see
result from whimsical or irrational forces. An example of
irrational discrepancy is the fact that men typically are paid
more than women for performing the same job, such as that
of bank teller. Usually there is no pretense that men can do
the job in question any better than women. In general, however, a logic of sorts is at work to try to assure our society,

through differential reward and recognition, a sufficiency of the scarce talents our society needs or desires.

Typically, a half-dozen factors combine to establish the prestige ranking of any occupation. And this prestige rank of the breadwinner's occupation, in turn, as we've seen, plays a major part in placing his family in the social-class system. These are the six main bases we use in assigning prestige to an occupation:

1. *The importance of the task performed.* Raymond Mack, sociologist of Northwestern University, and an authority on social stratification, made an analysis of the social system of a United States Air Force base. He queried airmen in thirty squadrons at two Strategic Air Command bomber bases to get their ideas on the "best" and "worst" squadrons to be in. Men tended to upgrade their own outfits, but overall an unmistakable pattern of prestige emerged. Squadrons engaged in the primary SAC mission, that is, in manning bombers, rated highest in esteem. Those in command at wing headquarters rated next. These were followed, much further down in status, by the various squadrons providing support for the primary mission, such as armament maintenance. And finally, lowest in prestige, were all the squadrons servicing the base, such as those in Medical, Air Police, and Food Service. Mack suggests that this same system of assigning prestige operates in industries such as railroading. There, he points out, "the prestige hierarchy runs from the operations personnel—engineers, firemen, conductors, and brakemen—to the command group—tower operators and signalmen—to the support people such as station agents, to the service personnel—repair and track maintenance section gangs. . . ."[1]

2. *The authority and responsibility inherent in the job.* With the growing importance of large corporations in our economic life, there has been a demand for "generalists" (experts in decision-making) capable of deciding what to do with large work forces and million-dollar budgets. Doctors wield little authority, but we grant them life-and-death responsibilities.

3. *The knowledge required.* Bernard Barber of Barnard College makes the point that to achieve high status one's knowledge must be of a special kind. It must be "systematized" and "generalized." A butcher, he points out, can be a storehouse of information about meat cuts, and yet doesn't have the kind of systematic knowledge of animal anatomy required of a biologist.

4. *The brains required.* Harvard sociologist Pitirim Sorokin has stated that the higher the intelligence called for in a task (along with the more social control involved) the higher we will rank its practitioners as a privileged group. Americans do not stand in awe of their more brilliant professors as most Europeans do, but up to a point they accept the notion that brains should not go unrewarded. "Brain" jobs offer more prestige, if not more money, than "brawn" jobs.

Success in most professional careers requires the kind of intelligence that is quite scarce. Lyle Spencer, President of Science Research Associates, has estimated that most good scientists and engineers have an I.Q. of around 135, which puts them in the top 1 or 2 per cent of the United States population.

Business executives, interestingly, do not need such brilliance, and, in fact, might find it a handicap in trying to communicate with associates if they did have such an I.Q. Spencer noted in one analysis he made of presidents of companies that they were less bright than the subordinates who headed research departments. On the whole, he finds that top executives have an I.Q. of about 120, or about the same as draftsmen, G-men, Army officers, and typical college graduates, and 20 points above the United States average. I might add the jocular observation that one of the hidden barriers to being a good businessman apparently is being too bright for the job.

Here are the brain-power ratings of men working in twenty different occupations (on the basis of scoring in the Army General Classification Test). The figures listed are average. There were, of course, men considerably brighter and duller in every category.

Lumberjack	85	Salesman	115
Barber	93	Radio repairman	117
House painter	99	Production manager	118
Auto mechanic	102	Pharmacist	122
Machine operator	103	General bookkeeper	122
Entertainer	108	Teacher	124
Salesclerk	109	Writer	126
Policeman	109	Medical student	127
Band leader	114	Mechanical engineer	128
Store manager	115	Accountant	129

5. *The dignity of the job.* Hollingshead found in Elmtown that one of the leading financial pillars of the town's churches and a person of considerable wealth and power held an exceedingly low prestige position. She was Polish Paula, the town's leading madam. In contrast, a notoriously skinflint banker held perhaps the highest position in prestige. In many cities, bookies and racketeers are among the communities' wealthiest citizens, and are frequently leading contributors to candidates for high political office. They, too, rank low in most communities (but not in some Italian-American and Negro lower-class districts).

Currently, some people in the high-income-but-low-prestige positions are striving mightily to remodel the public's image of them. The nation's 25,000 undertakers have undertaken a campaign to become known as "funeral directors," a title that conveys more dignity. They are striving to become accepted as professional men "on the same level as a doctor or lawyer." To this end, their academic requirements have been raised to include attendance at one of the nation's twenty-four mortuary colleges.

In Chicago, a labor union has succeeded in raising the income of janitors to the point where they make more money than many of the white-collar tenants of their apartment buildings. This has produced a delicate situation with not a little resentment, on the part of the tenants, of the expensive status symbols the janitors flaunt. Furthermore, the union has been endearing itself with members by a crusade to move the janitor and his family out of the basement into a first-floor apartment, bespeaking the new dignity the janitor so much desires. Many school janitors are now called "custodians."

6. *The financial rewards of the occupation.* This undoubtedly is the most important of all in influencing us to assign high or low status, since it is, as I've indicated, more visible to neighbors than some of the other factors. Therefore, let's pause and examine the variations of reward in some detail.

Our patterns of reward have been undergoing a profound change in the past decade. Occupations once thought to be highly rewarding are less so today, and occupations we once thought of as being poor sources of income are producing rewards far up the income scale. Seemingly startling inequities have developed. Some of these changes illustrate, at the same time, the great gains in income of many blue-collar groups in relation to white-collar groups.

It was only a decade ago that an economist, in explaining to congressmen the class and income structure of America, pictured a pyramid with a broad base of unskilled laborers at the bottom. Above that base he pictured ever-smaller layers upward in this order: semi-skilled, skilled, white-collar clerical and sales force, semi-professional and lower administrative positions, professionals and higher administrators.

That picture today is cockeyed. In fact, the long-favored concept of a pyramid is obsolete. Unskilled laborers no longer form a broad base. Their number is shriveling. Meanwhile, the better-paid blue-collar working people such as craftsmen and foremen are coming to dominate the middle-income position in our society. A clear majority of all families in the $4,000 to $7,500 bracket, long accepted as the middle-income range, now wear blue, not white, collars.

At the same time, groups such as policemen, bank tellers, firemen, clergymen, social workers, and, yes, income-tax collectors have been dropping to a lower relative position on the income scale.

I first became suspicious that our traditional ideas about the relative reward of different occupations were badly out of date while chatting with a dealer for a higher-priced line of cars (Buick) in Fall River, Massachusetts, in 1956. He was explaining to me who were the best prospects for his cars. The average sale price of his cars is $4,000. He explained that the most likely customers are "middle-class people . . . not the white-collar people such as you find uptown in the stores and offices." He went on to clarify that by "middle class" he meant primarily the workers at nearby plants and mills. They are the buyers, he said, who keep his firm in business.

Subsequently, I tried to assemble a reliable picture of what was happening within our reward system. After gathering statistics on a nationwide basis in Washington, D.C., I went into sixteen representative communities in the northeastern United States for a closer, flesh-and-blood look at the way people were living. I consulted moneylenders, realtors, insurance men, car dealers, boat-yard operators, tax consultants, local employment officials, and so forth to find who was making the money these days.[2] Since then, I have assembled some additional data. Here are six conclusions I believe we can draw about the income pattern now emerging.

Among the professions, your best opportunity, moneywise, is to be a doctor. In fact, when it comes to money, it is better to be an independent physician than just about anybody. General practitioners on the average net around $16,000 a year; surgeons average about $35,000. (Psychiatrists average only $17,000, perhaps because their patients individually take up more of their time than ordinary patients.) Most specialists average several thousand more. If your town has more than fifty doctors, the chances are excellent that at least one nets more than $75,000 a year. A few of the nation's more enterprising physicians net more than $200,000 a year.

(A medical employment agency recently promised $30,000 to the ear-nose-and-throat man accepting a position in an air-conditioned clinic near Chicago.)[3]

As you go from town to town, the occupations of the people in what is frequently called "the upper crust" vary. But, always, in the finest, most exclusive sections of the town you will find the residences of doctors. And many have their offices elsewhere. Brattleboro, Vermont, is built on the side of a small mountain, and the most exclusive residential area is at the crest of the mountain. When I was there, 40 per cent of the homes on the crest were owned by medical people. The most exclusive suburb of Washington, D.C., is Spring Valley. You will have extreme difficulty building a house there unless you have at least $60,000 to invest in it. Some executives, lobbyists, admirals, and senators live there, but when I asked a real-estate salesman who had the money to buy such houses now, his first response was, "Doctors." And the doctors do not use their homes for offices—that is not allowed.

The owners of a firm outside Trenton, New Jersey, that installs swimming pools on private properties said, "About a third of our customers this year are doctors." In four other towns, I heard spontaneous references to the special affluence of baby doctors. A lad at a Red Bank, New Jersey, boat yard, in ticking off the owners of thirteen big power cruisers by the dock, came to a thirty-foot beauty and said, "Another doctor . . . what is the one who takes care of babies before-hand?" I said, "Obstetrician?" He said, "Yeah, that's it."

Medical people usually justify their income on the grounds that they require a long and costly training and that they work long hours. It should be noted, however, that they have not always had such an enviable edge over other professionals. In 1929, lawyers were in first place on the scale of professional incomes, engineers and scientists second, and medical people third. Lawyers are now a poor second, and engineers and scientists an even poorer third. A realtor in Taunton, Massachusetts, suggested a possible reason why doctors have pulled a good $5,000 a year ahead of lawyers: doctors in the town are in short supply and lawyers are overabundant, more than sixty for a town of 40,000.

Dentists have not pushed incomes up as rapidly as physicians, but have gained faster than most other professionals, including lawyers. They net somewhat more than $12,000 annually.

As for engineers and scientists, the recruiting advertisements seeking them are misleading. We read a great deal about the high starting salaries for engineering lads fresh out of college. One advertisement for them cried: "CRAZY, MAN, CRAZY ARE OUR RATES." But while rates are high for beginners, close to $5,000, engineers soon find themselves up against a ceiling. The median salary for mechanical and electrical engineers now is a little above $7,000. They may, of course, earn more, especially those who advance to administrative positions. Physicists run about the same in income. The professional spokesmen of scientists and engineers blame their relatively low incomes—in comparison with those of doctors, dentists, lawyers, etc.—on the fact that they are so absorbed in their work, and are so unworldly, that they have never got tough in a collective way about money.

As professions become less "practical" (and are less likely to be in demand by profit-making organizations) they command less and less money. The median annual income for an anthropologist with a master's degree is approximately $4,700. At the bottom of the professional scale are clergymen. Protestant ministers are paid less than factory workers (but many of them have housing provided without charge).

In contrast, men now beginning careers as doctors can look forward confidently to a lifetime income of more than a million dollars. Why have medical practitioners succeeded in pulling so far ahead of other professionals? A major answer seems to be that they have been exercising collective birth control on themselves. A scarcity—an artificial one, some charge—has been created. In spite of the increase in our medical needs over the decades, the number of doctors available in a typical community has been decreasing. In 1900, there was one licensed doctor for every 578 people. By 1940, the proportion of doctors had shrunk to the point where there was one for every 750 patients; or, if you consider only those still in active practice, there was one active doctor for every 935 persons.[4] President Eisenhower in 1957 referred to "the already acute shortage" of medical manpower. At hospitals at least 2,000 intern positions have remained unfilled.

The birth control of the profession is exercised most often (whether by design or not) at the medical-school level. The acceptance of applicants at many schools has been on a highly selective basis. Expansion of facilities—which, it should be noted, is relatively expensive—to permit the training of more doctors has been approached conservatively. When the shortage of doctors was most widely claimed to be acute during World War II (40 per cent had been withdrawn from civilian practice), one medical school decried all the fuss about an alleged shortage and said the supply of doctors was adequate. A few years ago, the dean of a Midwestern medical school sought to explain the limitations on entrance to his medical school by saying there was a limited supply of cadavers!

Blue-collar skills are gaining on the lower white-collar skills in relative reward. In many cases, unionized working-class people, paid an hourly wage, have been earning more per week than the salaried, white-collared members of the limited-success class (or lower middle class) who identify themselves more with management and typically are not unionized.

At the United States Steel plant near Levittown, Pennsylvania, the top workmen have hourly-wage rates that yield them close to $7,500 a year. And this does not include overtime, incentive and fringe extras. One plant official stated, "A lot of people here who are not even foremen are making more than $1,000 a month."

In Newark, where building-craft incomes have been the highest in America, contractors report that some of their busy electricians make $200 a week, counting overtime. By way of contrast, in Newark I met a United States Internal Revenue agent who was working Saturdays as an appliance salesman in order to support his family. After twenty years of working at his white-collar job for Uncle Sam, he said, he still was not making $100 a week. Bricklayers, however, are the aristocrats of the building trade. Nationwide, they average $150 for a forty-hour week.

While bricklayers were advancing to $150 a week, a major airline advertised for white-collared reservation agents. It said it wanted "university graduates" with sales experience and good voice and diction. The pay: $65 a week.

The following scale, based on Department of Labor figures, indicates the startling differences that exist from industry to industry in the weekly-wage rates for average "production workers or non-supervisory employees." It is based on earnings as of November, 1957.

More than $110 a week
Building construction
Soft-coal mining
Electrical contracting work
Plumbing contract work

$100 to $110
Blast-furnace operation
Brewery jobs
Highway construction
Automobile production

$90 to $100
Shipbuilding
Aircraft manufacture
Jobs with security exchanges
Refrigerator making

$80 to $90
Local bus driving
Jobs with car dealers
Meat packing
Book printing

$70 to $80
Carpetmaking
Baking
Radio and TV manufacturing
Logging and sawmill work

$60 to $70
Food-store clerking
Furniture-store selling
Bank and trust-company jobs
Telephone switchboard operation

$50 to $60
Sea-food packing
Hatmaking
Footwear manufacture
Cleaning and dyeing work

$40 to $50
Hotel service jobs
Department-store clerking
Laundry work
Men's shirtmaking

It is not a coincidence that the white-collar jobs listed tend to be well down the list. That is where they appear most frequently on the complete Department of Labor tabulation. And outside the production field, it might be noted that United States schoolteachers average, on the basis of a forty-three-week teaching year, $94.30 a week. But, as most have no other income, the average weekly salary for the fifty-two-week year drops to $80.64.

Private industries tend to pay much better than public-supported institutions. One reason for this, perhaps, is that the private industries are major taxpayers and so keep a sharper eye on signs of "waste" and "frills" in public institutions than they do in their own (where frills can be deducted on their tax forms as a business expense).

At the professional level, industry pays approximately $1,500 more per year for engineers than the government does. And it pays $3,000 more for a Ph.D. economist than a university does.

Young physicists with Ph.D.'s often start to work with private firms at higher pay than their professors back at the university are making, who have been working more than twenty years—and who taught the neophytes most of what they know!

A psychiatrist can easily make twice as much in a year by treating two dozen private patients as he can in assuming responsibility for two hundred seriously ill patients at a state mental hospital.

The farm is a hard place to make a living these days unless you own a large one. Although farmers began enjoying a rise in income during 1958, the fifties in general have been most discouraging, especially to small farmers. Cash net income of farmers dropped substantially in the decade beginning 1947, with farmers who grow cotton, wheat, tobacco, corn, and peanuts having a particularly difficult time. An official of a firm dealing with farmers in Richfield Springs, New York, said he had reached this firm conclusion: "You've got to be bigger than average to make a decent living on the farm." (Farmers, incidentally, range from poor lower-class farm hands to upper-class multimillionaire ranch owners. Most, however, would fall in the limited-success class.)

One white-collar skill that is highly rewarded is salesmanship. The clerks who "wait on" people in a general-merchandise store average approximately $45 a week, whereas salesmen working for automobile agencies (where hard selling is called for) make nearly twice as much.

In this era of self-service, more and more attention is being paid to pre-selling products through advertising; and the experts in this highly competitive field of devising messages and imagery that will move merchandise are well rewarded indeed. The pay scale of the key people in thirty or forty leading advertising agencies in New York might make a $5,000-a-year college professor with a Ph.D. drool. Here are the ranges of rates in leading advertising agencies for the seasoned men and women who shape sales messages, according to a New York employment agency that places a great many advertising men:

Copy writers	$12,500 to $30,000
Copy chiefs	$27,500 to $60,000
Account executives	$15,000 to $75,000
Research directors	$15,000 to $35,000
Art chiefs	$30,000 to $50,000

The best way to assure oneself of a six-figure income is to be a business manager or owner. Lower-range, or medium-responsibility, business executives (those above the rank of foremen, but below the policy-making level) have been averaging approximately $12,000–$13,000 nationwide. When you move up to the heads of companies the positions pay primarily on the basis of the size of the company. Bank presidents as a group average $25,000, but the heads of the larger banks typically earn more than $100,000 by salary alone. As for the top men of our largest industrial concerns, they may earn anywhere from $50,000 to more than $500,000. A random sampling of the incomes of fifty presidents of the approximately one hundred largest corporations in the United States showed an average income of $183,355. *Business Week* reports that in 1957 there were 235 United States business executives who were paid more than $100,000.

While the big salaries went to the top executives of the large companies, it is, nevertheless, true that the fabulous fortune builders of our present high-tax generation are virtually all men who own or substantially control their own smaller firms. Such entrepreneurs, if highly successful, can end up with more income each year after taxes because, as already noted, they can have their profits taxed on the more favorable capital-gains basis. A few are managing to accumulate several million dollars in additional wealth each year. Even at the less grandiose level, successful individual entrepreneurs seem to be living more lushly than salaried executives of the large corporations. Of twenty-five new homes I saw in an ultra-elite area of Rochester, New York, off East Avenue (the houses averaged in price considerably more than $50,000), what stood out about the owners was that two thirds of them were in business for themselves.

Some observers are suggesting that businessmen of America are getting more than their share of the national income in comparison with non-business pursuits requiring considerably more training. And this prevails despite our urgent need for able scientists and teachers. Seymour E. Harris, the Harvard economist, has pointed out that, while one distilling corporation pays its chief executive close to $400,000, the highest-paid college president in the nation receives approximately $45,000, and the average president receives $11,000.[5]

Money, as they say, isn't everything—at least when it comes to social prestige. Among professionals, for example, a world-famous scientist on the payroll of a leading university at $10,000 a year may be the full equal in status of a corporation lawyer making $100,000. As Harvard's Talcott Parsons points out, the scientist "simply does not compete on the plane of 'conspicuous consumption' which is open to the lawyer but closed to him." And it may well be that the $100,000 lawyer's greatest ambition in life—now that he has his fortune and his yacht—is to walk, begowned, somewhere near the $10,000-a-year scientist in a Commencement Day ceremony that will culminate in the bestowal upon the lawyer of some sort of honorary degree.

Or consider the case of the successful small businessman who has made a small fortune selling appliances at a discount. In income, he is probably better fixed than most professionals and middle-layer corporate executives. Yet, in social status, he may rank well below most professionals and executives, and probably knows it. The chances are high that he comes from a working-class family, married a working-class girl while he was himself still a wage earner, and never went to college.[6] The chances are quite high that his wife didn't finish high school. A professional, in contrast, is typically already a professional by the time he seeks a mate, and chooses accordingly.

Several investigators have attempted in recent years to arrive at an over-all ranking of occupations by prestige. One obvious way to do this is to ask people how they, in their minds, rank different occupations. Mapheus Smith, while at the University of Kansas, asked 345 evaluators to imagine they were arranging a formal dinner for a celebrity, and had to seat one typical representative from each of one hundred occupations. Aside from government occupations, such as that of United States Supreme Court justice, the seven occupations entitled to seats closest to the celebrity proved to be college president, banker, medical doctor, captain of ocean-going merchant ship, criminal lawyer, architect, author. And the bottom seven in prestige for this dinner table, in descending order, were peddler, scissors grinder, odd-job worker, scrub woman, garbage collector, unskilled migratory worker, prostitute.

Prostitutes, it might be noted, have their own fairly rigid hierarchy of status. Call girls, who consider themselves the aristocrats of the profession (to use the word loosely), shun even for socializing restaurants and bars frequented by street-workers or "house girls" or even "chippies" (promiscuous amateurs). And a $50-a-trick girl wouldn't dream of swapping telephone numbers of prospects with a $30-a-trick girl. Anyone charging below $20 a trick is regarded in the trade as "a common prostitute."

Status among prostitutes is based in large part on the customary fee the female can command. It is also based on appearance, address, political connections. Finally it is based to a large extent on the style in which she maintains her pimp or "old man" (assuming she can afford one).

Harold Greenwald, Executive Director of the Association for Applied Psychoanalysis, found in his study of a group of call girls that the pimp, far from being a harsh exploiter, typically functions as a status symbol. The high-status prostitute will lavish upon her pimp (or kept man) fine clothes, first-edition books, and Cadillac convertibles in much the same way that a businessman may lavish upon his wife fine furs and jewelry as visible symbols of his success. Greenwald also makes the point that there is little inter-class mobility among prostitutes. A streetwalker doesn't work her way up to being a call girl (but an aging call girl may descend to being a streetwalker). The call girl starts out at that level. She comes typically from what he calls "upper or middle class" origin. Greenwald concludes that association appears to be easier when the class levels of customer and call girl are approximately the same. The overwhelming majority of call girls, he adds, are filled with self-hatred and are utterly unresponsive to the "Johns" who patronize them. Most have made suicide attempts.

The most imposing study of occupational prestige is that made by the National Opinion Research Center about a decade ago. It took a nationwide sample involving 2,920 people, who were asked to grade each of ninety occupations on their general standing. Again the job of being a Supreme Court justice ranked highest. Here are the rankings (in descending order) of twenty-five occupations that were scored above average in prestige and twenty-five that were scored below average in prestige.

ABOVE AVERAGE

	Relative Rank		Relative Rank
Physician	2	Sociologist	27
College professor	7	Accountant for large firm	28
Banker	10	Author	31
County judge	12	Army captain	32
Minister	14	Building contractor	33
Architect	15	Public-school teacher	36
Dentist	17	Railroad engineer	38
Lawyer	18	Farm owner	39
Large corporation director	19	Official, international labor union	40
Nuclear physicist	20	Radio announcer	41
Psychologist	22	Newspaper columnist	42
Airline pilot	24	Electrician	44
Owner of factory employing about 100 people	26		

UNDER AVERAGE

	Relative Rank		Relative Rank
Small-store manager	49	Night-club singer	75
Bookkeeper	50	Farm hand	76
Insurance agent	51	Coal miner	77
Policeman	55	Taxi driver	78
Mail carrier	57	Railroad section hand	79
Auto repairman	59	Restaurant waiter	80
Plumber	60	Night watchman	82
Factory machine operator	65	Clothes presser	83
Barber	66	Soda-fountain clerk	84
Store clerk	67	Bartender	85
Milk-route man	70	Janitor	86
Filling-station attendant	74	Street sweeper	89
		Shoeshiner	90

People in other industrial nations rate occupations in orders that are similar at many points with those made by North Americans (according to a comparative study of poll results in the United States, Great Britain, the Soviet Union, Japan, New Zealand, and Germany made by Alex Inkeles and Peter H. Rossi). The agreement in ratings by New Zealanders and United States residents was particularly high: .97 correlation. And ratings of Germans and Americans also have a startlingly high correlation: .96.

The NORC list above probably grants more prestige to academic occupations—and less to business executives—than people really feel. I suspect a distortion caused by people giving answers they think they ought to give, just as many people say they read high-prestige magazines when they really don't. We profess admiration for intellectual pursuits, but really reserve our highest envy and respect for successful businessmen. This is understandable, since our aspirations primarily are focused in the business world.

This American respect for business talent appears in a comparative investigation of attitudes toward community projects in a city in the state of Washington and in western England.[7] Influential people were asked to name ten people they would want to work with them if they were responsible for a community project. Two thirds of the people ranking highest on the American list were business people, whereas only one quarter of the Britons chosen were from business.

In Italy, university professors still command profound respect from the populace and there is a great deal of deference to them even on the campus. Industrialists, in contrast, tend to rank relatively lower than in America because they typically are weak on family background. Recently, an Italian girl was turned down for a fashionable finishing school because her father was only an industrialist. (In the Soviet Union, it might also be noted, a full professor is paid nearly twice as much as a factory manager.)[8]

Another impressive approach to establishing an over-all rank order of prestige for occupations is that reported by sociologist Bevode McCall on behalf of the Research Division of the *Chicago Tribune*. In this approach, sociologists from the University of Chicago arbitrarily assigned a status rating to each occupation, based on the skill and responsibility involved. The occupations are more precisely defined than in any other listing I've encountered. The ratings were for occupations found in the Chicago area, and were arrived at after the sociologists analyzed data supplied by the *Tribune* on a sample census of 3,880 Chicago households.[9]

In this approach, approximately 300 occupations were given a status rating of from 1 (highest) to 7 (lowest). Here are examples of occupations assigned to each of the seven groups.

Highest-status group

Licensed architects
Medical specialist
Executives, top level, large national concern
Stock brokers

Federal judge
Law partner in prestige firm
Flag-rank military officers
Bishop, D.D.

Second-status group

General medical practitioner
Editor of newspaper
Mechanical engineer
Top-level executive, local firm
City or county judge

Downtown lawyer
Colonel or Navy captain
College professor, prestige school

Third-status group

Bank cashier
Department-store buyer
Professor, small or municipal college
Advertising copy writer

Junior executive
High-school teacher
Minister (D.D.) from sectarian school
Office supervisor

Fourth-status group

Bank clerk
Carpenter, small contractor
Clerk, prestige store
Dental technician
Railroad engineer
Grade-school teacher

Factory foreman
Insurance salesman
Chain-store manager
Staff sergeant
Office secretary

Fifth-status group

Auto mechanics
Barber
Bartender
Carpenter, employed
Grocery clerk
Crane operator
Skilled factory worker

Hotel desk clerk
Telephone lineman
Mail clerk
Corporal
Policeman
Truck driver

Sixth-status group

Taxi driver
Semi-skilled factory worker
Gas-station attendant
Plumber's helper
Spotter, dry cleaning

Stock clerk
Waitress
Watchman
Riveter

Lowest-status group

Hod carrier
Dishwasher
Domestic servant

Gardener
Janitor
Coal miner, laborer

Scrub woman
Street cleaner

This ranking by status based on assessment by social scientists at least has the advantages of preciseness. All executives are not lumped together, nor are all teachers. Note, too, that the long-assumed status superiority of white-collar workers over blue-collar workers does not carry through in any definitive, straight-line way on the list. Bartenders reading this list can rejoice that sociologists, at least, rate them a notch or two higher than public opinion does, as revealed by the earlier NORC listing.

A few final observations might be made. The system of material rewards we have evolved for work skills seems to be to some extent out of kilter. If work roles are appraised objectively in terms of talent, training, and responsibility required, we seem in general to over-reward businessmen and under-reward those in intellectual pursuits. We seem to be under-rewarding people working for our many non-profit institutions and over-rewarding those with the same skills working for profit-making institutions. We seem to over-reward any occupational group that by collective action can control the flow of new, competitive talent into their field. Finally, if I may be permitted a bold suggestion, it would seem that any reward system that year after year pays a wailing crooner approximately one hundred times as much as the Chief Justice of the United States Supreme Court is somewhat out of balance.

8

pecking orders in corporate barnyards

"WANT TO MOVE UP AS A MANAGER? LEARN TO BE A FIRST CLASS SUBORDINATE."—HEAD-LINE, *Supervisory Management.*

◄─O─►·◄─O─►·◄─O─►·◄─O─►·◄─O─►·◄─O─►

THE HEADLONG TREND TOWARD LARGE ORGANIZATIONAL STRUC-tures in America—not only in business but in government, labor, and education—has in the past decade produced new built-in stratification systems across the landscape. Nowhere is this more apparent than in the great corporation, which can often impose its hierarchy of ranks—and symbols of differential status—upon the social structure of the surrounding community.

These hierarchical ranks are becoming as explicit as those of the United States Civil Service or those of the armed forces. Each corporation has its hierarchy of the "line" (first-line foreman, assistant general foreman, general foreman, assistant department superintendent, department superintendent, divisional superintendent, assistant plant manager, plant manager, and others responsible for production) and its vertically parallel hierarchy of staff specialists (such as designer, assistant supervisor, supervisor, general supervisor, assistant staff head, staff head). Topping these twin jungles of titles are the elect of "advanced management" or "elite nucleus."

Mabel Newcomer, in comparing the lives of modern business executives with those at the turn of the century, was deeply impressed by the fact that while two thirds of the executives in 1900 had once run their own enterprises, only 1 in 10 of the mid-century executives had; and the number who had spent their entire careers within the walls of one corporation had tripled.

One result of the growth of corporate bureaucracy is the intense preoccupation that has developed in the past decade with symbols of status. The *Wall Street Journal*, after a nationwide study of business trends, reported on its page 1: "At an increasing number of concerns, the corporate caste system is being formalized and rigidified." And *Time* magazine reported on its business pages that the "trappings of power and rank are normal incentives in U.S. business life." It quoted a Cleveland president as saying that "often the little privileges that go with an office are more important to an executive than a raise. You'd expect executives to be more mature, but they frequently aren't."[1] *Time* added that the trend is toward "more instead of less luxury" in executive trappings. (A corporation executive who read this present chapter suggested only that I make it clear I'm not being facetious, that status symbols have indeed come to play a most serious role in corporate incentive systems.)

This preoccupation with prerogatives—or "perks" as the British call them—reflects the special problems posed by bigness. In a small company, everybody knows who is who, and where the power resides. An executive can charge about in shirt sleeves issuing orders and use a battered desk in an open room as his office. In my search for men who had made at least $10,000,000 in the last twenty years, I found that almost all made their fortunes by starting and running their own companies (which makes them look a little like dinosaurs in this modern managerial era); and I found the ways of operating of these lone wolves startlingly different from the hundreds of corporate executives I have interrogated, over the years, behind their neat, polished desks. Several of the entrepreneur-multimillionaires worked in such modest cubicles that I couldn't believe I had reached my destination when I faced them. One shared a secretary with his two assistants. Another had odds and ends of furniture; a third had a "board" room less than ten feet square. Most impressive, at least eight relaxed by putting up their feet on their desks as they talked. I have strained my memory and I can remember only one executive of a large corporation who ever did that. He was a president, and even he did it uneasily.

In the large corporation, just as in the Army, the executive feels a need for highly visible signs of his authority, even though he feels a need simultaneously to act out the American Creed by showing what a nice, regular fellow he is.

The result is that the office managers of many corporations are trained in the nuances of status and systematize the apportioning of "perks."

First, there is the physical problem of assigning office space. This is often done by rule. Crown Zellerbach Corporation, in planning its move to a new twenty-story building, has arranged walls so that offices for executives of equal rank can "all be built to within a square inch of one another in size."[2] In a typical corporation, the head of the hierarchy assigned to a floor gets the corner office with the nicest view, and the offices of his subordinates branch out from his corner in descending order of rank. Physical closeness to the center of power is considered evidence of status; and nobody wants to be put out "in left field."

Desks, too, typically are categorized by rank. Mahogany, of course, outranks walnut; and walnut outranks oak. The man who is entitled to wall-to-wall carpeting is likely to have a water carafe, which has replaced the brass spittoon as a symbol of flag rank, and also probably has a red-leather couch. An executive with a two-pen set on his desk clearly outranks a man with a one-pen set. At one broadcasting company, executives above a certain level—and only they—are entitled to electric typewriters for their secretaries.

Several of the automobile-making corporations have highly formalized systems for bestowing status symbols. Here is how the *Wall Street Journal* described the ascent of one former Ford executive: "As his position improved, his office grew larger, his furniture fancier, his name went on the door, he received a rug for the floor and a spot in the indoor garage. Then came keys to executive washrooms, country club membership at company expense, and finally a free car." One of the added benefits of gaining a key to the executive washroom was that in it he could enjoy showers and the use of electric shavers and free cologne. In the town of Darien, Connecticut, where executives tend to congregate, 65 per cent of the membership fees of one local country club are paid by companies.

The private washroom, in many companies, is reserved for vice-presidents and up. Some have gold faucets. At a Midwestern oil firm, however, a fine line is drawn. The vice-presidents, like the president, have a private washroom; but it is literally that. Their washroom has no toilet, as the president's has.

An invitation to use the executive dining room is another "perk" that comes only when the employee passes a certain level on the company's hierarchical chart. At a steel plant I visited near Pittsburgh, there were two executive dining rooms side by side for different levels of executives. The one with tablecloths was for the higher group. A New York insurance company has, in its building, five dining rooms in ascending elegance, and personnel are assigned by rank. The democratic custom of eating with rank-and-file employees at a common dining hall has become so rarely observed by corporate executives that the president of a medium-sized company in Northeast City boasted to me that he did that. It helped morale, he felt.

The circumstances under which an employee arrives for work also are highly indicative of status. Does the employee have to punch a time clock or not? Does he or she come through the plant gate or the office door? At what time does he or she arrive in relation to others? Bosses typically make it a practice to arrive either earlier or later than their flock. In England, a government proposal to ease the rush-hour traffic by persuading some business firms to start their day a half hour earlier encountered a snob barrier. White-collar workers of one large company that was considering opening a half hour earlier (at 8:30) vehemently objected. When questioned, they reluctantly made the point that factory employees commonly started their work at 8:30, so that for them to do so would involve a loss of social prestige.

Perhaps the most precise assigning of status symbols—certainly the most visible to the general public—is seen in the way many corporations assign company cars. A large oil corporation divides its management people into five levels for the purpose of distributing all sorts of special "perks," including the company cars. A Class I person (division managers, etc.) is assigned a Cadillac or comparable limousine. A Class V person (salesmen, etc.) is confined in his choice to certain specific models of Chevrolet, Ford, and Plymouth.

Writer David Knickerbocker made an analysis of the systems used by large, nationwide merchandising firms in assigning cars. He found a six-level system most widely used, and commented that many of these systems are so highly codified as to make, model, and accessories that "you can tell your neighbor's annual income by a glance at the auto he uses for business."[3] He summarized the six groups as follows (and the prices, I should stress, are for 1957):

1. Salesmen: Inexpensive Fords, Chevrolets, Plymouths. ($2,200)

2. Sales supervisors: Higher-priced Fords, Chevrolets, Plymouths. ($2,500)

3. Assistant sales managers: Mercury, Pontiac, Dodge. ($2,800)

4. Sales managers: Oldsmobile, DeSoto, Buick. ($3,600)

5. Division managers: Chrysler, Lincoln, or a Cadillac in the $5,100 range.

6. Vice-presidents and up. According to one company official, "They can have any kind of Cadillac they want."

As for accessories, it is much the same: white-wall tires, air conditioners, power steering, etc., for vice-presidents; and nothing but a heater for salesmen.

The hierarchy of a company can often be noted visually by inspecting the name posted before each parking space in the parking lot reserved for management. At an Ohio rubber company's home office, the president's space is nearest the door (in case it rains), and the ranking vice-president's is next in line, and so on down the hierarchy.

For the executives living in one-company towns, even their private purchase of a family car must be done with a cautious eye on their company's hierarchical chart. Economist Leland Gordon reports the situation in one steel town where the chairman of the board drives a Cadillac, and the president has one of the more costly Buicks. Protocol in the town, he relates, "forbids any lesser executive to drive a Cadillac or a Buick. The only ones who have a free choice in purchasing automobiles are the independent trade people of the community."

In some European countries, presumably much more conscious of the trappings of class, you find less attention focused on the status meaning of cars than you do in America. When the King of Norway visited the King of Denmark in 1958, a ceremony was held at the town hall in Copenhagen. I noted with interest that one Danish Cabinet member was chauffeured up to the red carpet in an old Chevrolet coupe.

Some of the more eminent executives of the larger United States corporations still choose to do their official traveling in a private railroad car. That is, perhaps, the choicest of all status symbols, and can cost the company about $100,000 a year. One of the top executives of a major corporation still travels to conventions only by private railroad car. In contrast, the head of his company (a more modest, budget-minded man) goes "commercial."

The privilege of going to a distant spa for an annual or semi-annual free medical checkup that takes several days (you play golf in the afternoon) is granted only to those executives of high status. Rank-and-file executives can get their checkups at a local hospital. If you really rate, your wife goes along and gets a checkup, too. And you are permitted to put her on the expense account on company excursions. Wives, in fact, play a key role in all the pushing for the trappings of status at the office, because they need some way to indicate their husbands' importance when chatting with the girls; and it is easier to mention a free junket to a spa—or the number of secretaries a husband has—than it is to boast about how much he earns.

Behind the façade of elaborate courtesy shown one another by members of the management "team" of the typical corporation, a great deal of quite forthright elbowing for status takes place. Sociologist Melville Dalton of the University of California spent a great many months at three industrial plants studying the tensions within each hierarchy. He concluded that in all the plants the relations between members of management could best be described as "a general conflict system."[4] Two principal causes of the conflicts were the drives by many members to "increase their status in the hierarchy," and frictions between members of the two vertically parallel rank orders of officers: staff and line. This last source of conflict has been increasing because the trend is toward using more and more staff specialists—such as engineers, statisticians, public and personnel experts, chemists, and so on—who like to consider themselves agents of top management. They are typically younger, better educated, and smoother than the older "line" managers in charge of producing the goods. The latter may still have dirty fingernails and typically view the young "college punks," "pretty boys," and "chair-warmers" from staff with suspicion or annoyance; and they receive their most delicious pleasures from batting down or slyly sabotaging bright ideas staff men have for improving their own methods of operating. A young staff officer complained to Dalton, "We're always in hot water with these old guys on the line. You can't tell them a damn thing. They're bull-headed as hell!"

Upward progress within any corporate hierarchy of management depends, of course, in large part on talent. But a number of informal considerations—some of them social—often weigh heavily in promotions and hiring. In early 1958, the *Wall Street Journal* made another study of executives, and quoted one recently appointed vice-president as saying, "Naturally you have pride if you're socially accepted by your superiors. It does you an awful lot of good. You can have a wonderful personnel system, but the thing that determines where you go in the company is personal contacts."

Where your office is located also seems to be a factor of importance. Being on the same floor with the people at the "head office," so that you can be seen, helps. Other things being equal, you are far more likely to be advanced than a status equal whose office happens to be in another floor, another building, or (worse) another city.

Home life, too, is important. An advertising executive who stated publicly that he and his family couldn't live on $25,000 a year also stated why: "There is no denying that when a man starts to make a certain amount of money how he lives becomes a matter of concern to his employers. And the advertising business is an Ivy League, where clothes, manners and gracious living are an essential part of doing business."⁵ So, evidently, is the gracious wife. A top official of a Midwestern concern states: "Entertaining is one of the best ways to determine if the wife is good enough to enable a man to become a well-rounded executive."⁶ A member of a management-consulting firm in the Midwest recently found himself being considered for a top spot in one of the nation's larger food corporations. The scrutiny of him went on for what he felt was an indecently long period. Finally, he and his wife were invited to dine at an elite downtown Chicago restaurant with the president and the president's wife. The candidate and his wife dressed and behaved the very best they knew how. Two days later, without any further evidence of screening, he was advised that he had been hired. He had passed the final test.

Who you are, in terms of religion, ethnic background, and politics, also is important in influencing your possibilities for progressing in many, if not most, corporate hierarchies. Melville Dalton, in a study of informal factors influencing the career achievement of 226 people within a managerial hierarchy, cited these criteria of success as apparently exerting influence: not being a Roman Catholic, being Anglo-Saxon or Germanic, being a member of a local yacht club (114 were), and being a Republican. Virtually all the 226 except a few first-line foremen were.

In Northeast City, which I investigated, the top managements of the major industries in town were heavily Protestant, even though the city was almost 50 per cent Catholic. One president, an Episcopalian, confided, however, "Our treasurer is a Catholic . . . and it is hard for a Protestant to get a job in his office."

Jews were even more rarely encountered among the management personnel of the larger companies of Northeast City's major industries. (The only exception was in the textile field, where they headed their own plants.) This same general situation has many parallels in the United States. William Attwood, after spending several months for *Look* magazine investigating the status of Jews in modern America, concluded: "Most young Americans feel that the big corporations now offer the best opportunities for security and advancement. Because of invisible barriers, some young Americans would be forced to disagree."[7]

With the growth of more complex corporate hierarchies, we are seeing a growth in anxiety about status, partly because such systems call for superiors who are expert in applying pressure. And we are seeing a growing adoption of the military procedure of periodic ratings by immediate superiors. This latter forces every aspiring employee constantly to wonder how successfully he is impressing himself upon the superior.

Unwittingly he may eagerly assume for himself the known prejudices of the superior, and even his mannerisms.

Those who reach the top level of hierarchies are, increasingly, those who have successfully shed their rough edges of individualism. As the businessman's magazine, *Changing Times,* has noted, the trend is toward an upper level of businessmen and technologists who are "highly trained technically and less individualistic, screened for qualities that will make them better players on the team. . . ." The president of a major aircraft company, in speaking to associates over the intercom, addresses them as "Teammates."

Some corporate hiring agents are favorably impressed if an applicant has been through military training because that training, among other things, has taught him to accommodate to hierarchy. The director of technical recruitment of a leading oil company makes the point that one of the good returns of military service is the "experience with authority." He says, "Apparently the Armed Forces don't fool about authority. We have observed that veterans do not resent supervision; in fact, they appear to understand and to welcome it." On the positive side, it should be noted also that military service gives many young men from private-school and Ivy League backgrounds their first real contact with members of the supporting classes.

Few men who hope to reach the top today can be indifferent to the opinion of associates, as Henry Kaiser or old Henry Ford could be. The top power in modern business can be achieved only by those who are accepted by the members of the board and by the company's bankers as sound upper-class men like themselves. And even at the lower level of striving, the strain to prove oneself sound and amenable leaves its mark. C. Wright Mills, in his study of white-collar people, made this disquieting point: "When white-collar people get jobs, they sell not only their time and energy, but their personalities as well. They sell by the week, or month, their smiles and their kindly gestures, and they must practice the prompt repression of resentment and aggression."[8]

Some of these members of the management "team" are

never free, except in their dreams, when, as Orwell put it, they have the boss in the bottom of the well bunging lumps of coal at him. Others, at the more sophisticated level, and who live in metropolitan areas not dominated by their company's shadow, manage to become rebels at night. They become wicked wits and flaming liberals in the safety of their patios and favorite bars.

Meanwhile, some more thoughtful corporate managers are uneasily wondering if hierarchical growth has not got out of hand. The personnel director of Sears, Roebuck made a study of the impact of organization structure on employee morale and concluded: "We seriously question the necessity for much of our present high degree of over-specialization and over-functionalization."

The proliferation of hierarchy, of course, is not limited to private business. Our larger universities, where staffs number in the thousands, have developed social systems of their own, with low-status maintenance hierarchies and the higher hierarchies of faculty and administration.

With the growth of Big Labor, even labor unions, which once idealized the leather-jacketed, open-collared leader-worker, developed their own fairly complex hierarchies with many staff people in neckties, such as educational directors, publicists, and negotiators, who have rarely seen the inside of a factory or mine. And many of the union leaders began taking on the trappings of status favored by the industrialists they faced across the bargaining table.[9] They pressed for high salaries (a number are in the $30,000–50,000 range), built themselves kingly offices, demanded limousines or private planes for their travel, held their conventions in deluxe seaside hotels where they demanded the best rooms, lived in penthouses—and stopped putting their feet up on their mahogany desks. That extreme of the empire-building businessman-labor leader, the teamsters' James Hoffa, explained the fact that his union supplied him with not only a Cadillac but a private barbershop, gymnasium, and massage room by saying: "Just because I'm a labor leader, do they want me to go around in baggy pants, drive a three-dollar car, and live in a four-dollar house?" One labor leader who has tried to keep his own way of life, and that of his headquarter associates, not too remote from that of the workingman they represent is the fiery Walter Reuther of the automobile workers. At this writing, his United Auto Worker salary is less than $20,000. He will ride only in a medium-priced automobile on business, prefers coach when flying. When he found himself attending a labor convention in a luxurious Miami Beach hotel, he showed how he felt about it by insisting on sharing a double room with an aide. He, however, is a lonely hold-out from a trend among labor leaders to high-status living.

Our nation's most elaborate hierarchy unquestionably is that of the United States Civil Service with its eighteen grades. Virtually every civilian employee of the federal government, below the higher policy-making level, is labeled by grade. Most occupations have a spread of several grades, from least to highest skilled; but here are examples of white-collar occupations that seem most frequently to fall within the various grades:[10]

Grade 1	Messenger
Grade 2	Mail clerk
Grade 3	Stenographer
Grade 4	Accounting clerk
Grade 5	Secretary
Grade 6	Nurse
Grade 7	Construction inspector
Grade 8	Aircraft-engine inspector
Grade 9	Chemist
Grade 10	Social-insurance administrator
Grade 11	Electronic engineer
Grade 12	Agricultural economist
Grade 13	Dental officer
Grade 14	Legal administrator
Grade 15	Physical-science administrator
Grades 16, 17, 18	Higher-level administration

It would seem appropriate for the leaders of our big organization structures in all fields, with their neatly ordered hierarchies, to cast a searching eye on the human cost of stratified bigness. If, more and more, bigness is judged to be irrevocably destined, perhaps, at the least, efforts can be made to check the withering of individuality of the "teammates."

9

shopping for status

"Regardless of her ability to pay, each individual wants to feel that she will be 'comfortable.' If the store is too high-style, the blue-collar worker's wife's sixth sense tells her she will be subtly humiliated by the clerks and other customers because she is out of her depth classwise."
—**PIERRE MARTINEAU, Director of Research and Marketing,** *Chicago Tribune.*

OUR EXCURSIONS INTO SPECIFIC STORES—AND PARTICULARLY the excursions women make to fashionable clothing stores—indicate more than we realize about our status and our status aspirations. The clothing we buy says a good deal about our status. And, for that matter, the way we pay our bills for the clothing and other purchases varies to some extent depending upon our status in our community.

The *Chicago Tribune's* study of shoppers and their habits in three homogeneous communities outside Chicago reveals that many women see the shopping trip to a prestige store (regardless of any purchases made) as a ritual which, if successful, reassures the woman of her own high status. The trip, the *Tribune*'s investigators found, "enables her to test her self-conception status-wise against the conception" others hold of her.[1]

Such women dress up for the shopping trip. They strive to look their most chic and poised, and if the trip is a success they feel "pride, pleasure, and prestige" in patronizing the store and in the satisfaction of "looking down on the customers of the lower-status store" (where women typically don't dress up to shop). Some women said it made them "feel good" just to go into a high-status store. The investigators concluded that "shopping at a prestige store enhances the status of the shopper and vice versa."

On the other hand, women who get beyond their status in their ventures into stores feel uncomfortable. There is a widespread feeling among women that store clerks endeavor to maintain what they consider to be the proper tone for their store by snooting customers who seem out of place. The wife of a research physicist in Stamford, Connecticut, told me that one day when she "ran" into a high-prestige store about a block from her home to buy a blouse that she needed she simply "threw" a babushka over her head and wore slacks. The clerks pretended not to see her. When she asked for a specific blouse in the window, the clerk frozen-faced said it was sold. Next morning, dressed in her best, she went back to the same store, sought out the same clerk (who did not recognize her in her more elegant apparel), and without difficulty purchased the same blouse. Sweetly she gave the clerk a $100 bill. The clerk couldn't change such a large bill, and apologetically took the $100 bill to a bank a block away to get change. Our vengeful wife said she enjoyed every minute of the wait.

Or consider a somewhat different case. The wife of a very ambitious but hardly prosperous sales manager went into a fashionable Fifth Avenue store and asked to see "theater suits." A crisp saleslady, after appraising her, brought out a dress priced at $39.50. That price was the store's bargain-basement price. The wife saw only the price tag and was offended. After barely glancing at the suit itself, she asked with some haughtiness if the store didn't have something "better." The clerk, not to be out-snooted, said the only other appropriate suits were "quite a bit higher." With that she disappeared and soon came back with another suit. It was priced at $165. The wife showed visible signs of distress but said it was just what she wanted. She spent the next two months finagling the family finances to conceal her folly from her husband.

In the choice of any store for making an important purchase, we unwittingly seek out the store with a status image at or near our own status level. Pierre Martineau of the *Tribune* has found that many merchants are unaware of this. He asked a major Chicago retailer with a large store in the heart of the city about the socio-economic character of his customers. The man replied proudly that the entire range of economic classes was his oyster. He said he drew people from all social classes. "But an analysis of his sales tickets," Mr. Martineau states, "revealed that nothing could be further from the truth!" Although he was centrally located, the vast majority of his customers were drawn from the lower third of the economic scale, with addresses in the South Side or southern suburbs.[2]

Another market researcher in Chicago states: "You could classify Chicagoans socially by the stores they patronize." He went down a rather long list of major stores of descending social status. At the top of his list was Marshall Field & Co., which is unsurpassed in status among the major stores.

Pierre Martineau contends that the most successful stores are those that deliberately develop a clear-cut image conveying their socio-economic status, whether high *or* low. One way stores develop an upper-class image is to bear down heavily on antiquity in their decor. Dark woods are said to be more suggestive of an upper-class status than light woods. Mr. Martineau tells of a leading department store in the South that had old-fashioned lighting and fixtures throughout. The best families from the city's fine old homes seemed to love the store. Then a change came in one section of the store. The merchandiser of women's apparel set out to modernize his department. Mr. Martineau relates: "He introduced new fixtures and lighting, more high fashion styling, and a promotional flavor similar to any aggressive chain store in the field."[3]

The result? "The fortunes of the store declined in definite progression—first women's apparel, then children's, then men's apparel and finally all the hard-line departments." The trouble was traced to the women's-apparel department, which had been modernized, and the decline was checked when the store brought back into that department the ancient lights, fixtures, and other mood-creating paraphernalia.

When big downtown stores open suburban stores in shopping centers, care must be taken, Martineau has concluded, to open in areas with status images comparable to that of the downtown store. A lower-class department store that builds a branch in an upper-class suburban neighborhood will find itself under a cloud. And the reverse is also true. Many shopping centers, he states, are a hodgepodge of stores with different status appeals and are "pulling against each other."

Now let us examine the status meanings of the clothing we buy in these stores. The economic director of the Wool Bureau happily predicted, some months ago, that clothing was enjoying a resurgence as a symbol of status and would become more so in the coming decade.

Historically, clothing has been one of the most convenient, and visible, vehicles known for drawing class distinctions. In early New England, a woman was permitted to wear a silk scarf only if her husband was worth a thousand dollars. Medieval London had detailed specifications on the amount of affluence that was necessary before a person could wear ermine, cloth of gold, or silk. Rothenburg, Germany, still exhibits the heavy wooden collar that was locked, during the Renaissance, around the neck of any woman who tried to dress beyond her class. And during the French Revolution, the revolutionists, in their desire to abolish class distinctions, struck down the laws defining the dress appropriate to each class.

The elite long viewed clothing as a way to demonstrate both its superior wealth and its habitual abstinence from any productive form of labor. Some examples of the latter: the high hats, patent-leather shoes, and fluffy white collars and cuffs of the males; the high spiked heels, hobble skirts, and bound feet of females. Developments of recent years, however, weakened the effectiveness of clothing for these two purposes. The mass production and mass marketing of fine fabrics—including nylon stockings—weakened the first function; and the lessening significance of leisure as a symbol of high status, due to the shorter work week, weakened the second one.

It develops, however, that class distinctions persist in more subtle forms. Sociologists Bernard Barber and Lyle S. Lobel made an analysis of clothing preferences of women at different social levels by analyzing fashion material in a number of women's magazines covering a twenty-year period.[4] The classes studied ranged from "old money" upper class down to lower middle class.

They found, for example, a significant difference in emphasis as you moved from the "old money" rich, or true elite, to the "new money" rich, or unseasoned elite. The women of "old money" families tend to be relatively indifferent to swings in fashion; and their taste is oriented more to that of the British upper classes than to the French. They like woolens and prefer a tweedy look to a daring look. All this, Barber and Lobel conclude, reveals a "concern for birth distinction and English heredity as against the distinction of occupational achievement." They respond to fashion messages that use such words as "aristocratic" and such phrases as "well-bred looks" or "a trumpet flare at the hip."

In contrast, the "new money" women are fascinated with high fashion, especially as it is dictated by Paris. They strive for a chic, sophisticated look while at the same time, with an eye on the goal of gaining acceptance from the "old money" rich, they strive for an appearance of quiet, assured elegance.

As you move down into the range of the typical American

woman, the aim is to follow whatever "smart" style is "sweeping the country" provided that the style permits the women to emphasize their "respectability" and prettiness. These women are more likely to look for guidance in their dress to Mrs. Earl Warren than to the Duchess of Windsor.

A woman of some wealth amplified for me the difference of attitude of "old money" women and "new money" women when she told of an evening she spent attending parties on the North Shore of Chicago. The first was at a club dominated by wealthy "new money" families. The second was a more elite club for "old money" millionaires. She had planned, for convenience, to wear the same outfit to both affairs, a dramatic black gown accentuated by diamond accessories. Her hostess, however, admonished her to change before going on to the "old money" affair. They looked through her wardrobe and the hostess pointed to a dark-brown woolen dress as being ideal. My acquaintance explained, "It was the thing I had been wearing to come down to breakfast."

The objectives women typically have in mind when they dress also vary from class to class. Women who are really secure in their upper-class status may become fond of a really good outfit and wear it for years as a favorite costume. The fabulously well-dressed Mrs. Winston Guest recently took with her to Europe a suit she has been wearing for eight years. She was reported as explaining, "Good suits simply do not wear out if you hang them up." When you drop down to the semi-upper-class level, however, you find a great deal of striving to demonstrate variety of wardrobe. This is particularly true among club women in the Midwest. As they go to their various club activities, they keep running back home to change their outfits so that they will be more in keeping with the setting, time, and mood of the occasion. They tend to think of their dressing in terms of self-expression. My family once had such a lady as a house guest. She changed her costume five times in the course of one day. The wife of a corporate executive is a former Kansan now living in the New York suburbs. She states that when she goes back to her home town in Kansas she has to plan on wearing more outfits per week than she does in New York. The women in the Kansas town, she states, seem to be more dress-conscious.

Social Research, Inc., has found that lower-middle-class women (limited success), on the other hand, dress primarily to make a nice impression on other people, particularly other women. And the lower-status woman, it found, likes to dress up for still a different reason. She wants most the fantasy of the experience. She is eager to get away from the drudgery of housework and children, and wants to become a Cinderella and so escape for a moment from her troubles. She doesn't dress particularly for men because most of the males she sees at parties are her relatives and in-laws.

Men, too, despite their resistance to attempts to change their styles, exhibit certain distinctive modes of dress as you move from class to class. Upper-class males are much more likely to wear vests than males of any other class. And they have strong ideas about shirt collars. My wife, Virginia, recently painted the portrait of a striking-looking young man of seventeen who attends, most of the year, an elite New England boarding school. The portrait revealed him clean-cut in his open-collared white shirt. When Virginia showed him the portrait for suggestions, he said it was very nice. Something, however, was obviously bothering him, and he finally confessed the cause of his uneasiness. He asked if she would mind putting buttons on his open collar. The button-down collar, it seemed, is mandatory with boys at his boarding school.

Many grown men would feel uncouth if they ever had to appear in public without their Brooks Brothers suit. They've been buying them ever since their own boarding-school days. The importance of the upper-class label and "look" to males can be seen in the fact that a Third Avenue merchant in New York has developed a highly successful business selling cast-off "snob label" clothing, for around $35 a suit, to men who have momentarily come upon hard times. The most sought labels include Brooks Brothers, Burberry, Chipp, Stadler & Stadler, and J. Press.

Perhaps the most visible differentiation between males of the upper cluster of classes and those of the lower classes is the elaborate casualness of the upper-class dress for most occasions outside work and the faith in formality of those in the lower groups. A now famous Hollywood actor still reveals his lower white-collar origins every time he sits down. He pulls up his trousers to preserve the crease.

A sixteen-year-old boy from a limited-success family was invited to attend a dance for young folks at a yacht club on the New England coast. His mother was thrilled and bought him a new blue serge suit for the occasion. The boy spent a miserable evening. Every boy at the dance except himself was wearing khakis and an old sports jacket. Among the yacht-club set this casual uniform was *de rigueur*. This same distinction apparently applies in England. The aristocrats dress down on weekends, wear dirty sneakers and go tieless. Meanwhile, the gardener, when he goes for a walk, dresses up in his Sunday best with stiff collar and hat even when the weather is very warm.

In clothing as in other matters, the really rich prize age, whereas men well below them in status prize newness. The New England aristocrat clings to his cracked shoes through many re-solings and his old hat.

The shape of our clothing varies in another interesting way by class. As you go up the class scale, you find an increasing number of fat men. Among women the opposite is true. You rarely see a really plump woman on the streets of the well-to-do suburbs surrounding New York. The slim figure is more of a preoccupation with women of the two upper classes. As you go down the scale, the married women take plumpness more calmly.

The way we spend our money and pay our bills—for clothes and other items—also is to a considerable degree a reflection of class-induced attitudes. William Foote Whyte found in his interviews with Chick and Doc, the two contrasting young men of the Italian slums, that attitude toward money has a lot to do with the possibility of rising in the social scale. Chick went on to "Ivy University" and law school to become a successful lawyer. Doc, in contrast, made little progress, continued to hang out nightly with the street-corner gang. Whyte, who came to know both men well as to their intelligence and ability, observed: "Clearly difference in intelligence and ability does not explain the difference between Chick and Doc. There must be some other way of explaining why some Cornerville men rise while others remain stationary." He found that those who later went on to college and became successful began showing signs of thriftiness even in boyhood. Whyte concluded:

"The college boy must save his money in order to finance his education and launch his business and professional career. He therefore cultivates the middle-class virtue of thrift." In contrast, Doc, to maintain his prestige as leader of his street-corner gang, had to be a free spender. "It is not possible," Whyte said, "to be thrifty and yet hold a high position in the corner gang."[5]

Aside from the lowest class, the worst credit risks in America appear to be the upward strivers of the semi-upper class. The *Chicago Tribune* study of "The New Consumer" quotes a dweller of its high-status community, Golf, as explaining: "You must spend just a little more than you can afford to progress high in life." (In late 1958, an insurance company began promoting a policy that, it said, was ideal for highly paid executives. The New York State superintendent of insurance soon felt it necessary to issue a warning stating that many men of moderate incomes [$10,000–$15,000] had been buying it— and had no business doing so.)

A builder in suburban Detroit cited one higher-income suburb favored by middle-level automotive executives as having "the worst credit rating of the Detroit area." And he added, from sad personal experiences, "I want no part of the market for the high-priced home in the $25,000–$40,000 bracket. The most dangerous group to do business with are these people who have salaries between $10,000 and $20,000. Specifically I'm talking about junior executives who have higher-class tastes but still don't have the money. They've got to join the country club and buy a second car and probably a boat and have a regular cleaning woman. I call them the Second Louies of Industry. You can have them!"

The people with salaries ranging from $7,000 to $10,000, he said, are far better credit risks. They are more solid and don't "lush up" at the country club. "Above $10,000 you're taking a chance." That income figure of $10,000, he said, "is the breaking point."

As you go up the class scale, you find that people tend to develop, as a status right, a more delaying attitude toward monthly bills. A workingman's wife who neglects to pay a bill by the fifteenth is likely to find her credit cut off at the butcher's and, if delinquent more than a few days, to find a collector on her door step. A semi-upper-class wife, in contrast, is likely to consider it "plebeian" to pay bills promptly and expects tradespeople to maintain a patient, hat-in-hand attitude. The man and wife are much too busy with larger matters to bother with bills. Actually, of course, they often are strapped.

In the real upper class, you are likely to see a monumental casualness about bills. The local tradespeople pretend that money really is a nuisance and often make a point of seeming negligent and offhand about submitting bills. And the customers frequently take three or more months to pay. When you reach the higher levels of the upper class, the casualness about bills becomes a source of wonderment. Gloria Vanderbilt recalls, in her autobiography, which she wrote with her twin sister, her surprise at learning that the family butcher bill had reached $40,000.

behavior that gives us away

"The upper classes LIVE in a HOUSE . . . use the TOILET, the PORCH, LIBRARY or PLAY-ROOM. The middle classes RESIDE in a HOME . . . use the LAVATORY, the VERANDA, DEN or RUMPUS ROOM."—E. DIGBY BALTZELL, University of Pennsylvania.

❖─o─►◄─o─►◄─o─►◄─o─►◄─o─►◄─o─►◄─o─►❖

WHILE AMERICANS ARE CEREMONIOUSLY EGALITARIAN IN their more conspicuous behavior patterns, they reflect, sometimes wittingly and often unwittingly, their class status by the nuances of their demeanor, speech, taste, drinking and dining patterns, and favored pastimes.

In the matter of demeanor, the upper-class ideal is one of cool, poised reserve. This demeanor serves the double purpose of rebuffing pretenders and demonstrating one's own competence to carry the torch of gentility. The model for genteel behavior is the pre-World War II British aristocrat, who wore a wooden mask and, in the male version, cultivated a mustache to hide any emotional twitchings at the mouth when the owner was under stress.

The stiff upper lip must be maintained regardless of the provocations. Some months ago, I happened to attend a very proper upper-class tea. The guests included members of several old, moneyed families, a university dean, etc. The hostess exuded cool elegance. In the midst of the tea sipping her young son burst in excitedly to exhibit a mongrel pup he had just bought for $2 at an auction. The hostess, presumably, was appalled by his intrusion and by the long-term implications of his impulsive purchase. But she smiled, murmured "How nice," and went on talking to a guest. The flustered pup, meanwhile, lost bowel control in the middle of the Persian rug. In a lower white-collar home, such an untoward incident would have occasioned gasps, blushes, and howls of embarrassed merriment. At this tea, the incident seemingly passed almost unnoticed. Guests continued chatting on unrelated subjects. The hostess acted as if this was the most natural thing in the world to happen at a party, raised a window, calmly asked her son to please remove all traces of the pup, and went on chatting about the forthcoming marriage of one of her guests' daughters.

In speech, too, the upper-class members copy the British model, at least to the extent of striving for a cool, precise diction, and by pronouncing the "a" of tomato with an "ah." The British upper-class members still have such a distinctive form of speech that, not long ago, a nationwide argument developed over claims that the Royal Navy, in its screening of officer candidates, was favoring candidates with upper-class accents, other things being equal. *The Evening Standard* headlined one article: "Is There a Sound Barrier against Your Son?" and added that "It might hang on a dropped 'h.'"

With Americans, choice of words is more indicative of status than accent, although the New England boarding schools nurturing future upper-class boys have long fostered the Harvard, or Proper Bostonian, accent. In general, both the upper classes and the lower classes in America tend to be more forthright and matter-of-fact in calling a spade a spade (for example: organs of the body, sexual terms, excretory functions, etc.) than people in between, members of the semi-upper and limited-success classes. In this respect, at least, we are reminded of Lord Melbourne's lament: "The higher and lower classes, there's some good in them, but the middle classes are all affectation and conceit and pretense and concealment."[1]

Persons who feel secure in their high status can display

their self-assurance by using unpretentious language. Old Bostonians are notably blunt (often to the point of rudeness) in their language. A well-established society matron of Dallas and Southampton gave the appropriate upper-class answer when asked about the "secrets" of her success in entertaining. She responded, according to *The New York Times,* with: "Why, I just give them peanuts and whisky."

Sociologist E. Digby Baltzell of the University of Pennsylvania has compiled a table[2] of upper-class and middle-class usage of language as he found it while making a study of Philadelphia's elite. Here are a few examples:

Upper Class	Middle Class
Wash	Launder
Sofa	Davenport
Long dress	Formal gown
Dinner jacket	Tuxedo
Rich	Wealthy
Hello	Pleased to meet you
What?	Pardon?
I feel sick	I feel ill

Also, I might add, as you move from the upper class to those somewhat below, sweat becomes perspiration, pants become trousers, jobs become positions, legs become limbs, and people "go to business" instead of "go to work."

When members of different classes address each other, we see a recognition of the differences in the language used. Ostensibly, we use first names with each other because first-naming is symbolic of equality. Actually, it is a little more complicated. Anyone is uncomfortable if his expectations are not met, and a social inferior expects his superior to act superior. However, it must be done in a nice, democratic way. The superior calls the inferior, democratically, by the first name; but the inferior shows deference in responding by addressing the superior more formally. Amy Vanderbilt, the etiquette authority, for example, advises me that even though the wife of a boss may address the wife of a subordinate by her first name, the subordinate's wife should not address the wife of the boss by her first name until invited to do so.

A sociologist, investigating salutations in shipyards, discovered that, while supervisors invariably addressed workers by their first names, the workers only addressed each other by their first names. They addressed their foreman as "Brown," and front-office supervisors who came through the yard as "Mister Brown," and often took their caps off while doing it. One worker, when addressed formally as "Mister _____" by the investigating sociologist who had got to know him quite well, confessed that it embarrassed him to be so addressed. "It's like you were making fun of me somehow, pretending I'm more important than I am."[3]

Experts in communications are finding that the maintenance of good communication between different levels, as between management and workers, is far more difficult than assumed. Meanings become lost or distorted, especially when workers try to communicate upward. One investigator makes the figurative point that communication between management and workers is filtered by a funnel with the large end facing upward. The workers, he said, must try to get their thoughts "through the small end of the funnel. Sometimes the results are fantastic."

Our very modes of communication, furthermore, differ from class to class. This is seen in a study made of responses of people in Arkansas when they tried to relate to investigators what had happened when a tornado struck their community. The interviews were gathered by the National Opinion Research Center.[4] A comparison was made between responses from an "upper group" (some college education and an income of at least $4,000) and those of a "lower group," composed of people with little schooling and income. The sheer problem the lower-class person encountered in trying to communicate across class lines his tale to the college-trained investigator was in itself a strain. Aside from language difficulties, communication was complicated by the fact that the lower-class person had different rules for ordering his speech and thought.

The lower-class narrator related the events of the tornado entirely in terms of his own perspective. His story was like a movie made with a single, fast-moving, and sometimes bouncing, camera. Other people came into the story only as he encountered them. His account was vivid and exciting, but often, to the listener, fragmented and hard to follow. (Example: "We run over there to see about them, and they was all right.") In contrast, the narrator from the upper group is more like the director of a movie who is commanding several cameras, as he tries to give the listener the big picture of what happened. He tells what other people did, what organizations did, and even what other towns did. His account becomes so generalized and full of classifying, however, that it is less concrete and vivid than the lower-class account.

Now we turn to other areas of behavior where characteristic class patterns emerge.

Drinking habits. Social Research, Inc., made a comparative study of patrons of twenty-two cocktail lounges and twenty-four taverns in the Chicago area, and found that they represented different worlds socially.[5]

The cocktail lounge is primarily an upper-middle-class institution serving primarily mixed drinks made of hard liquor, and operating in a commercial district primarily between the hours of 12 to 8 P.M. In contrast, the tavern is a neighborhood social center, and operates from early morning till late at night. Its patrons are almost entirely from what I call the supporting classes, the lower three. As you go down the scale, the number of hours that people who frequent drinking establishments spend in those establishments increases. Upper-lower-class people (essentially working class) who frequent taverns spend fourteen to twenty-three hours a week there. Pierre Martineau has made the interesting observation that many taverns catering to this group use, as a name for the establishment, a title combining the names of the proprietor and his wife. Examples: "Vie & Ed's," "Fran & Bill's," "Curley & Helen's."

As might be surmised from the foregoing, patrons of the tavern see the tavern as a place where they can obtain social and psychological satisfactions—and not just a fast drink.

Most of the patrons live within two blocks of the tavern. Each tavern has its own social system. "Regulars" come in at the same time every day; they have their own rules about who is acceptable as a member of their in-group, and what constitutes proper and improper behavior in a tavern.

Each tavern caters not only to a specific social class but often to a special group within that class. Many of the taverns studied turned out to have a clientele consisting almost entirely of either Old Poles, New Poles, Italians, hillbillies, or Germans. One of the taverns catering to Polish-Americans had on its walls posters announcing events of interest to Polish-Americans, such as meetings of Polish-American war veterans, and the juke box offered primarily polkas. This tavern's proprietor said of a nearby tavern, "No, the tavern across the street is not like this one . . . all hillbillies over there . . . never come in here—don't want them in here. . . . We never have any trouble, and we don't want any. . . . They stay in their places. . . . No, they just learn fast when they move in here that this is not a place for them."

That hillbilly tavern across the street, catering to recent white immigrants from the South, featured on its juke box rock 'n' roll, hillbilly, and Western music. While the big drink in the Polish tavern is beer, the big drink with the hillbillies is a "shot" of whisky.

In general, however, the preferred drink of tavern habitués is beer. A glass of beer can be nursed a long time and, further, it is less likely to threaten self-control. Pierre Martineau, in mentioning this fact, referred to beer as a "drink of control." He went on to say that the tavern customer, usually a solid workingman, has a "terrible fear of getting out of control and getting fired." You find the least concern about self-control, he added, at the top of the social structure. People there don't worry when they drink. They can do no wrong. This may explain something I noticed in Northeast City. The most notorious lush in town was a playboy who had inherited his father's wealth. Many people reported having seen him sloppy drunk in public.

Sociologists studying behavior patterns of the social classes of a South Dakota town, Prairieton, found the people of the top class and the bottom class had an interesting grievance against each other. Both accused the other of drinking too much!

In this connection, the attitude of Jews toward drinking might be noted. Among Jews, drunkenness is unforgivable. It is viewed not simply as in bad taste for a Jew to become drunk but degrading and sinful. An older Jew will rarely drink anything at all except an occasional sherry. The younger Jew, if he lives in a Gentile area, will serve martinis to guests before dinner, and may even, to be congenial, have a bar in his house. However, if he lives in a predominantly Jewish area, he drinks very sparingly; and if a Gentile visits his home he is, out of habit, more likely to offer food than drink as a refreshment.

Two considerations seem to account for the Jewish aversion to drinking. The first is the Jew's tremendous respect for intellectual accomplishment. Drunkenness, of course, undermines—at least for a time—one's intellectual capacity. More important, perhaps, Jews see alcohol as a threat to self-control. Historically, Jews, as a persecuted group, have had to be alert constantly to threats to their family and their life. Drunkenness has seemed to make about as much sense for them as it would for an antelope in lion country.

Dining patterns. Tastes in food vary considerably from one end of the social scale to the other. Harriet Moore, of Social Research, Inc., tells of interviewing a man who had, in his lifetime, undergone an interesting series of changes in his food and drink preferences. As a lad, this man had grown up in a poor family of Italian origin. He was raised on blood sausages, pizza, spaghetti, and red wine. After completing high school, he went to Minnesota and began working in logging camps, where—anxious to be accepted—he soon learned to prefer beef, beer, and beans, and he shunned "Italian" food. Later, he went to a Detroit industrial plant, and eventually became a promising young executive. This was in the days when it was still fairly easy for a non-college man to rise in industry. In his executive role he found himself cultivating the favorite foods and beverages of other executives: steak, whisky, and sea food. Ultimately, he gained acceptance in the city's upper class. Now he began winning admiration from people in his elite social set by going back to his knowledge of Italian cooking, and serving them, with the aid of his manservant, authentic Italian treats such as blood sausage, pizza, spaghetti, and red wine!

In general, conceptions about what foods best serve as treats become more elaborate as you go down the social scale. Bakeries in working-class neighborhoods sell birthday cakes that exhibit spectacular creations with a variety of flowers made of icing and a figure standing in the middle. Hors d'oeuvres will most likely consist of little sandwiches covered with a bland, green cream cheese and decorated with roses. I once saw an upper-class group, accustomed to casual hors d'oeuvres such as peanuts, blanch when offered a tray of decorated sandwiches at a party. Patrons of metallic diners— most of the patrons are from the three lower classes—can have their choice of pie or cake but all will be buried in whipped cream.

Tastes vary to some extent, by class, on the hard-soft scale. An executive of a leading bread company told me that only the upper classes like hard, firm bread, and that people in the lower classes prefer the loaves that are so soft that they seem to be made of sponge rubber. When you go into a restaurant, you can typically tell what kind of people patronize it just by glancing at the bread basket. Only restaurants catering to sophisticates will place hard-crust rolls in the basket. Restaurants striving for a mass appeal will emphasize soft buns and soft breads.

Finally, acceptance of strange, offbeat foods is much more common with the two upper classes than with the three lower supporting classes. The average person of the lower group feels anxious in the presence of strange foods, and considers them fraught with danger. A Midwestern society matron reports her astonishment to find that her maid will not touch many of the very costly foods she serves the guests, such as venison, wild duck, pompano, caviar. Even when these are all prepared, steaming and ready to eat, the maid will cook herself some salt pork, turnip greens, and potatoes. They are the foods she knows.

Most of us like sweet-flavored foods, and many of us like sour-tasting dishes. But a liking for the other main flavors— dryness, saltiness, and bitterness—has to be developed; and only people interested in demonstrating their superior tastes will go to the bother—or have the curiosity—to investigate such items as anchovies. Foods also become cherished by the social elite as they become more expensive, rare, or difficult to prepare. Social prestige derives thus from knowing the difference between a burgundy and a claret, or serving caviar, abalone, or lobster. Harriet Moore states: "As a person strives to gain entree into a more sophisticated social group, he will almost invariably be alert and receptive to food preferences and dietary habits of its members. Failure to do so may well mean failure to get 'in.'" They learn, for example, to prefer to have their coffee served in demitasse cups. An acquaintance relates that he recently attended a supper given by socially elite wives for their town's volunteer firemen (largely drawn from the three supporting classes). The firemen were fascinated with the dinky cups placed before them by the ladies, but later seemed chagrined when their tiny portions of coffee were poured. The person striving to gain entree into a select social group also soon perceives that one never asks for ginger ale with his whisky (a favored drink at the limited-success level).

Games and pastimes. Interest in developing perfection in dancing skill goes down as social status rises. If you drive along the lower-income stretches of Chicago's Archer Avenue, you will note large establishments, conspicuously advertised, devoted to teaching dancing. They promise high levels of skill not only in ballroom but also "toe, tap, ballet, and acrobatic" dancing. Working-class parents, particularly those of East or South European backgrounds, have been persuaded that helping their children acquire grace through dancing will help them escape to a higher class, and so is worth considerable financial sacrifice. On the other hand, if you look in on a higher-class dance, say at a New England boarding school, you are struck by the dancers' lackadaisical, offhand approach to dancing. Some, in fact, shuffle like zombies. This same contrast has been noted in Great Britain, where millions go in for dancing, or watch dancers on TV, each week, and where millions are taking dancing lessons.

According to one investigator, zest there for stylish dancing is definitely "non-U," or not upper class.[6] The editor of the *Ballroom Dancing Times* states: "The quality of dancing goes down as you go up the social scale. You will find much better dancing at the Hammersmith Palais, than at the Savoy." (An additional explanation for this greater interest in dancing skill at the lower social levels is that lower-class young people have fewer places they can go to socialize and meet the opposite sex.)

The magazine *Mademoiselle* has found, in a comparative study it made of the lives of women who went to college and those who didn't, that college-educated women are seven times as likely to play golf and eight times as likely to play tennis as women who never went to college. On the other hand, the non-college women are more likely to go bowling, fishing, and boating.

Others have noted that bridge playing is largely confined to the upper two classes, and bingo playing to the lower three classes. While poker playing cuts across class lines, some of its most passionate devotees are Negro "society" women. They talk about their latest game for hours over the telephone, and some even stake their automobiles on the turn of a card. Sociologist E. Franklin Frazier, in exploring this phenomenon, sees their obsession with poker as an attempt to escape the frustrations (sexual and other) of their lives. One woman said that winning at poker was in some ways similar to the release of sexual orgasm.

Entertainment and "culture." Although most United States families now have television sets somewhere in their houses, television was originally most enthusiastically embraced (and still is) by people in the lower classes. When television was an innovation, the percentage of class members buying a set rose with every move down the social-class scale. At one stage, nearly three quarters of the members of the two lower-class families had television sets, while only one quarter of the upper-class families had them.[7] One explanation—taste aside —for the greater popularity of television with people of the lower classes is that they are more confined to the house. They have no country club to go to.

A similar descending growth in popularity exists in the pattern of attendance at motion pictures, sports events, and other "spectator" types of recreation. In contrast, members of the two upper classes show a marked preference for active, creative activities such as playing tennis, visiting friends, and carrying on programs of serious reading. The upper classes read non-fiction as well as fiction. The lower-class members who read books at all strongly prefer fiction. A study made a few years ago of readers of *Harper's* and *Atlantic Monthly* magazines (mostly executive and professional families with an average yearly income of $13,150) revealed that they bought seventeen books a year, on an average; and half of them owned collections of long-playing classical recordings (average value of collection: $150).

The old class lines that preserved "culture" as a monopoly for the aristocrats, it might however be noted, have slowly been crumbling with the growth of literacy, democratic forms, and mass-production processes. Opera is being marketed in the hinterlands, and reproductions of art masterpieces are hanging on the walls in tens of thousands of American homes. The result has been the emergence of "mass culture," which Dwight Macdonald calls "a debased form of High Culture." Mass culture, he points out, is imposed from above: "It is fabricated by technicians hired by businessmen; its audiences are passive consumers, their participation limited to the choice between buying and not buying."

Fascination with culture among the two upper classes seems to have regional variations based on distance from a major cultural center such as New York, Boston, Chicago, or San Francisco. A semi-upper-class couple living within fifty miles of New York may never go to the opera or a concert or a ballet during their entire marriage and may rarely go to a play. In Texas or Iowa, on the other hand, such a couple is likely to travel hundreds of miles to see a road performance of a noted opera, orchestra, ballet, or play. Possibly, in such an area, people feel a greater thirst for culture because it is not readily available. Quite possibly another factor is that it is easier to achieve status in Texas or Iowa by being an opera- or ballet- or theater-going enthusiast than it is in New York.

Magazine reading. The editorial content of any magazine pretty much selects its audience. We are drawn to the magazines where we can find self-identification with the situations, characters, or authors presented. Social Research, Inc., found this to be true in terms of class in its study of blue-collar vs. white-collar wives. As I indicated in Chapter 1, it found an "invisible wall" between the ways of life of the two groups. This carries over, it was found, into their selection of magazines. The blue-collar or Wage Town wife, who reads the "family behavior" magazines (sometimes called "romance" or "confession" magazines), very rarely reads the "women's service" magazines such as *Good Housekeeping*.

The report by Macfadden Publications, on Social Research's findings, states: "You might find a story about a truck driver and a diner waitress in either *True Story* or a women's service magazine. But in the service magazine the atmosphere is apt to be light and airy, the characters even treated as faintly comic. In *True Story,* these people are hero and heroine. . . ." (And the hero or heroine, if I may intrude a thought, is usually caught in some ghastly dilemma involving sexual waywardness on someone's part.) Here are examples found of typical contrasts in title treatment between the white-collar "service" magazines and the Wage Town "behavior" magazines:

Service Magazines	*Behavior Magazines*
YOUNG LOVE	
"To Catch a Man"	"I Want You"
BIGAMY PROBLEM	
"One Wife Is Enough"	"Which Man Is My Husband?"

ETERNAL TRIANGLE
"Remember He's a Married Man"   "Lovers in Hiding"

The "behavior" magazine article typically is illustrated with photographs, rather than drawings, to enhance the reader's feeling that this is an honest-to-gosh true tale.

Instinctive differences of behavior patterns by class will probably always be with us. Watching for the differences can in itself be a game that challenges our perceptiveness.

11

the sociology of sex appeal

"For nonmarital sex relations the ideal girl is a one-man 'lay,' blonde and fair-skinned, belonging to a socially superior old-stock group. . . . For marriage, preference is for the virgin, a dark brunette, of Italian extraction."—WILLIAM FOOTE WHYTE, **on the preferences of corner boys in Cornerville, an Italian-American slum.**

◄─○─►·◄─○─►·◄─○─►·◄─○─►·◄─○─►·◄─○─►·◄─○─►

PERSONS IN THE UPPER CLASSES TEND TO ASSUME THAT sexual behavior becomes more and more promiscuous as you move down the social scale. They often express shock and disgust at the way the lower classes, wed or unwed, make love like "animals," to employ a frequently used word. On the other hand, people in the lower classes often express shock at what they feel to be the "wild," depraved love-making habits of the upper classes.

It might be fruitful to examine what each group considers to be shocking in the other group's behavior. Much of the general disapproval springs from the fact that people in the different social classes have distinctive courtship patterns; tend to marry within their own class; and develop distinctive patterns as far as stability, fidelity, and dominance are concerned after marriage. Many of the differences that seem so shocking, it should be noted at the outset, develop from the single fact that marriage is delayed more and more as you go up the class scale. Girls in the lower classes start marrying soon after their mid-teens, whereas girls in the two upper classes are usually well into their twenties before they marry. They are waiting for men who must complete their higher education and launch themselves in careers. The years of delay after both the girls and men are physiologically ripe for marriage force them to develop inhibited rituals of courtship that will still supply them with token gratifications.

Let us begin by looking at the love-making practices of the lower classes that shock the upper classes so much. Three studies are of particular interest.

August B. Hollingshead, in his study of the high-school-age youth of Elmtown in Illinois, concluded that at the high-school age the "sex mores were violated far more frequently" by adolescents in the two lower classes than in the upper and in-between classes.[1] Girls in the lower classes also talked more openly about sex, and were believed to be more "full of sex."

The boys in the lower classes who had already dropped out of school derived much of their prestige among their peers from their skill in "making" girls. The boy who had not "made" a girl was likely to lie and say that he had, because failure to do so made him a "pansy" with his clique mates. However, he was subject to severe condemnation if he fell into "trouble," either by "knocking a girl up" or "getting a load" (venereal disease).

As for the girls of the lower classes, many had learned to develop an expectation that affectionate responses to physical advances were the natural and reasonable *quid pro quo* for their acceptance of material favors such as a movie, a ride, a gift, or candy. Many considered all this as "having some fun before settling down." The girls insist that they be "treated as a lady," but they interpret this quite broadly as "not being manhandled" in a muscular way by boy friends. A lower-class boy who really treats a girl as a lady, Hollingshead pointed out, is not respected by the girls and is hooted at by the boys.

The second study of pertinence is William Foote Whyte's on sex life of young Italian-American men in Cornerville, a slum area of an Eastern city.[2] The young men spend a great deal of time in sexual exploration and most of those of high-school age regularly carry "safes" or condoms. Yet, although superficially there seems to be a great deal of laxness about sex behavior, Whyte found "an elaborate and highly developed sex code." For example, the young man is careful to meet even a "good girl" on street corners for dates, rather than at her home, because it is assumed by all concerned that the moment he steps a foot inside her home he intends to marry her. The corner boys, furthermore, have a code of honor that prevents them from ending a girl's status as a virgin.

Whyte offers this incident related by Doc, a gang leader, to indicate how deeply the taboo against deflowering virgins is ingrained. It involved Danny, a gambler, and Al, who was "a hound, after women all the time." Doc stated: "One time Al and Danny went out with a girl—she said she was a virgin. She had one drink, and she was a little high. They were up in a room and they had her stripped—stripped! She still said she was a virgin, but she wanted them to [be intimate]. But they wouldn't do it. . . . Can you imagine that, Bill? There she was stripped, and they wouldn't do anything to her. . . . The next day she came around and thanked both of them. They can't be such bad fellows if they do that."

The most-sought girl for Cornerville boys to date casually, from a prestige standpoint, is what they call a "one-man lay." She is faithful for the time being. Preferably she should be as non-Italian looking as possible. The "real McCoy" is a blonde of "old Puritan stock." Rated below the one-man lay in desirability are, in order, (1) the promiscuous girl, (2) the prostitute.

When it comes to choosing a girl for marriage, however, the requirements are quite different. Now the ideal is a "good girl" and virgin, from a background much like his own. An Italian girl is desired because "she would understand my ways." Readers may wonder that there would be any virgins left in view of the male preoccupation at this level with sex. Actually, a majority of the girls are likely to remain chaste. The fact that twenty-five young men in a neighborhood are promiscuous doesn't mean there are twenty-five promiscuous girls. Only eight or ten girls may be promiscuous. The males compete for them as sex partners, but not usually as marriage mates.

Finally, we have the findings of Indiana University's Institute for Sex Research. In its investigations it has been, as one aspect of its studies, analyzing sexual behavior encountered at different class levels (on a ten-class scale).[3] It has found that the boy destined to become a semi-skilled worker later on is fifteen times as likely to have intercourse by the time he reaches his mid-teens as the boy destined to go to college and become a professional or "upper white-collar" person. The Institute reports that in some lower-level communities it had been unable to find a single male who had not, by the time he was seventeen, had sexual relations. And, in such lower-level communities, the occasional boy who had not had such relations proved to be either physically or mentally handicapped, homosexual, or a bright, ambitious lad destined to go to college. Premarital intercourse for males is accepted as such a normal and natural occurrence at the lower social levels that some lower-level clergymen, according to the Institute, preach against profanity, smoking, drinking, gambling, and infidelity, but will not include premarital sex in their listing of sins to guard against. Even in the matter of extra-marital sex relations there is general, if bitter, acceptance that, although such activity is disapproved, boys will be boys. Whyte made the same point about Cornerville men.

When we turn, however, to the behavior of the girls of the lower classes, quite a different morality prevails. This contrasting morality is supported by the men who take it for granted that a double standard should prevail. Although the young men at this level are almost unanimously experienced sexually, 41 per cent of them insist that they wouldn't consider marrying a girl who wasn't a virgin!

Whatever the reasons, girls in the lower educational classes show just about the same restraint in waiting as girls in the upper classes. The girls not going beyond high school who transgress the moral code are likely to start their transgressing earlier than the girls who go on to college. On the other hand, the girls going on to college have a much longer wait before marrying after the onset of puberty than the girls with grade-school or high-school educations. That presumably helps account for the seemingly contradictory fact that, among girls who do not go beyond the lower-grade school, 70 per cent are virgins at the time they marry whereas the proportion drops to 40 per cent for girls who go to college. The girls at the lower educational levels show somewhat more proneness to become pregnant before marriage; but this may derive from the fact that their transgressions occur while they are at a younger, more naïve age.

The upper classes, viewing much of the sexual behavior of the lower classes as morally abhorrent, often consider it their moral duty to impose their own code, as far as possible, on people in the lower classes under their domination or influence. So let us look at the sexual behavior pattern of the two upper classes.

Unmarried males of the upper educational and vocational levels certainly do show more continence than males at any lower level. On the other hand, they engage in many expedient practices the lower classes consider to be unnatural if not perverted. Two thirds of the upper-level men going to college masturbate, according to the Institute for Sex Research's investigation, while fewer than a third of the men the same age at the lower level do. The contrast is even more extreme in the matter of petting to orgasm.

A lower-level male may have intercourse with dozens of girls he casually encounters and not kiss any of them, at least more than superficially. In contrast, the college-level male, while continent as far as intercourse is concerned, engages in deep or tongue kissing with dozens of girls. Nearly nine tenths of all college men are tongue kissers, according to the Institute, and yet many of these same men would recoil at the thought of sharing a common drinking glass. Lower-class people consider such wallowing about at the mouth as filthy and unsanitary.

Similarly, upper-level males show considerably more fascination with the female's breasts, both as objects of beauty and as objects for manipulation during intimacies, than males from the lower classes. The latter tend to associate them more with their feeding function.

When the upper-level people marry, their sexual behavior again often seems odd to people at the lower level. Perhaps the upper-level people just have livelier imaginations. At any rate, they are more experimental in their love-making: they make love in the nude (a thought that appalls many in the lower level) and they occasionally make love in the light (an even more appalling, indecent arrangement in the eyes of people of the lower level).

While upper-level couples devise a variety of ways, before marriage, to handle their impulses short of coitus, there is some evidence that after marriage they feel less urgent concern about the sexual side of their union than lower-level couples do. Certainly the husbands are less demanding. Many have restrained themselves so long—more than a decade after puberty—that they are far less likely than lower-level males to be sexually unfaithful after marriage. Not only are they inhibited sexually, but they wouldn't know how to go about plotting and carrying through a seduction.

Furthermore, there is evidence that a sizable proportion of men who have gone to college are relatively unaggressive as partners and love-makers.

Robert F. Winch, sociologist at Northwestern University, directed an exhaustive psychodynamic exploration of twenty-five college men and their recent brides. He found most of the couples felt that sex was not so very important in their marriage relationship. Both partners seemed to like the idea that their spouse was not more demanding sexually.

Most of the men Winch studied showed some uneasiness about the fact that they were not more aggressive in their general approach to life. Winch concluded from an analysis of their life histories that a number of the men had been reared by a "castrating" mother who frightened them out of their aggressiveness and made them "over-controlled," passive adults.

Winch was so impressed with the evidence of male passiveness—in his intensive study and from more general studies—that he suggested the "Thurberian" marriage may be one of the commonest types of marriage among modern college-educated people from middle-class backgrounds. In these marriages, he noted, the brides tend to be active, pleasantly directive girls who need passive young men whom they can nurture and control. (He suggests that mate selection is to a large extent the search for a person who can supply our complementary needs.)[4]

If we drop to the limited-success or lower-middle-class level (usually non-college), we still find a wide prevalence of wives who take charge of their marriage relationship. Hollingshead found that such Elmtown wives typically exert the deciding influence in all matters affecting home, children, and social life.

Two different investigators of radio's soap operas (which appeal very largely to limited-success women) have been impressed by the fact that the males depicted tend to be weak characters.

One psychology expert, a European refugee, who spent many months listening to soap operas as a part of his work, confessed the experience depressed him so much he almost began wishing that Hitler had got him. Typically, he found the soap opera built around a female Fuehrer who manages the affairs of the rest of the characters, who tend to be spineless men and sexless, glorified women.

Social Research, Inc., in its analysis of the "invisible wall" between white-collar and blue-collar wives living in the same neighborhood, placed considerable stress on this matter of dominance. The white-collar wives, it found, tended to look upon their husbands as rather easily handled and well housebroken as far as being "family-oriented" is concerned. On the other hand, it found that the blue-collar wives of Wage Town see "all men—whether husband or men in general—as more powerful figures: dominant, independent, sexually active and demanding, and, over all, as actually more *mature* than women."[5]

And the women, when married, are much more active sexually than the white-collar wife. The young blue-collar wife, even after marriage, may still have adolescent love fantasies.

One possible explanation for this tendency of working-class wives to see men as powerful is that workingmen's wives include more foreign born than the general population. They came from countries such as Italy, Poland, and Puerto Rico where husbands of most classes still want it to be known they are the bosses of the family.

It has long struck me as intriguing that motorcycling as a boy-girl pastime has not caught on in America as it has in Europe. In America, only women of the lower classes take Sunday excursions on motorcycles with their husbands or boy friends. In Europe, couples from the more successful and prosperous classes go in for this extensively. Even celebrated playboys take their girl friends for rides. One explanation, of course, is that automobiles are more prevalent in the United States than in Europe and offer a more luxurious, dignified ride. But another explanation, I suspect, is that American women above the working class would resist assuming the dependent position necessary for a motorcycle outing. The woman sits behind the man, who is masterfully guiding the cycle with both hands while she clings to his waist.

When people of different class levels marry, they face a considerable problem in adjusting themselves to a mutually agreeable mode of expressing love for each other. And that is just one area where there are deep differences between the social classes. Two social scientists of the University of Chicago, Julius Roth and Robert F. Peck, who have investigated the problem of cross-class adjustment in marriage, found the differences "deep enough to make it relatively hard for two people of different classes to live together happily as man and wife." To illustrate, they cited the adjustment problems of an upper-level man dedicated to accumulating an estate for the future marrying a lower-level girl who has always been taught to believe that money is meant to be spent, and as quickly as possible. Similarly, a man in the limited-success class, who typically has firm ideas on the proper rearing of children, may find himself frequently exasperated by a wife from a lower class who is likely to take an indulgent, easy-does-it attitude toward child rearing. Because of such difficulties, these two investigators found, "cross-class marriages . . . are a poorer risk than same-class marriages." Low happiness scores, they added, are particularly common in cross-class marriages in which the wife is conspicuously superior to the husband in education.

Here are the findings of Roth and Peck on the prospects of a "good" marriage adjustment for couples, based on social classes from which each spouse came:[6]

	"Good"
Both from same class	53.5%
Spouses 1 class apart	35 %
Husband from higher class than wife	35.3%
Wife from higher class than husband	27.7%
Spouses more than 1 class apart	14.3%

Girls and men from opposite sides of the railroad track do fall in love and marry, and some adjust very successfully. Pretty daughters of miners marry millionaires, and the public rejoices. Most, however, suffer the frustration of the fictional Kitty Foyle, who found the ordeal of adjusting to her man's wealthy, sedate oh-so-well-bred family exasperating beyond her endurance.

For better or worse, such cross-class marriages are uncommon in America. A college girl is six times as likely to marry a college man as a non-college girl. Even dating across more than one class line is likely to create comment. Hollingshead tells the poignant fate of Joan Meyers who belonged to an elite girls' club, called God We're Good, in Elmtown, where 96 per cent of all dates were with youths of the same or adjacent classes. Joan accepted a date with Melvin Swigart, a Class IV (or, roughly, working class) boy. At the dance, her club members shunned her conspicuously. She "sinned a second time" a few days later by going for a ride during noon hour in Melvin's jalopy. A week later, a club member was asked about Joan and she said, "We do not have anything to do with her *now!* There's a wall there."

In dating, the crossing of class lines is condoned, typically, only when the boy dates down, not the girl. James West found, in his Plainville, that it was inconceivable for an upper-class girl to date a lower-class boy. In marriage, too, the girl is far more likely to do the advancing socially, if any class lines are crossed, than the man.

Sociologist Richard Centers made a study of marriage pairings by seven occupational classes (executive, professional, small business, white-collar, skilled manual, semi-skilled, unskilled).[7] At every level, girls married a higher percentage of men from the same level as their fathers than from a higher or lower level. Significantly, however, the girls in the lower classes were much more successful in marrying upward than men. Of the men in the three lower or manual classes, only 1 in 33 managed to marry a girl whose father was an executive or professional. In contrast, 1 in 4 of the girls made such a marriage. The comely daughter is still an asset to be prized by the lower-level family that finds most other routes to social advancement blocked.

Our dating and marrying is even more clearly compartmentalized by the vertical stratifications of religion, national background, and, of course, race. W. Lloyd Warner relates the case of a lovely, gracious, brilliant Polish Catholic girl attending Jonesville High School. A popular high-school boy was trying to explain why he had never dated her, or even thought of dating her. He spoke of an "invisible barrier" between them.

He said that if he didn't know she was Polish he undoubtedly would regard her as beautiful. Frankly, he said, he wished he could be above such attitudes; but if you try to be, other people think you're "peculiar."[8]

In some American cities, the overwhelming majority of marriages take place within the boundaries of religion or national background. Two studies of marriages in New Haven, Connecticut, emphasize this.[9] One showed that 91 per cent of all white marriages were within the same religious group. Another showed that two thirds of the marriages took place within the same national-background group.

Nationals who intermarry tend to do so within the boundaries of religion. Protestants with British, German, or Scandinavian backgrounds intermarry; Catholics from Ireland, Italy, and Poland form another intermarrying group; and Jews of whatever background marry almost completely among themselves.[10] In recent decades, the Irish-Catholics in New Haven have been marrying more and more Italian-Catholics, because the prestige of Italians in New Haven has been rising rapidly. In some other Connecticut cities, however, the Irish have tended to remain aloof.

Intermarriage rates between Catholics and non-Catholics have been considerably higher in cities less conspicuously ethnic than New Haven. In a city such as Raleigh, North Carolina, where barely 2 per cent of the population are Catholic, three quarters of all Catholics enter into mixed marriages. On the other hand, in a city such as Santa Fe, where the majority of people are Catholic, less than 10 per cent of the Catholics enter into mixed marriages.

Barriers in the form of intense public disapproval prevent all but a very few whites and Negroes from establishing relations of courtship and marriage. Casual sexual relations, however, are quite a different matter. Here the barriers work in some complex and peculiar ways.

Sexual barriers affect only half the adult Southerners in a mandatory way. White women and Negro men are sternly prevented from amatory pursuits across the caste line. White men and Negro women know that the taboo does not apply, at least strictly, to them. In 1958, newspapers featured a story from North Carolina that, in one paper, was entitled: "Negro Boy Jailed for Kissing White Girl." It is most unlikely that a white boy would be jailed for kissing a Negro girl, or vice versa.

Some years ago, Yale's social psychologist John Dollard explored these barriers while studying in depth Southern Town. Officially, Dollard found, it was only the no-good poor white or "red-neck" males who went prowling with sex in mind in the Negro section of Southern Town after dark. Dollard heard from informants of both races, however, that some of the highest-class males in town had consorted with Negro women, and that a great many of the local white boys began their sexual experience with Negro girls.

One white woman, who believed that most white men in the town "had to do" with Negro girls, told Dollard of one of her own unforgettable courtship experiences. She was in love with a white boy and gave him a very warm farewell kiss. An older woman observing this admonished her afterward never again to kiss a boy so warmly. She said such a kiss might inspire him to go to "nigger town" afterward.

That incident illuminates the dual attitude many Southern white men have toward women. They have idealized the Southern white women to the point where many come to regard them as untouchable. At least this was so at the time of Dollard's researches. Negro girls, then, become the lightning rods for their unsublimated sexual feelings; and in their fantasies the white men often picture the Negro women as seductresses who live for the moment of sexual expression. Needless to say, many Negro women, particularly the educated ones, deeply resent this concept and have had to learn to be forthright with amorous white males who have come to believe their own fantasies.

With the recent economic upheaval and the great movement of population into, and out of, the South, Southern men appear to be moving toward the American norm in their attitude toward women. They seem to be breaking away somewhat from the tradition that the white girl must be placed on a pedestal and left there to be admired from a distance until the veil of marriage is lifted.

Relations between the sexes at all levels and in all areas have distinctive characteristics that deserve our sympathetic interest. These distinctive patterns are not the result of whim or "wildness" but of fairly fundamental facts in the people's lives. Professional people who seek to guide or regulate relations between the sexes, in particular, I feel, would be well advised to act only after achieving a breadth of understanding of our mores.

12

who can be a friend?

"And if I am observed talking to him will it make me seem to belong or not to belong?"—LIONEL TRILLING.

◄─o─►·◄─o─►·◄─o─►·◄─o─►·◄─o─►·◄─o─►·◄─o─►

THE PEOPLE WHO ASK US BACK TO DINNER ARE ALMOST AL- ways those who regard us as approximate equals in social prestige. I'm referring here to the social evenings that are relaxed and spontaneous. For better or worse, most people feel more at ease with their own kind. An early sociologist, F. H. Giddings, developed a concept to explain this, which has be- come known as "consciousness of kind." Certainly it is true that many people find that trying to socialize across class bar- riers can be a strain, because ingrained habits, outlooks, tastes, and interest, especially if they are people of low curiosity, typically differ by class. Sociologist Joseph A. Kahl has stated that the fellow who owns a yacht is likely to think he cannot have much fun with a townsman who owns a rowboat. When people find themselves in a cross-class social situation, they are likely to put on their best behavior and strain to make pleasant conversation.

Furthermore, most of us confine our socializing to members of our own social class because we feel that status is attached to the act of socializing. What will people think if we are seen at so-and-so's house? People a notch higher than we are, socially, may hesitate to come to our house, despite all our charming qualities, because someone might interpret this as meaning they had slipped down to our social class. Thus it is that we usually end up confining our socializing to our own kind of people.

In Hollingshead's Elmtown, an informant, Mrs. Daniels, told about her neighbors, the Joseph Stones, whose home backed up to her own. The Stones, she said, "are above us socially" in a clique known as The Little Eight. She said, "We talk back and forth as neighbors in the yard," and she added that Mrs. Stone had invited her for some afternoon bridge, but then she remarked, "Mr. Daniels and I have never been invited to any of their parties, and we never invite them here." Another family in the neighborhood was the Hewitts, who belonged to a still higher social clique, The Big Eight. The Hewitts, she felt, were downright snooty. "We have been neighbors for seven years, but she has never asked me to one of her parties, and she has them all the time."

Actually, Elmtown is an old-fashioned community, where people of the different classes do at least see each other around the neighborhood. Even this is becoming unlikely in the newer, stratified development-type communities. There, we see only people whose husbands make an income close to our own—within a quite narrow band, say $6,500 to $8,250. Such a family rarely sees the family of a factory worker, an industrialist, or even a schoolteacher.

The people we are willing to declare are our "friends" persistently come from our own social stratum. Some years ago, a fund-raising campaign in Boston ran aground because of this fact. The women's auxiliary of the Boston Symphony Orchestra conceived the idea of using a chain letter to raise money. Each woman in the auxiliary was supposed to write a letter to ten "friends." It was assumed that, in no time at all, such a chain letter would swirl over Boston and produce a windfall of dollars. Unfortunately, that didn't happen at all. The women in the auxiliary were all upper-class women, and the chain letters to "friends" never got out of the relatively small upper class, and down into the city's other classes.

At the bottom of the scale, much the same situation prevails regarding friends. The majority of textile workers in Paterson, New Jersey, reported that they had no friends in any social class but their own.

Perhaps the most illuminating study of friendship patterns is that conducted by Bevode McCall in a study of the social structure of his Georgia Town.[1] He concluded: "The way people choose their friends is a part of the functioning of social class." In his Georgia Town, at least, few mutual friendships crossed the lines of the classes he found there. McCall asked more than 2,000 persons to name their "three best friends." Many people named one of two bank presidents as their best friend. A druggist and an eighty-year-old lady also were named as "best friend" by many people. With the exception of the very bottom class, the people in each class named as "best friends" more people in their own class than in any other.

Altogether, McCall had 5,200 choices listed for "three best friends." He sorted out all the cases where a "best friend" was named across a class line. Then he checked the list of the persons named to see if the feeling was mutual. (Often it was not.) He found only 140 cases out of the 5,200 where there was a mutual choice across class lines—or less than 3 per cent!

The stratification of our socializing patterns is seen most vividly in situations that parallel the company town. I have in mind those socializing systems confined to employees of one company, or to people of a military base, a university campus, or a one-industry town such as Hollywood. Let us look at examples of the four in order.

Company entertaining. Management officials of a company, living in the same area, will almost always devote most of their home entertaining to one another. Partly, perhaps, this is "consciousness of kind" at work. Partly it results from a deliberate encouragement by management of off-hour socializing to promote, it hopes, team spirit. Also, it reflects an anxiety on the part of the officials to keep an eye on one another even during off hours. And much of it is a reflection of ambition. One account of Neil McElroy's rise up through the echelons of Procter & Gamble states that he and his wife, both ambitious for higher things, "limited their entertaining primarily to important P & G people. . . ."[2]

The *Wall Street Journal*, in a study of executive entertaining, noted that men are quick to deny they have fallen into any corporate mold or "just live for the company." One young sales executive, who made that protestation, stated a few minutes later, however: "My wife and I decided a long time ago not to waste too much of our leisure time with casual entertaining. When we have people out to the house, it has to be those who may be important to me as contacts."

Some companies not only encourage home entertaining within their ranks, but have some pretty explicit rules on how it must be done. The *Wall Street Journal* quoted the wife of a middle-management executive of a great chemical concern as griping: "I know of at least four couples who have left our company recently because of the unwritten rules of protocol that must be observed when entertaining company officials. We can never entertain anyone higher or lower in rank than my husband; when the husband of a friendly couple receives a promotion, then we can no longer socialize; except for formal open houses, or yearly cocktail parties, higher officials never entertain anyone below them."

The vice-president of a sizable company in a small western Pennsylvanian town told me of an awkward social problem he had. He brought in, from the "field," a promising man of Hungarian extraction to head up a sales department under him.

The man persisted in asking the vice-president and his wife to his house for dinner. Each time the vice-president and his wife begged off, pleading other engagements. The president, similarly invited, also declined. After three months, although he was performing brilliantly at his job, the new subordinate grumbled to associates that the local "society" situation was too sticky for him and quit.

Recently, *Nation's Business* carried an article, "Friendship Can Ruin Your Business," by a business writer who cautioned executives to keep a sharp eye on fraternization patterns developing around the office to prevent fraternization from becoming "excessive." He cited positive values such as "group spirit," but his concluding paragraph pointed out that precautionary watchfulness "will prevent an up-and-coming manager from carrying around his neck a millstone of personal commitments, loyalties and friendships . . ." and help him perform his job better.

Below the management level of companies, you find somewhat similar stratification in entertainment. Although members of the white-collar force may work only a few yards from blue-collar workers, they almost never intermingle with them, either on or off the jobs. As for the blue-collar workers, they apparently just want to get home. They rarely invite their colleagues to come to their houses for supper; and most of them wouldn't dream of asking their foreman to their houses. It is not that they would be afraid to. The idea simply would not occur to them.

Military towns. Officers in the regular services, of course, are accustomed to putting the business of behaving according to one's rank openly and precisely on the line. They aren't inhibited by the requirement imposed on corporate officers to maintain, ostensibly, democratic forms. Actually, there is quite a bit of unofficial intermingling at the casual level across the lines of rank. In any social event of consequence, however, the lines are drawn firmly by rank; and seating is by date of rank. An invitation that comes from a higher-ranking officer, or his wife, has the force of a command. And, if it is a large affair where both tea and coffee are to be poured, the officer's wife invited to pour the coffee must outrank the wife invited to pour tea. This, apparently, derives from England, where coffee is regarded as a higher-status symbol than tea.

A perceptive young wife, who has just completed a tour of several years' duty as an Air Force lieutenant's wife, relates that as an Air Force wife she had to forget her ideas about democratic sociability. And the Air Force social pattern is not as rigid as that of the older services. She and her husband dutifully attended an orientation course during which they were warned of the dangers of familiarity with men of lower rank—or the men's wives.

While stationed in Enid, Oklahoma, this couple lived next door to a sergeant and his wife. They talked affably across the few feet of yard many hundreds of times—but never did they have supper together or play cards together. The wife explains, "Between enlisted men's families and officers' families there is no social passing. You do not invite them to your house and you do not socially go to theirs."

Whenever the base commander gave a party or reception, she added, attendance was mandatory. Every officer was required to leave his calling card (as proof of attendance). If the couple neglected to attend, the husband had to fill out an RBI (reply by endorsement) and that went into his permanent record.

My informant has concluded that wives of superior officers are more likely to "wear their rank" than the husbands. The line at the commissary always gave way when the colonel's wife appeared. My informant relates that, unfortunately for her, she and the colonel's wife became pregnant at approximately the same time. As the delivery dates approached, she found that her appointments to see a base doctor—which always involved an exhausting wait in line—fell on the same day as those of the colonel's wife. The colonel's wife asserted her prerogatives and was always ushered directly into an inner office whenever she appeared. My informant waited an average of two hours each visit. The colonel's wife never spent more than fifteen minutes at the clinic.

University towns. For all their broad-mindedness, college

professors are almost as careful about observing rank in social matters as the most anxious corporate executive. They have their own tight hierarchical structure for socializing, especially if the college dominates the community. Associate professors, on many campuses, are people who still haven't arrived; assistant professors are a big step further away from arriving; and teaching fellows at the bottom of the scale have no status at all. They might as well be janitors. A man who went to the University of Michigan, at Ann Arbor, from the West Coast, as a full professor, expressed pleasant surprise to an associate professor in the same department at the speed with which he and his family had been accepted socially in the community. He attributed it to the community's democratic spirit. The associate professor sourly suggested it was more likely due to the fact that he came with the rank of full professor.

A former faculty member, who served as an associate professor at Michigan for some years, told me he made several overtures to seek membership in a "discussion and drinking" faculty club on the campus. More than two hundred faculty members belong. He kept receiving evasive responses to his overtures. Finally, a friend, a full professor, advised him: "You need to be a full professor, or the equivalent in status, to belong."

Even the full professor has his social limitations. He would not invite a dean to his house socially, or the president or the vice-president. However, he might invite a department head if it was a large affair. At larger, more official, parties, where a dean is the top ranking guest invited, he or she will be careful to be the last to arrive and the first to leave. That situation prevails at Michigan. Some time ago, while visiting Penn State University, I found myself being escorted to a party by a dean. I mentioned to him, good-humoredly, that at Michigan deans were expected to arrive last and leave first. He laughed, and said they didn't believe in that sort of fancy protocol at Penn State. He went on to say, however, that at some colleges where he had served they had simply frightful rules of etiquette regulating social intermingling. When we arrived at the party, I noted that the party was in full progress. I noted, further, that no guest arrived after we did. We had been at the party for what seemed a short time when the dean came up to me and said he was ready to leave any time I was. There were about sixty people there. We were the first to leave.

Students, too, at the universities are evidently showing keen interest in being seen only with the right people. *Parade* magazine quotes one of the biggest men on campus at Iowa State University as stating: "You have to be careful not to associate with the wrong clan of people, an introvert group that isn't socially acceptable, guys who dress in the fashion of ten years ago, blue serge suits and loud ties. These people are just not accepted. And if you associate with them, you're not accepted either." This man, who was on the Student Council, said he aspired after college to go to work for a large corporation. As for the secret of his success in becoming a campus leader: "You've always got to be in there pitching and smiling."

Hollywood. My informant here is a high-ranking, creative artist who has been in Hollywood more than twenty years, and has attended "hundreds" of Hollywood parties. "Hollywood is the most class-conscious place in the world, and getting worse," he said. "It's brutal." Surprisingly, to me, it is not the stars who throw their rank around. They tend, he said, to be rather naïvely democratic. He called them "jay walkers." Rather, it is the movie makers (producers, writers, technicians, and staff people, etc.) who draw the lines. A $120-a-week secretary would not think of associating with a $70-a-week one. "A $1,000-a-week writer will not associate with a $2,000-a-week writer," he said. "If they associated when they both made $1,000, they stop associating. The man being promoted in income may associate once or twice after the promotion with his old $1,000 friend—he doesn't want to seem an utter heel—but no more." All creative artists, such as composers and writers, who are permitted to work at home, are automatically of higher status than those who are expected to report in regularly at studios.

Anyone giving a party in Hollywood, he said, draws the

guests from his social level. He indicated four of the major levels by listing the kind of people you inevitably see at the parties of each of the four levels:

First level: "Your party here will be made up of directors, producers, a couple of stars (probably of pre-1940 vintage), a famous columnist, perhaps the wife of a famous writer, now dead. You will never find a cameraman, important as he is, at this level, nor a set designer unless he is awfully famous, brought in especially for a film from New York."

Second level: "Most of the composers, writers, top cameramen, set designers. I'm at this level. I've been to hundreds of parties and I've never seen a cutter, even though he makes more money than many of us, and can be terribly important— some say the most important—in making or breaking a picture. He's not 'creative.'"

Third level: "The cutters, top electricians who handle the lights, skilled technicians of all kinds, the 'effects' men who make the miniatures. When the Oscars are handed out each year, these effects men are the two little guys who run up early in the evening, when no one is paying any attention, to get their prize."

Fourth level: "The lower levels of prop men, the higher level of secretaries, etc."

As with the faculty people of universities, the Hollywood motion-picture people, from top to bottom, socialized almost exclusively within their own fantasy-building world. The outside butcher, brakeman, and candlestick manufacturer may pass them every day, but are seen only as blurred figures.

To return to the over-all view, ideas about what constitutes a good party vary from class to class. At the upper-class level, the cliques tend to prefer a good deal of relaxed informality, with the emphasis on sociability laced with whisky rather than show. Food typically is offered casually. There may be amiable and fairly open flirting, and talking. Weaving figures may offer toasts. Other parties at this level are carried on with quiet decorum. It depends on the personalities. Publicity, in the newspapers, in either case is not sought. It is considered a sign of social weakness to seek publicity. The people having the party at the upper level usually aren't trying to prove anything.

At the semi-upper-class level, members of the cliques frequently are trying to prove something, and it shows. More thought and effort go into decorations and food preparation. Allison Davis and Burleigh B. and Mary R. Gardner, describing party life in a Southern town they studied, noted that, at the upper-middle-class level (as they call it), there was a great deal of vying to serve the most unusual delicacies, and a great deal of preoccupation with decoration and display of status symbols.[3] There is less emphasis on drinking or flirting. There may be card playing, or some cultural treat such as a Tchaikovsky recording just acquired. The hostess will often see to it that news about her party will somehow reach the attention of the local society editor.

Clique parties in homes of the still lower limited-success class are likely to be even more decorous, if less ostentatious. These are the people who show the greatest fondness for church suppers, and when they have parties at their homes prefer the same type of festivity. Frequently, at least in smaller communities such as Elmtown, each couple will bring a dish. They call it "potluck," but when the hostess gets around to writing her piece for the local paper, as she is very likely to do, it will become a "covered dish party."

At the working-class level, most of the socializing is done with siblings, siblings-in-law, or very near neighbors, and is quite random. The parties are often spur-of-the-moment affairs. In fact, the clique, as we've known it in the above classes, a pack of people running together, virtually disappears at the working-class level. A study of fifty working-class couples in the New Haven area disclosed that only two out of the fifty couples belonged to a clique of non-relatives who took turns giving parties. And two fifths of these working-class couples confined their intimate friendships entirely to kinfolk. At this level we see, too, the beginning of a tendency of the sexes to split up in their socializing. The women have their auxiliaries and their "hen" circles. The men get away from their wives by chatting or drinking with male friends and relatives.

The real-lower-class people depend even more than the working class on relatives for companionship. Their idea of festivity is to idle on Main Street Saturday nights, chatting with people they know, or to congregate in the taverns. In any case, the tendency for the sexes to split up in their chatting becomes even more marked.

One interesting way people reveal their class status in a simple act of socializing is the way that two married couples, on their way to a festivity, get into an automobile. If they are from one of the two lower classes, the men will climb into the front seat together and the women in the back. If they are from the limited-success class, where respectable behavior is cherished, each man will typically get in beside his wife. If they are from one of the two top classes, each husband will most likely, with a show of gallantry, get in with the other man's wife.

We shall explore in the following chapter the more organized aspects of socializing.

13

clubs, lodges, and blackballs

*"The private club is becoming the businessman's
castle. . . . It seems convenient, somehow fitting,
to come to important decisions within the exclusive
club."—Business Week.*

←o→·←o→·←o→·←o→·←o→·←o→·←o→

WITH THE RISE OF NATIONAL OPULENCE PERMITTING PLUMB-
ers to drive limousines and foot doctors to buy mansions, the
private club has looked more and more attractive to status-
minded people as a place to draw lines. In the private club,
you can sit, as in a fortress, in judgment of pretender-appli-
cants. They can pound the wall in vain if you have your
blackball and a good, sound membership committee in front
of you to do the preliminary screening.

One thing you'll want to see from an applicant is the list
of his other clubs. Has he achieved membership in clubs of
comparable prestige? Lacking that, has he served time (or
better still, did his father serve time) in one of the proper
waiting-room clubs? Every city has its elite clubs and its
waiting-room clubs. In fact, there is usually a well-understood
hierarchy of clubs. Among the men's city clubs of New York
and Philadelphia, you have at the pinnacles of prestige the
Knickerbocker Club in New York (favored by several Rockefeller brothers, etc.) and the Philadelphia Club in Philadelphia.
Just slightly below them in prestige are the Union Club (New
York) and the Rittenhouse Club (Philadelphia). Below them,
in both cities, are the waiting-room Union League and Uni-

versity Clubs; and at a level below these, at least in these two cities, are the Athletic Clubs. And below these are many others of varying prestige. An informed clubman can, by a glance at any applicant's list of clubs, place him just as surely as he could by reading a long biography of the man that included his present position and income.

A man of unsurpassed prestige, however, does not confine himself to the most elite club. He is likely to continue holding membership in the better clubs of somewhat lesser status. This enables him to become a "status-lender," to use a phrase coined by sociologists. By lending his status to the slightly lesser club, the man has the quiet satisfaction of having in his debt—and exercising dominion over—some really nice chaps who simply need to mature a little. And it all helps promote a sense of orderliness in an otherwise uncertain world.

While I was exploring the elite structure of Northeast City, I talked with two dozen business and social leaders who were described to me as the "real powers" of the city. Most of them talked with considerable pride about their clubs. And they were in substantial agreement on the prestige meaning of each club. The "real aristocracy" of the city's business and social life belongs to two clubs, the Pioneer's Club (city) and the Gentry Club (country). Most of the current aristocrats or their families belonged to waiting-room clubs during their rise to power, and may or may not continue membership in them, along with their membership in the elite clubs, depending on their inclination to be status-lenders. The lowest-prestige bank president I saw (a newcomer in the smallest major bank) had just been accepted finally for membership in the Pioneer's Club, and in talking with me he said he "used" to belong to the lesser-status University Club. Evidently he still felt so precarious in his new role that he feared to remain in the University Club, which is well recognized in Northeast City as a waiting-room club. Another city club generally recognized as a waiting room is the Downtown Club.

One of the city's leading brokers, Mr. Dunlap, gave this appraisal of the prestige meaning of the several country clubs ringing the city, and other informants gave a substantially identical rank order:

"The highest socially is the Gentry Club. It looks sort of shabby and moss-covered, but the members like it that way. Everyone who is a climber strives to get into Gentry. Failing that, they try to get into the Mohawk Club, which also isn't much to look at, but it has the comers of the business world, many really high-grade people. The third is Grandview Manor Club. This might fool you because it has the best golf course—national tournaments are held here—it has the biggest clubhouse and it has a big swimming pool. Grandview has to have a lot of members to keep it out of the red. It is fine physically, but still lacks the prestige of the other two. Fourth would be Apple Creek Club. Now we're getting down into the middle class. It is a nice enough place. Fifth is the Rolling Hills Club. It is a good place to belong if you're a salesman or a plumbing contractor. Sixth is the Oak Falls Club. This used to be nice. Mostly Italian today. Anybody can get in. Seventh, the Winding Acres Club. Actually this isn't seventh. I just don't know where to place it. Anyhow, it has the higher-level Jews, many very fine people."

The elite individuals I consulted were quick to deny that there was any significant relationship between club membership and their success in business. The clubs, they said, were "just social." And most of them saw no handicap to Jewish businessmen, who are barred from most of the leading city and country clubs of the area. The Jews, they kept saying, have their own country club. The main city club accepting Jews, the Downtown Club, is considered more "business" than "social." In other remarks, however, these people revealed that their club memberships did make important contributions to their business effectiveness. Mr. Thompson, one of the city's leading bankers (he is also on the board of one of the larger corporations), said, "An active banker belongs to every damned club in town. It is part of the game."

A second bank president, Mr. Hall, said, "We pay the dues of any bank officer who belongs to a good club, and uses it for business." A third banker, Mr. Parsons, said, "Our officers are encouraged to be active in clubs where they can have contact with leaders of the community." Mr. Parsons listed the club affiliations of each officer of his bank, and it was clear that, as he went down the list of officers, the prestige of the clubs they were permitted to join declined. He and his executive vice-president belonged, of course, to the two elite clubs (Pioneer's and Gentry) as well as the yacht club. But none of the other officers belonged to the two elite clubs. The chief loan officer belonged to Grandview Manor and the University Club. The vice-president in charge of consumer loans, a Catholic who never went to college and who began as a messenger, simply belonged to the Downtown Club.

The women of Northeast City, I should add, have their hierarchy of clubs, too, topped by the Martha Washington Club, housed in a remodeled old mansion. It is highest in prestige and is composed of older women from the older first families. There is also the Cheerio Club for the younger wives of comers. This dual pattern seems to be typical in metropolitan centers across the nation. The screening of applicants required by the constitution of the Martha Washington Club offers abundant reassurance that unworthy pretenders will not get past the door. These are the safeguards:

1. Each applicant must be recommended, in writing, by four members.

2. The Membership Committee shall have a "reasonable amount of time" to consider applications.

3. At least two members of the Board of Directors must be "personally acquainted with the applicant and vouch for such applicant."

4. When the board finally votes, "two blackballs shall be sufficient to exclude any candidate."

In most metropolitan centers in America, an elite women's club comparable in prestige to the Martha Washington Club can be found. In Boston, it is the Chilton; in Philadelphia, the Acorn; in New York, the Colony and Cosmopolitan. Also, across the nation in each metropolitan center, you find the elite have a preferred men's club comparable to the Pioneer's Club of Northeast City. The men's club is typically considered by males as a better refuge than the country club because at the country club you not only encounter women and children but, because of the compromises often required by high overhead, you run the hazard of encountering the *nouveau riche*. High dues are not a sufficient barrier in these days of material abundance. (It costs $4,000 to get into the Brook Hollow Country Club of Dallas. A Jewish country club outside Detroit charges initiates $6,000. And, according to one report, membership shares in the River Oaks Country Club of Houston have sold for as high as $17,500. Many have paid $9,000. A Texas millionaire who explained this situation to me said simply, "It's the cost of getting on the team."

Dixon Wecter sums up the greater appeal of the men's social club, with its mahogany paneling, mellow leather chairs, and vast fireplaces, in these words: "Here is his peculiar asylum from the pandemonium of commerce, the bumptiousness of democracy and the feminism of his own household."[1] The Philadelphia Club has permitted female guests inside its premises only rarely. During a recent one-hundred-year period, women were permitted inside on an average of once every thirty-three years.[2] The Athletic Club of Milwaukee requires women to use a side door. A few years ago, one lady created a scandal by fortifying herself with stimulants, and brazening her way right through the front door.

The Harvard Club in New York has a separate entrance for ladies; and the Yale Club of New York requires them to skirt the lobby by following a side passageway. Both clubs let down their outright barricade against women only begrudgingly during the forties under pressure to put their food and liquor services on a larger volume basis. The Yale Club went through an internal crisis a few years ago when observers professed to have seen an elderly member in an upstairs bedroom of the club with a nude woman. This was certainly off bounds for ladies. Officials investigated the allegation and proved to their satisfaction that the observers had actually been seeing a reflection superimposed on the Yale Club window of a bedroom in the Biltmore Hotel across the street.

Author Cleveland Amory has suggested that one of the

motives in barring womenfolk from clubs in the old days was that it kept wives out of the place. The male members who had mistresses were thus able to receive notes from them in their sanctuary without worrying about prying eyes.

More alarming than the invasion of women to many older club members is the growing commercialization of the town clubs. Many no longer are social sanctuaries where congenial fellows relax over cards and billiards but rather are luncheon clubs where corporate executives take clients for business talks on the expense account. An official of the Chicago Club, according to the *Wall Street Journal*, has reported that 90 per cent of the checks it received are company checks. A member of the New York Links Club has complained of members "who bring in the type of businessman who will spread his damned papers and contracts all over the luncheon table."

According to my information, the most elite men's clubs in these nine metropolitan areas are:

Houston: The Eagle Lake Club. You have to inherit your way in. It has a ramshackle barn for its clubhouse.

Boston: The Somerset Club.

New York: The Knickerbocker Club.

Detroit: The Detroit Club.

Chicago: The Chicago Club.

Cincinnati: Queen City Club.

San Francisco: The Pacific Union Club.

Philadelphia: The Philadelphia Club.

Atlanta: The Piedmont Driving Club (memberships largely inherited).

The Piedmont Driving Club, incidentally, sponsors a Halloween Ball every year at which the debutantes of Atlanta's leading families are presented. The men's Idlewild Club in Dallas performs the same function of unveiling the properly reared daughters of proper Dallas families. Dallas also has a "Party Service" for the debutante-age set, made up of society people, which maintains eligibility lists for society's whirl of winter parties.

Society, in most United States cities, supplements the private "coming-out" debutante parties with at least one mass ball that stamps a girl with the imprimatur of Society. This has become necessary, especially in Texas, because so many ambitious, new-rich, free-wheeling mothers have tried to bring out daughters with flossy parties, sneeringly called "climbers' balls," without anyone's permission. Thus it is that a girl in Houston is not really a debutante unless she has been presented to society at a ball of the Allegro Club. In Boston, she must be honored at the Debutante Cotillion held each June at the Sheraton Plaza. In San Francisco, the important ball is the Cotillion. In Charleston, South Carolina, the most proper launching still takes place at the St. Cecelia Society Ball. And in New York there are several mass balls, but the best one is the Grosvenor Ball. Bringing out a daughter at one of these New York functions costs the parents $1,400 minimum. But if the parents really want to make sure their daughter is well launched after this official recognition, they should stage a private ball costing no less than $5,000. And in New Orleans, girls permitted to sit in the "call-out section" at Carnival balls during Mardi Gras are being recognized in a way that is roughly equivalent to an official "coming-out" ball.

To assure a proper launching into society, a girl needs, as a first requirement, a father with plenty of money or a high business position. As a second requirement, she needs a mother with a good deal of shrewdness, persistence, and, if she is slightly weak on the money requirement, a good deal of aggressiveness. At the very latest, the mother must start mapping plans by the time the girl is ten years old. Age six is preferable. The girl must be enrolled in the acceptable schools (see Chapter 16), because they become the key to everything in many cities. She must also be enrolled in the right dancing school. As the girl fulfills these requirements she must be invited to the right sub-debutante parties. To achieve this, in the New York area, the mother must send a letter of application to the invitations committee of each dance she wishes her daughter to attend, along with three letters of recommendation from people who are personal friends of three different members of the committee. This is where the climbing mother must display her social skills on the telephone and at parties. She must win commitments to write letters from insiders without seeming guilty of gall and aggressiveness. At one of these sub-debutante dances in 1958, a girl (or her parents) had to pay $40 admission if the girl could get a male escort from the approved list of schools. If in desperation she had to go outside the approved list of boys' schools, she had to pay another $40.

When the girl of proper background approaches marriage-able age, she and her mother start the maneuvers necessary to win an invitation from the local Junior League. Among old families, these tend to be handed down unofficially from mother to daughter. Daughters of families that have been in the community less than a generation face a challenge. You don't just apply. That would be unforgivable. You must be proposed by a member and seconded by another member. This often takes persuasion because members must hoard their proposing and seconding privilege. They are restricted to us-ing each only once a year. Once the proposal is made, your qualifications are most carefully examined on such points as "congeniality" by a screening committee. New members must be between eighteen and thirty-four. Those accepted must face the prospects of spending considerable time not only at high-level play but in engaging in charity, worthy causes, and other good works.

In Los Angeles, a well-established socialite caustically com-mented on the large number of new groups dedicated to worthy causes that have appeared there by saying, "I know of some cases where the groups were formed before they found a disease to work for." The aspiring socialite knows that the way to recognition is to work like fury on a minor subcom-mittee for some worthy cause. Eventually the day will come, if her social credentials are adequate, when she will achieve an important committee post and have her picture taken for the newspapers beside the socially eminent status-lenders heading up the drive. And all this tireless striving, it should be noted, does indeed raise money for worthy causes, and it does get bandages wrapped. Daughters of the well-to-do are taught from girlhood that proper people devote themselves to proper causes. An extremely wealthy father on Chicago's North Shore, who had sent his daughter to Northwestern University, was trying to explain to a friend one area of her course of study. He said, "She's taking some handicraft courses. . . . You know, to prepare herself for volunteer work later."

Social clubs and associations that offer their members prestige usually stress how exclusive they are. To be exclusive you must exclude. Some exclude on the basis of undesired character traits, or lack of money, or failure to attend proper boarding schools. Whatever other bases they use, most exclude on a religious basis.

The most elite clubs, such as the Knickerbocker in New York, the Somerset in Boston, or the Pacific Union in San Francisco, are so particular on this point that an applicant not only has to be a Protestant but the right kind of Protestant— usually Episcopal. When you get down to the mass of non-elite country and city clubs, however, where Lutherans and Catholics are not necessarily excluded, the exclusiveness regarding religion is typically limited to one specification: no Jews. We shall explore later what seems to be behind this aversion of the upper and semi-upper Gentiles toward Jews as club members. At this point, we shall merely note that it is a nationwide phenomenon involving thousands of clubs. Some of the more elite New York clubs draw no line on religion at all; but in most American cities the line is quite firmly drawn. Atlanta is an example of a city where most of the country clubs and city clubs are either 100 per cent Gentile or 100 per cent Jewish.

With the help of a Rockefeller grant, two Cornell professors, Robin M. Williams, Jr., and John P. Dean, directed a study of social discrimination that reached into 248 cities, small and large. In each city they made three tests of social acceptability: admission to the Junior League; admission to the country and city clubs; and admission to exclusive residential areas. In more than eighty cities—or one third of them—Jews were denied admission to all three. In only 20 out of 248 cities were even some Jews accepted in all three of these categories.

These investigators note a paradox on a nationwide basis that I noted in Northeast City. Many cities welcome and encourage Jews to work with Gentiles in the leadership of programs for community improvement and in community fund-raising drives. Many of the Gentile leaders in Northeast City told me admiringly of the wonderful way all religions worked together to better the community. Yet in Northeast City—and throughout other cities in the country, according to the Williams and Dean study—the social barriers against Jews are in full force. In fact, there seems to be an odd, inverse relationship. Dean states: "The communities that score *low* on social acceptability of Jews score *high* on Jewish participation in community affairs." The situation undoubtedly is not only perplexing, but discouraging, to Jews. Dean quotes one Jewish community leader as saying, "I sometimes feel like a prostitute. They'll call on me to lead their Community Chest campaign. . . . But when it comes to the country club, I'm not good enough for them."

A few years ago, when a world-famous New York Jewish businessman died, the newspapers devoted several columns to describing the honors that had been bestowed upon him, to his many public services, and to his known philanthropies that had run into the millions. In passing, the stories stated that he belonged to two clubs. Both were definitely non-elite.

The service clubs of America, such as Rotary and Kiwanis (which rank about halfway between community and social clubs), typically do not exclude Jews, although some are believed to confine Jewish participation to a select few.

Until this point, we have been examining club life at the higher level of the larger metropolitan areas and their suburbs. Tens of thousands of the nation's clubs, of course, are in the small towns: service clubs, garden clubs, Optimist clubs, secret fraternal orders, women's clubs, veterans' posts, union clubs, and so on. Americans are tremendous joiners, especially among the three higher classes. Some of this joining, unparalleled in the world, is a symptom of our gregariousness in the face of growing loneliness. And, possibly, it may reflect a growing inability of Americans to draw upon their own inner resources. Much of it, however, clearly represents an effort to improve one's social standing. Max Lerner, the social historian, makes the point that the elite and the middle classes typically join clubs for different purposes. The elite use the associations "chiefly as instruments for the strategic manipulation of the life of the community—through their control of the country clubs, the eating and discussion clubs, the civic associations, the fund-raising drives. . . ." The middle classes, he added, use the associations "largely as a way of improving their social status and for training themselves in articulateness and leadership."[3]

When these club-joining habits of Americans in typical towns are subjected to class analysis, we see that the primary split—as in many other areas of life—is between the two upper classes and the three lower classes. Until recent years, we had social associations such as fraternal orders that covered the spectrum of our classes. Today, the two upper classes have substantially abandoned all associations, such as the lodges, that would bring them into contact with members of the three lower classes.

The two upper classes in their joining habits today prefer clubs that are by invitation only. This is especially true of the upper class, which participates primarily in social and charity clubs. The upper-class person in our smaller cities and towns is likely to belong to the country club (as a status-lender). The woman will belong to the garden club. In Jonesville, the W. Lloyd Warner group found that virtually all the upper-class women belonged to one of these three: a charity club to support the local hospital, the local chapter of the Daughters of the American Revolution, and a social club called the Monday Club. All three, it should be noted, have devices for restricting membership.

At the semi-upper-class level—or upper-middle, if you prefer the conventional terminology—you have the bulk of the country-club membership. In Elmtown, Hollingshead found that 85 per cent of his Class II members belonged to the local country club. Some country clubs in the smaller communities, for economic survival, draw members from the lower, limited-success class. This is a fact widely bemoaned by the members of the two upper classes.

A major purpose of the semi-uppers today in their joining, however, is to prove to the world—and particularly to the upper class they aspire to—what fine, sound-minded, reliable citizens they are. Their clubs are devoted to local uplift. The women have their Woman's Club, and the men their Rotary and other civic luncheon clubs, where they rejoice in their own solidarity, receive inspirational addresses, tell dirty stories, and map plans for community or business betterment. In the larger towns, where you find more than one civic club, the clubs are usually well understood to have differential prestige. Rotary typically draws the cream of the community leaders. The Lions, when in the same town with Rotary, sometimes draw members from a more modestly successful level. In Elmtown, the Superintendent of Schools and the high-school principal were Rotarians; the elementary-school principal belonged to the Lions Club. In some communities, the Lions Club is primarily a limited-success-, or lower-middle-, class organization, made up of small shopkeepers, company white-collar people, etc.

Now let us drop from the elite to the level of the three supporting classes to examine their joining habits. The situation appears to be much as W. Lloyd Warner found it in Jonesville. He reported: "There is, in general, a sharp break between the upper-middle and lower-middle classes, with respect to the kind and amount of participation in associations. . . . There is little participation between the upper-middle and lower-middle classes."[4]

At the supporting-classes level, the clubs joined are mainly of the patriotic and mystical type with a higher mixture of secrecy and emotional symbolism than the upper classes consider to be dignified these days.

The fraternal orders reached their peak of popularity in the 1920's, when most of the adult males of America belonged to one or more. Their secrecy and rituals and costumes may seem a bit juvenile today, but these orders did make one important contribution to democracy. Like the Roman Catholic church, they embraced the span of the American social order. The lodge hall was an excellent place for people of all classes to become acquainted, and to understand each other's problems and aspirations. Such an opportunity to make oneself known to people of the superior class is an essential precondition to winning acceptance into their class, in case one has ambitions. The fraternal orders performed, at least, that vital function of providing a common ground for intermingling. A generation ago in Jonesville, W. Lloyd Warner points out, "every important man in the community was a Mason, and often an Odd Fellow or a Woodman."[5] And the man who managed to become a high-degree Mason was taking a long, sure stride toward social success. Today, the situation has changed abruptly not only in Jonesville but throughout America. The members of the two upper classes have abandoned the lodges almost completely in favor of their exclusive civic-type groups; and, typically, the lower classes have not been able to follow them into these. Nowadays, the Masons and the Knights of Columbus draw their membership predominantly from the limited-success class; and the Woodmen of the World, the Odd Fellows, Eagles, and Redmen draw a very large part of their membership from the workingman class.

Even among the three lower classes the fraternal orders have lost much of their fascination. In Northeast City, I was told, the Moose were having a "hard time," and were running what amounted to restaurants. Other towns have Elk headquarters that seem to be frequented primarily as restaurants or taverns. Many men at the lower levels keep up their lodge affiliations because of insurance and other advantages. Oddly, while the male lodges have, in general, been declining, their feminine auxiliaries (and here, again, we see the sexual apartness common at the lower-class levels) have been thriving.

To summarize, it would seem that our socializing patterns, both informal and organized, are characterized by a confinement to one's own kind and a carefulness to avoid or exclude those who might be construed to be of lesser or different status. The example of our leading national folk hero, Abraham Lincoln—who relished mingling with all kinds of people and enjoyed pricking the pretentious—is evidently no longer considered relevant by a very large proportion of our people.

14

the long road from pentecostal to episcopal

"Individual Protestant churches tend to be 'class churches,' with members drawn principally from one class group."—LISTON POPE, Dean, Yale Divinity School.

◄─o─►·◄─o─►·◄─o─►·◄─o─►·◄─o─►·◄─o─►·◄─o─►

AMERICA, WE KEEP READING, IS UNDERGOING A TREMENDOUS religious renaissance. Membership is growing by a million a year, and is now up to more than 104,000,000. Per member contributions are up. Nearly a billion dollars' worth of new structures are going up in the United States each year. Moreover, issues of morality would seem to be uppermost in our minds, because, as anthropologist Clyde Kluckhohn has noted, "no people moralize as much as we do."

In the face of all this, we see some puzzling bits of evidence. In the study of Elmtown's youth, it was found that religion was remote from the lives of the great majority of them. And the exceptions were mostly youngsters from Norwegian and

Lutheran families. To most students, Hollingshead concluded, "the church is a community facility like the school, the drug store, the city government and the bowling alley."[1] And this is in the heart of the so-called Bible Belt. Many of the youngsters attend church functions regularly, but carry their status feelings with them, often in a most un-Christian manner. He said that a socially select gang of girls attending the Sunday night "Fellowship" meetings at the most elite church (Federated) "deliberately make any girl of whom they do not approve feel so uncomfortable" that she will not attend again.

Going to church is a deeply felt, soul-searching experience for many millions of Americans. And religious faith still dominates and guides the lives of millions of people, some of whom may not be regular churchgoers. Many still kneel in fervent prayer at night. For the majority of American Christians, however, going to church is the nice thing that proper people do on Sundays. It advertises their respectability, gives them a warm feeling that they are behaving in a way their God-fearing ancestors would approve, and adds (they hope) a few cubits to their social stature by throwing them with a social group with which they wish to be identified. And even those who take their worshiping seriously often prefer to do it while surrounded by their own kind of people.

The status implications of attending a particular church are especially perceivable among the Protestant churchgoers. In our frontier days, the Protestant churches outside the settled coastal towns and cities were institutions where brotherhood often truly prevailed. I remember, from my own boyhood and young manhood—long after all the frontiers were settled—attending Protestant churches that drew their congregation from virtually the entire community. Today, such churches are becoming harder and harder to find. The trend toward more rigid stratification in the Protestant churches is proceeding apace with the general trend in that direction. This is perhaps not surprising, because, as Liston Pope points out, "every American community . . . has some pronounced pattern of social stratification, and religious institutions are always very closely associated with this pattern."

In earlier days, people who moved to a new community typically chose the church that came closest to harmonizing with their own doctrinal viewpoint. And these doctrinal viewpoints were often passionately felt and held. Today, the doctrinal meaning of joining a particular church is far less important in the decision than the social or business meaning.

Let us then look at the social meanings—from the most elite downward—of the various Protestant denominations. There are, of course, variations, particularly in the South, and churches, like country clubs, draw their members from a band that covers more than one class. Also, it should be noted that individual churches built more than twenty years ago may find that, while they start out as high-status churches, population shifts have left them in a sea of lower white-collar or working-class homes. Actually, every denomination if not the individual church has some members from all the social layers. With those qualifications, there does seem to be a definite prevailing pattern in the ratio of distribution of church preferences among the various classes.

The upper class in most United States communities is drawn more powerfully to the Episcopal church than to any other. Consider the evidence:

—A sociological analysis made of the leading wedding announcements involving socially prominent families in *The New York Times* revealed that three quarters of the weddings taking place in known Protestant churches occurred in Episcopal churches.[2]

—E. Digby Baltzell found, in his study of Philadelphia society, that two thirds of the Philadelphians who were in both the *Social Register* and *Who's Who* were Episcopalian.

—Corporate executives are ten times as likely to list "Episcopal" as their religious preference as are Americans at large.[3] Episcopalian, in fact, is by far the preferred denomination of executives.

—In Northeast City, the church favored by more of the city's business and social leaders than any other (just under half of the Protestants) was St. John's Episcopal, whose rector had a staff of twelve and a wife who was active in the Junior League.

Recently, while I was visiting an elite club in southwestern Michigan, the head of the local radio station explained to me that the area there was overwhelmingly Lutheran. I asked him what his religious preference was. He said, "I'm Episcopalian. Used to be Lutheran." I then turned to the local Republican leader on my right. It turned out that he, too, was Episcopalian.

The upper-class fascination with the Episcopalian church seems to stem, at least in part, from its close kinship ties with the Church of England. As we have noted in other connections, the upper class in the United States feels a strong pull to all things British, especially upper-class British. In Britain, the Church of England is itself divided into "high" and "low" church, and the division—while ostensibly theological—often has a strong social basis. The Episcopal churches in the United States, reflecting the English model, have, as E. Digby Baltzell points out, a style of architecture, a "dignity of breeding of its clergy and richness of ritual" that reflect values cultivated by the upper class.

One might assume that Episcopal churches, in view of their many rich parishioners, would be rolling in financial clover. That, oddly, is not the case. Episcopalians are notoriously tight with a dollar when the collection plate is passed. At the end of 1957, the National Council of Churches of Christ in the United States of America published a list of "per member contributions" by fifty-two reporting denominations. Protestant Episcopalians ranked thirty-ninth in average contributions to their church. They ranked thirty-eighth in contributions to foreign missions. The average Episcopalian's total contributions amounted to $52.79 for the year. In contrast, members of denominations with lower social status but, evidently, far higher religious zeal, averaged considerably higher. Seventh-day Adventists—who lead the list—contribute, on an average, four times as much as Episcopalians; and Friends contribute nearly three times as much; as do Mennonites.

Three other denominations strongly favored by the two top social classes of America are the Presbyterian, Congregationalist, and Unitarian. Corporate executives, for example, favor Presbyterian churches second only to Episcopal. They are six times as likely to be Presbyterians as are Americans at large. Every fourth corporate executive you meet, in fact, is likely to be Presbyterian. (In Bevode McCall's study of Georgia Town, two thirds of the college graduates were Presbyterian.) The New York suburb of Westfield, New Jersey, is a wealthy "bedroom" town favored by Wall Street commuters and other nearby executives. Its Presbyterian church virtually overwhelms the center of town, with several structures built around a vast park. The church has to hold three services on Sundays, has four ministers and, at last report, needed a fifth. Wives of economic titans, who have homes staffed by servants, wait on table at church suppers.

As you go north into New England, the Presbyterians tend to become Congregationalists. The Congregational churches _____ ____ ___ ____ __ mill towns. And in many New England villages they have congregations that ___ _____ ___ entire churchgoing population. But, in larger cities and growing suburbs, these churches tend to be especially appealing to people from the higher socio-economic and educational levels. An earnest, forthright Congregational minister of the socially elite church in a western Wisconsin town (overwhelmingly Lutheran) told me, "It has often bothered me that we don't have a single farmer or workingman in the congregation." The Unitarian church, tiny in total number, outranks all denominations in the number of eminent Americans who have claimed it as their church.

Whatever the denomination, care is taken, in many American churches having a strong element of wealthy socialites in the congregation, to see that the socialites are visited, in the church's annual canvass, by someone of their own social standing rather than by a volunteer chosen at random from the general committee. Also, care is sometimes taken to see that downright lower-class people don't wander in on a lovely Sunday morning. The W. Lloyd Warner group reports that, in Yankee City, the two churches with the heaviest upper-class membership "devised a method of limiting the number of persons from the lower parts of the class hierarchy." St. Paul's Church (Episcopal) and the Unitarian Church established branches in the lower reaches of town that served as missions for people of the two lower classes.[4]

Sociologist E. Franklin Frazier reports finding that some Negroes in professional occupations maintain two church memberships. They will maintain their colored Baptist or Methodist membership as they themselves move up the social ladder because most of their clients are still in those churches. This, Frazier points out, has financial advantages. At the same time, they may affiliate with Episcopal, Congregational, or Presbyterian churches, usually colored, "because of their social status."

As we drop down the social scale, we come to the denominations that have the largest (and usually the most enthusiastically active) followings. Methodism probably comes closer to being the choice of the average American than any other. There are 12,000,000 Methodists in the United States today. It has many elite churches, especially in the South, but overall it has only half as many upper-class members, on a percentage basis, as the Episcopal church. Nearly two thirds of all Methodists are either farmers or manual workers, according to an analysis made by the Federal Council of Churches of a nationwide sampling (Office of Public Opinion Research).[5] In Jonesville, the Methodists were categorized by one citizen in this way: "Some are pretty well-to-do, but there's no really rich people in that church . . . [they] are pretty well dressed, and have better cars than the Baptists."

A shade below the Methodists, in the Federal Council analysis, are the Lutherans. In a three-class breakdown—upper, middle, lower—the Lutherans show a distribution of 11 per cent upper class, 36 per cent middle, and 53 per cent lower. The Lutheran church is particularly strong with farmers and skilled workers of Scandinavian or German backgrounds.

And somewhat below the Lutherans come the Baptists. In

many communities, and especially in the South, the local Baptist church is the highest-prestige church in town; but, nationally, it is predominantly a workingman's church. The Federal Council analysis shows it to have this distribution in its three-class scale: upper, 8 per cent; middle, 24 per cent; lower, 68 per cent. It has less than one third as many college graduates, per one hundred members, as the Episcopal, Congregational, or Presbyterian churches.

At the bottom of the social scale you find few churchgoers. They suspect—and correctly, Hollingshead found in Elmtown—that they are not wanted by the congregations of the so-called respectable churches in their town, and often not by the ministers. One Class V woman commented bitterly on the "Everyone Welcome" signs in front of several Elmtown churches.

Increasingly, in the past quarter-century, Liston Pope reports, people in the lower classes have turned to the new Pentecostal and Holiness sects. They represent, on the one hand, he says, "a protest (couched in religious form) against social exclusiveness, and, on the other, a compensatory method (also in religious form) for regaining status, and for redefining class lines in religious terms."[6] Other studies have shown that a dominant theme in some of these new lower-class revivalist and fundamentalist religions is that faith and righteousness make their adherents holier-than-thou; and will entitle them, when they get to Heaven, to sit in the high places (and be waited on by servants). At the same time, however, their ritual typically says, "Have mercy upon us, miserable offenders."

While the lower-class religions offer consolation for failure, many (but not all) upper-class churches tend to generate the pleasant feeling that everything within the social system is pretty fine just as it is. As you go up the social scale, services become less emotional and evangelical, and more intellectualized and restrained. Even Baptists and Methodists tend to think of Episcopalians, Congregationalists, and Presbyterians as chilly, dried-up types. When they visit an Episcopal church, they are bothered by what, to them, is the unresponsive, very proper way Episcopalians leave the church after a service with, perhaps, a few polite nods and chats with old friends. The Baptists and Methodists like to chat, in a spirit of good fellowship, with their pew neighbors, friend or stranger, after the service.

Dr. Walsh, rector of St. John's Episcopal in Northeast City, tried to explain to me why the Episcopal church is one that wealthier people "naturally adhere to." He mentioned that the Episcopal ministers preach "literate" sermons that appeal to the more highly educated, and that the church has a kinship with the Church of England. To the non-educated, he said, the Episcopal service may seem "dry." And then he added rather sadly, "The more churches become filled with the conservative and wealthy, the more reluctant they become to make faith more relevant to all kinds of people."

In this connection, Yale theologian H. Richard Niebuhr reminds us that Christianity began as a religion of the poor, of disinherited people such as fishermen, peasants, publicans, and outcasts who had been denied a stake in contemporary civilization. Whenever Christianity has become the religion of the fortunate and cultured and has grown "philosophical, abstract, and ethically harmless in the process," the lower strata of society find themselves religiously expatriated by a faith that neither meets their psychological needs nor sets forth an appealing ethical ideal. "The rise of new sects of Christianity," Niebuhr explains, "to champion the uncompromising ethics of Jesus and 'to preach the gospel of the poor' has again and again been the effective means of recalling Christendom to its mission."

Now let us move on, for a moment, from the Protestants to the other major United States religions. The Federal Council found that the distribution of Jews in the three-class scale is quite similar to that of Episcopalians. One reason for this, undoubtedly, is that few Jews ever become manual workers or farmers. Viewing Jews on the basis of their occupations, they lead all religious groups in the proportion of their total engaged in "business," "professional," or "white-collar" occupations. Their total here is nearly three quarters. The

Episcopalians have 57 per cent in these categories, and the Baptists 26 per cent.

Jewry, too, has its denominations: Orthodox, Conservative, and Reform. And they are differentiated somewhat by social class. Lower-class Jews tend to remain in Orthodox synagogues. The upper-class Jews, especially those with higher educations, tend to move on to the Conservative and Reform denominations.

The Roman Catholic church, of course, does not have denominations, and so has escaped the trend to stratification by social classes that is becoming so conspicuous in the Protestant churches. Catholic parishes are organized on a geographic basis, and each parish is expected to minister to all Catholics in its area. The more conspicuous divisions within the Catholic church, if they might be called that, are on the bases of vertical ethnic divisions rather than horizontal economic divisions. Thus, in adjoining parishes, you may have churches—because ethnics tend to cluster in their home addresses—that are predominantly Irish Catholic, Italian Catholic, French Catholic, or Polish Catholic. In areas where one parish includes several ethnic clusters, the priest often has a desperately trying time in organizing auxiliary church activities that bring together the various ethnics. Frequently, there is more than a little holding back, and occasionally some unChristian elbowing. One general source of tension is the fact that traditionally the hierarchy of the Catholic church has been dominated by the Irish. In recent years, the Italians, in particular, have been challenging that dominance. The residential neighborhood comprising each parish, of course, powerfully reflects class lines.

As for the social-class profile of the Catholic church as a whole, it resembles that of the Baptists more than that of any other Protestant denomination. According to the Federal Council analysis, it divides on the three-class scale as follows: 9 per cent, upper; 25 per cent, middle; 66 per cent, lower. According to Mabel Newcomer's analysis of the religion of corporate executives, the Catholics make up a third of the United States population, and supply one out of ten executives. Catholic industrialists have particularly favored railroads and public utilities. On the other hand, Catholics have a higher percentage of people in the trade-unions than any other religious body. Catholic journals follow the events at major trade-union conventions with close interest.

The explanation for the predominantly working-class composition of the Catholic church is easy to find. A large proportion of its members are descendants of immigrants who, as a group, arrived later on this continent than the national groups, especially English, that largely make up Protestantism in the United States.

One interesting current development in the Catholic church is its mild success in recruiting Negro converts. This has several explanations, including this church's continuing desire to minister to all who declare themselves members of the faith. In addition, a real-estate factor has been making a contribution to this trend in some areas, such as certain sections of Chicago. As children and grandchildren of Irish, Italian, and Polish immigrants have prospered and moved out of the working-class districts into suburban developments, Negroes, also prospering at a lower level, have been leaving their confines of the slums to replace them. The parish churches have, of course, been unable to follow the flocks. They have welcomed the incoming Negroes.

To date, the proportion of Negro church members who are Catholic is small, about 1 in 25. At least one third of them are affiliated with mixed parishes. The rest are in segregated churches. But even that record of integration is far higher than that of the Protestant churches. Until a few years ago, barely 1 per cent of the Protestant congregations with white members had any Negro members. By a variety of techniques, about as gracious as that of the white waitress who spills soup in their laps, the white members have succeeded in making those Negroes who have ventured to approach white churches feel unwelcome. When a Negro persisted in coming to a church in one Kansas town, the minister took him aside and said that, of course, he was welcome but wouldn't he be happier in his "own" colored church of the same denomination on the other side of town, a mile's walk from his home?

While great strides were made during the 1940's in lowering the color bans in business, sports, politics, entertainment, and education, Protestant churches did little, actually, and remained 99 per cent Jim Crow. For the last few years, however, Liston Pope tells me, considerable progress has been made in reducing the segregation in the Protestant churches. This forthright and courageous dean has been in the forefront of those seeking to pierce the color barrier in the churches. The proportion of Protestant churches that now have at least a few Negro members is approaching 10 per cent. A Congregational church in the Boston area has recently had a Negro Sunday-school superintendent of a mixed congregation. Among Protestant churches, the Congregational and Episcopal churches have been particularly active in seeking an end to racial barriers in the churches. Relatively few Negroes belong to those two denominations, even on a segregated basis, and those who do belong—just as among whites—are the more educated, sedate, and prosperous. Some leading Negro Episcopalians are: Thurgood Marshall, famed attorney for the National Association for the Advancement of Colored People; Nat King Cole; Richard B. Jones, United States Ambassador in Liberia; Cab Calloway. The overwhelming majority of Negroes are Baptist (65 per cent) or Methodist (22 per cent).

Congregationalists are making perhaps the most wholehearted effort to desegregate their churches. They have backed their drive with cash. Any church that is threatened by withdrawal of financial support for integrating will receive aid from the national church's Board of Home Missions. Furthermore, the Congregationalists have made an honest effort to understand the problem they face. They have surveyed ministers and laymen in more than one thousand churches. The finding: 12 per cent of the churches have accepted Negro members; a slight majority say they wouldn't want to. The most depressing finding concerned the attitude of members of the congregations toward the efforts of their pastor to promote desegregation. A large number said they would be more willing to support him in efforts to promote desegregation in the community at large than in any efforts he made to support desegregation in their own church! But only 1 member in 9,000 has walked out of a sample group of churches that became integrated.

All of the foregoing indicates, I believe, that Christianity in mid-century America shows a sizable gulf between practice and preaching. The minister of the most fashionable church in Jonesville told W. Lloyd Warner, "The whole trouble with this world today is that for all the talk about Christianity, our society is not organized on its principle." Liston Pope, while noting all the very real efforts being made to reduce class barriers in the churches, adds: "But, unless a drastic transformation comes about in the churches, and especially in their idea of what a true Christian church really is, they will probably continue for the most part to adapt to class divisions— and even to intensify them—as they have done in the past."

It may reasonably be argued that some of the social stratification of Protestant churches arises from the composition of the neighborhood surrounding the churches. A minister in Levittown, Long Island, has little opportunity to broaden the social reach of his church. His stratification is built in. Also, it may be argued that some people can worship more serenely and at ease if they are surrounded by their own kind.

But still the question persists: Should one be worshiping in a setting that makes a mockery of one of the core values of Christianity: the brotherhood of man? At present, the brotherhood of man is in danger of becoming merely a nice intellectual concept.

a sociological peek into the voting booth

"The Negro Pullman porter who owned his home and four shares of stock valued at about $80 . . . declared that he was against the policies of [the Democrats] because they taxed men of property like himself in order to assist lazy working men."—E. FRANKLIN FRAZIER, Howard University.

◄─○─►·◄─○─►·◄─○─►·◄─○─►·◄─○─►·◄─○─►·◄─○─►

OUR ATTITUDES TOWARD THE WORLD AROUND US ARE TO A very large extent shaped by our particular standing in the social structure. This is perhaps most conspicuously evident in our political predispositions. More and more, our voting habits are determined by status factors within ourselves rather than by specific issues and party programs at stake in an election campaign. Increasingly we vote as our friends, neighbors, and business associates vote. Political sociologist Paul Lazarsfeld of Columbia University has summed up the situation in these five blunt words: "Social characteristics determine political preference."[1]

One of the candidate's most challenging problems thus is to pull together—by such acts of symbol manipulation as eating pizza pies—a winning combination of status groups from within his particular electorate. This may help explain why an increasing number of professors of political science, knowledgeable in what it takes today to be elected, are running for office, and winning.

Have you ever wondered how someone is going to vote in a coming election—or what his "politics" really is? What follows is a handy guide that, while perhaps not as accurate as a Univac machine, will in most cases whir up the right answer for you. (Also, if you have any doubts, it can probably whir up how you are going to vote yourself.) Because of the fact that there are still a few rugged individualists left in our society who persist in the old-fashioned habit of voting cerebrally—conceivably you may be one of them—100 per cent accuracy is not guaranteed. Also, it should be noted, Southerners are regulated by a somewhat different set of factors. With these qualifications, let us proceed.

Five factors in the average voter's life pretty much determine how he votes and thinks on political issues. They are:

1. *The money factor.* It is hardly news that upper-class rich people tend to be conservative, show a reverence for the status quo, and prefer the Republican party; and that working people tend to be liberal or radical and to show a bias in favor of the Democratic party. However, two facts are noteworthy about the money factor. One is the precision with which political attitudes change as you move down the stratification scale of occupation. The other is the fact that this tendency is increasing.

Richard Centers, who analyzed the political attitudes of 1,100 Americans in a nationwide sample, concluded:

"There exists some fairly convincing evidence in the data obtained from this survey that the political alignments of our population are shifting steadily in the direction of cleavage along stratification lines."

He compared the political preferences of the 1,100 people interviewed with those of their parents. "The parents' voting habits do not show so great a difference along stratification lines as those of the younger generation," he said, and added, "The cleavage has grown."[2]

Centers asked his subjects a series of questions designed to uncover their position on a radical-conservative scale. (Wanting change vs. wanting to keep things just as they are.) Here are the results by seven major occupational groups:

	Conservative or Ultra Conservative	Radical or Ultra Radical
Large business	87%	2%
Professional	70	11
Small business	74	8
White collar	56	16
Skilled manual	39	27
Semi-skilled manual	21	49
Unskilled manual	23	38

These columns, you will note, follow a fairly regular progression as we descend Centers' occupational scale. There are two mild (and interesting) distortions, and both can be accounted for. Professionals tend to be somewhat less conservative than small businessmen. Although professional men typically have relatively high incomes and status, they typically don't feel as much of a stake in preserving the status quo as businessmen, big or little. The other distortion is that semi-skilled manuals rather than the unskilled at the bottom are our most radical group. Presumably the explanation here is that the semi-skilled are more likely to be organized and militantly led by labor unions.

Paul Lazarsfeld, in analyzing the voting habits of several hundred people, found much the same neat progression. He reports: "And with each step down the SES [socio-economic scale] the proportion of Republicans decreased and the proportion of Democrats correspondingly increased."[3] He devised a three-scale index that included SES for assessing political predisposition in a community.

More recently, the Opinion Research Corporation has found much the same progression but with a general shifting of the populace toward the Democratic side. In the eight years from 1950 to 1958, the proportion of college-educated Americans who considered themselves Republican dropped 8 per cent. This presumably includes many professionals and businessmen. Other studies show the shift away from the GOP reached into both well-to-do and poor neighborhoods.

One executive of Democratic origin relates that he remained, out of habit, a Democrat while stationed in Chicago, where his private life was pretty much his own. When he went into an Iowa corporation as sales manager, however, he had been on the job only a few weeks in 1956 when the board chairman dropped by. The chairman affably asked for the usual bi-annual $250 donation to the Republican party, which, it seems, was always collected from whatever sales manager was occupying the office at the time. When the newcomer confessed he was a Democrat, the chairman was incredulous. It was such an implausible situation that he kept shaking his head in disbelief. He finally saw the humor of the situation and went away with no hard feelings. By 1957, however, the sales manager had become a liberal Republican and spoke of his new allegiance with conviction.

One of the nation's most astute feelers of the nation's pulse, Samuel Lubell, has been ringing doorbells for more than a decade to sample political attitudes. He quotes a lawyer in Sweet Home, Oregon, as explaining:

"Almost everyone on Main Street but the postmaster is Republican. Just about everyone else in town, all the working people, are Democrats."[4] Lubell adds that Sweet Home is a particularly interesting spot for a political analyst to prowl because it has grown from a tiny hamlet of 350 persons to nearly 4,000 inhabitants within two decades. The townspeople of this melting pot, in short, virtually all came from somewhere else. Lubell makes this point:

"Sweet Home furnishes dramatic evidence of the underlying class consciousness which permeates American politics today. Both its businessmen and workers must have brought a consciousness of class interest with them from wherever they came." And he goes on to say that the same kind of class voting can be noted in every American city. "Simply by looking at the homes along a street," he has found, "or by noting the incomes and occupations of the people living there, one can determine with fair accuracy how any particular urban area has voted in recent Presidential elections. There is no mistaking a heavily Democratic from a heavily Republican district."

The parallel between our voting and our economic status, he has observed, has remained so constant that the divisions are coming to be accepted as normal by politicians. And the politicians now tend to keep out of each other's way in their campaigning. This tendency to abandon the opponent's strongholds should speed the trend toward an even more complete class stratification in American politics.

One interesting paradox on this rich-poor axis of American politics is that the sons of fabulously wealthy families who aspire to high office have usually appeared as Democrats. The names of Roosevelt, Harriman, Biddle, Lehman, and Kennedy come to mind. A noted plutocrat who ran as a Republican, it seems, would be automatically suspect. Political writer Leo Egan reports that Nelson Rockefeller gave a great deal of thought to this hazard before finally deciding to run for Governor of New York on the Republican ticket. One Republican county boss warned him, "Only the Democrats can get away with running somebody who has inherited a lot of money."[5]

Rockefeller ran, but he hedged. He sought to disassociate himself in an almost scandalous way from the Republican label and from that party's national policies and leaders. In some of his display advertisements, there was no mention at all of the fact that he happened to be the Republican party's nominee. He was running as plain Nelson Rockefeller.

2. *The ancestry factor.* There is a strong tendency for descendants of early arrivals in America to be Republican and the descendants of later arrivals to be Democratic. This situation first developed in the decades after the Civil War when the new Republican party, reflecting the laissez-faire mood of the violently expanding country, became the favorite of the well-established. The Democrats found themselves recruiting voters among the newcomers and the less contented.

The break point regarding newcomers appears to be in the 1840's, when the Irish began arriving in large numbers. They might be called our first immigrants. Those who got here before then were "settlers" or slaves. The Irish seemed so different because they were Catholic, and back home were subjects of the English. Natives of other Catholic nations who followed, of course, were Italian, Polish, Hungarian, etc. And there were also the large Jewish contingents.

According to the Federal Council of Churches analysis of the 1944 elections, Catholics were 12 per cent more Democratic than the nation as a whole. And Jewish voters were 33 per cent more Democratic. Centers found Catholics to be more inclined to radical solutions to national problems than the United States norm. The official Catholic policy, of course, has been vigorously anti-Communist.

Among the Protestant denominations, according to the Federal Council study, only the Baptists produced more Democratic than Republican voters. Methodism produced a slight preponderance of Republicans and the Lutherans a substantial preponderance. The massive majorities of Republican votes were produced by the Presbyterians, Episcopalians, and Congregationalists.

There has been a growing tendency in recent years for the two national parties to play politics with the ethnic blocs. They have set up divisions and committees to play upon the dissatisfactions of the various major ethnic groups. In this the Democrats, because of the ancestry factor, have had the best of it. But there have been exceptions. The Republicans were able to make sizable inroads with Italian-Americans after the Democratic Administration declared war on Italy in World War II. And, in 1952, the Republicans won many Polish, Czech, and Hungarian votes by indicating that liberating Communist-held Poland, Hungary, and Czechoslovakia would be one of their first concerns. The lessons of the 1956 Hungarian revolution—when the Republican Administration refrained from military intervention—largely wiped out this gain.

3. *The distance-from-center-of-city factor.* In general, the closer one's home is to the center of a metropolitan area, the more likely he is to be Democratic. And the farther out you go toward exurbia (to use A. C. Spectorsky's phrase) and surrounding farmland, the more likely a person is to be Republican.

Two forces appear to be at work to account for this. The

first is economic. The poorest houses, as we've seen, tend to be those ringing the downtown area; and the value and desirability of houses tend to increase every quarter mile as you move outward. Also, home owning, in contrast to renting, increases. Nothing makes a person a Republican faster than acquiring a mortgage.

As the waves of prospering urban masses from Democratic precincts move outward into Republican country, they tend to become Republican. William H. Whyte, Jr., in his study of Park Forest, the Chicago suburb, found settlers there voting 7 to 3 for General Eisenhower in 1952 even though many had migrated from Democratic districts in Chicago.[6] Republicans delightedly attributed this change to the beneficial influence of country air. Whyte suggested that a more likely explanation was the striving of the newcomers to win acceptance by proving they were politically safe and sound. Democrats tried to counteract the tendency by staging very proper teas, etc., to convince the newcomers that it was socially safe to remain a Democrat.

As the Democratic newcomers in the suburbs have become acclimated and found many people undergoing the same adjustment as themselves, they have tended to declare themselves Democrats. The Women's Activities Division of the Democratic party reports that in seven suburban counties surrounding Boston, New York, and Washington the Democrats showed quite uniform gains of 4 per cent in each county from 1952 to 1956. But this may just have been a part of the general swing away from the Republicans. A symposium of Democratic women leaders came up with a proposal that ways be found to give the Democratic newcomers to the suburbs "a sense of belonging."

The second force that seems to be at work to produce more Republicans and fewer Democrats as you move out from the center of a metropolis is the farmer vote (although in the late fifties this was becoming less and less assuredly Republican). Farmers have traditionally voted Republican. Partly, perhaps, this is family habit. Partly it is the farmer's faith in going it alone vs. the city dweller's conviction that many of his problems are beyond the power of singlehanded solution and require unified action. This tendency shows up even among Negroes. Although preponderantly Democratic, rural Negroes tend to be distinctly more conservative in their outlook than city Negroes. Farmers in recent years have had to do a great deal of rationalizing to square their traditional faith in the leave-me-alone approach with their eagerness to receive federal support for farm prices in our now more-or-less chronic times of glut. There is a growing suspicion that the foxy farmers are rising above tradition and playing power politics in their voting. They have found they can apply more leverage on farm policy if they make sure that the same party—whether Republican or Democratic—is not in control of both the Administration and Congress.

4. *The egghead factor.* If the person you are trying to diagnose politically is some sort of intellectual, the chances are 2 to 1 he is a Democrat. The intellectuals constitute the great exception to the money factor. Many are at least moderately well off, earning $5,000 to $20,000; and yet do not turn Republican. *Time* magazine reported in 1958: "An overwhelming majority of the key reporters and pundits who write the day-to-day political stories for the U.S. newspapers, radio and television are down-the-line liberal Democrats." Other sources supply evidence that three quarters of the nation's social scientists are Democrats; and so are most literary figures and librarians.

Why? Republicans are likely to say it just proves how muddleheaded, visionary, and impractical they are. The eggheads themselves, of course, like to think their choice is the result of intellectual deliberation. Possibly so, but other factors also seem to be at work. Some of the eggheads subconsciously resent the fact that they seem as bright as (or brighter than) the prosperous businessmen who are so fond of the GOP image but make much less money. Also, the eggheads can be more carefree on matters of public spending because they are not, as businessmen like to say, meeting a payroll.

Personality factors also undoubtedly play a part. Intellectuals tend to glorify traits that are the opposite of those reflected by leading Republicans. The Republican, wherever you find him, is likely to cherish such traits as orderliness, respectability, practicality, self-achievement. And he is fairly likely to take a wary view of the outside world. Eggheads, in contrast, tend to cherish such traits as nonconformity, playfulness, worldliness, bias for the underdog, and even untidiness. Observers who have spent a great deal of time visiting Republican and Democratic campaign headquarters around the country find the Republicans' characteristically more neat and businesslike.

At any rate, for the egghead, being a Democrat is the chic and daring thing to do.

In recent years, some Republican leaders have shown signs of regretting their party's traditional policy of scorning eggheads. Around 1956, in fact, the Republicans rather plaintively expressed concern that they were not loved by eggheads and set out—not too successfully—to win this love, perhaps to enlist their help in trying to communicate effectively with the public. Their concern was practical. Even though numerically eggheads don't count for much in the national picture, a few sharp-witted eggheads on your side, like a few millionaires, can go a long way in helping along a campaign.

The four factors thus far cited—money, ancestry, distance of home from center of city, and eggheadedness—can, viewed in combination, give you an excellent hunch as to the way 9 out of 10 Americans will vote. If most of the factors point in the same direction, your chances of coming up with a correct guess are especially good. Lazarsfeld found in a study of voting in the Sandusky, Ohio, area that 90 per cent of the Catholic laborers living within the city limits voted Democratic while 75 per cent of prosperous Protestant farmers voted Republican.

As Catholics prosper and rise on the economic scale, they tend to become Republican. Many affluent Irish and German Catholics are Republicans. Still, Catholic executives with $15,000 salaries, while far more likely to be Republican than Catholic steelworkers, are not as likely to be Republican as Protestant executives sitting in the next office and also earning $15,000. According to one study, while only 30 per cent of Protestants above the working-class level are Democratic, 45 per cent of Catholics above this level are Democratic. Perhaps we can summarize this situation by saying that Catholics have to become richer than Protestants do before they suddenly realize that they are not Democrats at all but really Republicans at heart.

When you see a person of clearly upper-class economic status who is a liberal politically, the chances are high that he is not fully accepted socially by the upper classes. He is not accepted because of the handicap of ancestry or other complicating factors. Gerhard E. Lenski, sociologist at the University of Michigan, made a study of people who are held back from full social acceptance by their economic peers because of ethnic or other background factors. These people, he found, tend to be in an ambiguous position socially. They frequently encounter rebuffs and embarrassments. And, he noted, they tend to support liberal political movements in the hope of somehow modifying "the existing social order which they often come to view as the source of their difficulties."[7]

This factor, which Lenski calls "low status crystallization," helps account for the strong liberal tendencies, previously noted, of Jewish people. If you judged them by their economic position alone, they should be mostly on the side of Republicanism-conservatism.

Thus we see counter-pressures pushing people one way and the other on the conservative-liberal scale. The four factors I've thus far cited will, in most cases, suggest a definite political inclination that can be accepted as a reasonably safe assumption. When the counter-pressures of status balance out so neatly that the person is left near the center of the political spectrum in his inclinations, a final factor can usually resolve the confusion as to which lever the hand will firmly grasp.

5. *The frustration-boredom factor.* This final element, although not a status factor, arises largely from the voter's own life, and is becoming more significant with each campaign.

It works to the disadvantage of any party in control of the national Administration for more than two years.

The atomic stalemate helps account for the frustration part of it. American voters and columnists alike bemoan the "eternal shilly-shallying over foreign policy," to use the phrase of one columnist. With the world split into two massive camps, this shilly-shallying is likely to continue—short of a generalized nuclear searing of the planet—into the indefinite future. Americans are accustomed to setting disagreeable situations straight in a hurry. Since this is no longer feasible, our foreign-policy makers, whoever they happen to be at the moment, are likely to be the butt of our irritations. The result is a yearning —more intensive with each year an Administration stays in office—for a housecleaning and new faces.

Another factor conditioning the public to yearn for "new faces" is the growing tendency of voters to be bored with any face they've seen around on the billboards before. Advertising has conditioned the public to expect new models and to desire to trade in the old.

The tendency, then, is for those voters near the center of the political spectrum, as a result of a balancing of status factors, to vote for the appealing face, and to vote against the party that has been in control of the Administration, faces being equal. And the longer the party has been in power, the more compelling this urge becomes.

Both parties, it is being frequently observed, are coming to look more and more alike to the voter. This is because both know victory lies in swaying the political neuters in the middle of the spectrum. (Most frequently, these neutral voters tend to be members of the limited-success class—skilled workers and white-collar workers.)

In their soliciting, both parties—and especially their public-relations consultants—are convinced they must offer these swing voters a new look and fresh personalities to counteract the boredom-frustration factor. Even the Democrats after the 1958 landslide agreed, according to *Newsweek*, that they would do well to pin their faith on new faces. It also appeared more and more obvious that sex appeal should be taken into account because of the larger women's vote. *Life* magazine, commenting on the Democratic sweep, noted that the plus qualities of the Democrats at the polls were the youthful look and sex appeal of candidates. It described one Democratic victor as looking like a "blond Greek god." Another was reported to be hard on the "hormones" of ladies. And it quoted one woman voter in Wyoming as saying she got a "buzz" just from watching the handsome young Democrat running (successfully) for governor. With television becoming such a decisive factor, candidates with lean, young faces were favored because TV tends to fatten and age a face. James Reston of *The New York Times* reported after the 1958 votes were in that the professional politicians were starting to show an "almost pathological fascination" with any candidate who is "good" on television. And *Newsweek* reported that the White House had come up with a plan for rebuilding the GOP. It reported, "The plan: Get more of the party's younger, attractive office holders on television."

As the situation now stands in mid-century America, former successful candidates who lacked the toothpaste-ad look such as Abraham Lincoln, John Adams, George Washington, John Calhoun, William Howard Taft, and Herbert Hoover would find campaigning a pretty discouraging business.

While at the University of Wisconsin recently, I came upon the trail of a political-science major, Jim Wimmer, who has earned a reputation in the Midwest as a "political prodigy." He conducted the campaign that put the first Democrat (a handsome, forthright, young family man) in the Wisconsin governor's chair in two decades. The blunt views of this young political expert on the trend in United States politics are illuminating. He states that he has noticed a new type coming into prevalence among the younger political leaders: "a personality that is very cold and calculating. These men are not fire-eating leaders in the image of the Roosevelts or 'old' Bob LaFollette, but are superb technicians."

Talking of the evident new trend of voters to vote for personalities rather than issues, he states: "I think probably the most important thing a politician can do, under our present system, is to establish a public personality, rather than establish a set of issues." In appealing to the voters, particularly the middle-of-the-spectrum voters, he says, both parties take public stances pretty close together. He calls it "middle-of-the-road mediocrity."

Concerning the assumed superior political acuity of his own generation of recent college graduates, Wimmer said: "Those that graduate from college generally enter the ranks of the Republican party: their wariness of the Democratic party is almost amusing. Actually, they differ very little from the rest of our society: they make decisions more on the basis of imagery than on thought."

As for the long-glorified typical American voter and his recent surge to the polls in record-breaking numbers, Wimmer stated: "I believe that the American voter is not interested in the issues of today; he is as sluggish as the political system. Larger numbers of the voters turn out, not because of interest, but rather because the mass media have constantly drummed into their heads the notion that they *should* vote."

In short, they vote pretty much as they go to church. It's the thing to do.

And they have, for the most part, accepted Groupthink while posing as the thoughtful, issue-weighing voter-citizens so glowingly depicted on the billboards. I think we could feel better about the democratic process as it is practiced in the United States if voters in general would start looking beyond personalities and predispositions, and make searching analyses of the core issues involved and the commitments of the candidates.

the molding of tender minds

*". . . there are more bright children in lower class
families than in middle class families because the
lower class has more children. . . . It is of great
importance to stimulate and encourage those able
boys and girls. [Yet] the school . . . speaks a
language foreign to the bulk of the lower group."*
—LEE J. CRONBACH, University of Illinois.

CLASS DIFFERENCES BEGIN IN THE CRADLE. WHITE-COLLARED
mothers are likely to make quite a personal drama of being a
new mother and lavish their baby with protective love. The
working-class mother is likely to have mixed feelings. She'll
be matter-of-fact with occasional spontaneous expressions of
joyous love.

Interviewers for the *Chicago Tribune* in a motivational
study asked young mothers to state the first thought that
leaped into their minds when the interviewer said the word
"baby." Women in the upper half of the population would
make such exclamations as "darling," "mother," or "sweet."
Those in the lower half were more likely to say "pain in the
neck" or "darling but a bother."

During the first years of life when, psychiatrists say, our
personality is largely molded, youngsters in the lowest class
learn to do what comes naturally. They are breast fed whenever they feel in the mood for a nip. They learn bowel and
bladder training in a permissive way. As you move up into the

higher levels of the working class and into the limited-success class, you encounter much more effort to exert control and guidance, according to studies made by a number of sociologists at the University of Chicago. For example, mothers of this class begin to train their babies in bowel control at the age of about seven and a half months, or nearly three months before the lower-class mothers do. Interestingly, final success is achieved by both sets of mothers at approximately the same age level, eighteen months. Apparently it is just physiologically impossible for most youngsters to achieve control earlier. Interestingly, too, boys are slower than girls in both groups in learning control.

The more success-conscious mothers at the somewhat higher level also begin earlier than women in the lower level in trying to wean their babies. One possible result of this is that twice as much thumb sucking was observed among their children as among children of the lower group.

These mothers at the higher level also work much harder at training their children to restrain their emotions and to accept responsibilities around the house. Training to "make good" begins early.

One result of all the training is that at least the middle-class child appears to be more orderly, organized, and inhibited than his counterpart in the lower classes. A comparative study of the reactions of four-year-olds of "middle" and "lower" classes in the Boston-Cambridge area to finger painting is illuminating. The lower-class youngsters dived in, seemed to enjoy messing with the paint. Higher-level youngsters were more inclined to hold back from dabbling in the paint, and when they did they tended to do it daintily.

As you go up into upper-middle-class (or semi-upper) families, you find, according to investigators Eleanor Maccoby and Patricia Gibbs, some parental relaxation, at least in terms of expressing hostility, toilet training, and sexual curiosity.

When toddlers grow into youngsters, the class differences become more clear-cut. Three sociologists focused their scrutiny on a one-half-square-mile area in Chicago that was chosen because it included the whole class gamut of families from real lower to real upper. All the youngsters thus had access to the same community facilities: movies, libraries, playgrounds, Y.M.C.A., Boy Scouts, parks, churches, settlement houses. All children in three grades (fifth to seventh) in a local school were asked to keep diaries of their daily activities. An analysis of these diaries revealed that, out of school, the youngsters from the lower classes lived in a world largely different from that of the so-called middle classes.[1] After school they went to the clubs and centers specifically designed for the so-called underprivileged. They spent much time at the movies, and they tended to have considerable freedom to roam and to come and go at home.

In contrast, youngsters at the higher level spent much of their time at self-improvement activities such as taking lessons and reading, indicating the future-mindedness of themselves and their parents. And they took part in great numbers in Y.M.C.A. and Boy Scout activities. In Elmtown, Hollingshead found the two upper classes had ten times as many youngsters in the Boy Scouts, in proportion to the number eligible, as did his Class IV, predominantly working class. And in the Camp Fire Girls, the proportional representation was about 20 to 1 in favor of the upper classes.

In another laboratory town, Plainville, U.S.A., sociologist James West was repeatedly told that "you don't find any classes here." Classes were felt to be "wrong." And children from better-class homes, he found, were cautioned repeatedly "never to show" they "feel any different" from the lower-class youngsters in town. Yet the parents were constantly admonishing the children in ways that showed the differences were very much on their own minds. The parents of the "better class" warned their children not to play with "people like that" (lower-class children).[2] For example:

"You don't want to play with Johnny Jones. People like that don't know how to play right. The Joneses keep hounds . . . are dirty . . . live back in the timber . . . don't go to church . . . are not *our* kind . . . people would laugh if they saw you at the Jones house."

The lower-class parents tried their best to prepare their

children for the rebuffs they knew would come. They told their youngsters:

"You're just as good as anyone. . . . I wouldn't want to go where I wasn't wanted." Slights received by children are explained with: "They're stuck up, uppity people . . . cold people . . . they have no manners . . . they're church hypocrites." And the youngsters are furnished with compensatory thoughts: "You know how to shoot and trap better than any Smith boy; you could outfight any Smith boy your size."

In the disciplining of children, class differences also appear. Among the lower classes, the youngster deemed to be guilty of serious misbehavior is flogged or deprived of privileges. And the punishment is most likely to be administered by the father. When you get up into the so-called middle classes, the mother is likely to dominate in the disciplining. Father, who typically gets home late from business, is likely to busy himself trying to prove in the few fleeting moments available with children that he is a real pal. At this level, the punishment most commonly inflicted is withdrawal of love.

Penn State's sociologist Arnold W. Green relates that he spent several years in a predominantly Polish-American industrial town in Massachusetts. The streets of dilapidated row houses rang with the screams and wails of youngsters being flogged by fathers trying to enforce obedience upon children contemptuous of their parents' Old World ways. Yet, Green points out, "those children do not become neurotics. Why? Because parental authority, however harsh and brutal, is in a sense casual and external to the 'core of the self.'"

Green points, in contrast, to the incidence of neuroses among youngsters reared in "Protestant, urban, college-educated middle-class" homes where a hand may never be laid on the children in anger. Such children, he points out, often find their personality absorbed by their parents. There is often a "physical and emotional blanketing of the child, bringing about a slavish dependence on the parents."[3]

The mother, in particular, may "absorb" the child's personality as her life may be dominated by care of the child. In cases where the child actually is a bother and a burden to a man and wife because it interferes with their dominant values and compulsions—career, social and economic success, hedonistic enjoyment—withdrawal of love occurs for prolonged periods, or indefinitely. The child is thrown into a panic and develops guilt feelings. Other investigators point out that parents of the major white-collar classes continually seek to arouse in the child a fear of losing parental love as a technique in training the child.

"In such a child," Green points out, "a disapproving glance may produce more terror than a twenty-minute lashing in little Stanislaus Wojcik."

Growing youngsters, we should also note, develop different life values, according to their class. The most impressive investigation in this regard is a study of the personalities of Harvard freshmen conducted by Harvard psychologist Charles C. McArthur. By using thematic apperception tests, he sought to find if there was a fundamental difference between upper-class boys coming from private schools and boys from the "middle classes" coming from public high schools.

The public-school boys—reflecting the dominant success culture of America—saw their father as a figure they were expected to surpass occupationally. These boys were oriented to *doing*, to accomplishing. To them, the significant time dimension is the *future*. They see college as a road to success.

The upper-class, private-school boys, in contrast, were oriented to *being* rather than doing. They expected to be evaluated for what they already were. And in terms of time, the important dimension was the *past*. Such a boy accepts his father as a model who probably was so successful that there is no point in striving to surpass him. Going to college, to this boy, offers the opportunity to live out his predetermined life role of a gentleman. And his collegiate interests center around the club and around congenial friends he will find there. As for collegiate study, his goal in marks is likely to be "the gentleman's C," which shows he is above striving. He knows that, for him, college grades have little relevance to his future career.

Psychologists, meanwhile, are finding that the lower classes are oriented to the *present*, the here right now. The people in the lower classes are the hedonists. They show little interest in thrift. They live for living's sake because tomorrow, if it ever comes, will probably be tougher. This contrasts with the prevailing white-collar youth's attitude of proper behavior and straining to make a nice impression. In surveying these two states of mind, Lee J. Cronbach, one of the nation's leading educational psychologists, asks of our educators:

"Can the school be sure that punctuality and self-control and effort are better values than casualness and self-expression and enjoyment of the moment?"[4]

With that blunt question in mind, let us turn to the role of our educational system in creating and nurturing and coping with class differences. First, the public schools.

America's public schools are often said to be a force for democracy. And when compared with private schools, they undoubtedly are. At the elementary level, the public schools often are class melting pots, particularly in old-fashioned-type communities that embrace the spectrum of income groups. But as Bevode McCall points out: "It is a fallacy to say that we have mass education in this country." Even the public schools reflect the class feelings of the teaching staff, parents, and school board.

By the time youngsters reach the senior-high-school level, two of the five major social classes have pretty well disappeared from the picture. The youngsters from the upper class have to a large extent gone off to private schools (particularly in the East). And virtually all youngsters from the real lower class—and in many towns most of the working class—have quit school. Only a little more than half of all adolescents ever complete work for a high-school diploma.

Youngsters, by the time they reach the fifth or sixth grade, have absorbed the social-class origins of their playmates, and know whom they shouldn't associate with, except on a polite basis. A mother in Fairfield County, Connecticut, relates that she heard her ten-year-old daughter say to another ten-year-old girl that one member of their class couldn't "get into dancing school because she is a Jew."

Awareness of the social status of one's classmates becomes more intense as the youngster gets into junior high school and starts dating. The lower-class youngster, almost universally looked down upon, often becomes a "problem" student, and typically counts the days until he can legally quit. Once he quits, of course, his class status is likely to be frozen for life. The Institute for Sex Research, for example, has found that the level at which one terminates one's formal schooling is the most precise single indicator of social level.

With most of the upper class gone off to private schools, the student bodies of our high schools are dominated by the semi-upper- (or upper-middle-) class youngster. And as McCall points out: "Teachers tend to kowtow to upper-middle-class children." Middle-class parents tend to be firm allies of the teachers because they are eager for their children to get ahead. Being human, the teachers like this. In contrast, lower-class parents tend to view teachers as authority figures and approach them, if they must, warily. The teachers, again being human—and often untrained in class behavior patterns—react negatively.

In many schools, the youngsters from the higher-prestige families form tight cliques. An eighth-grade teacher in a Connecticut school voiced to me her discouragement because she had in her home room "a snippy little clique of girls" from the upper level of classes "who outlaw everyone who doesn't seem to belong to their group and do what they do." One girl in the clique fell by the wayside because her parents neglected to send her to dancing school. "She was dropped from everything," the teacher relates.

The public schools of America are in general not only dominated by upper-middle-class thinking but make intensive—if unwitting—efforts to reinforce values cherished by such classes. Efforts are made to hammer proper grammar into the minds and speech of the lower-class youngster even though his use of such proper language in his own neighborhood will cause neighbors to snicker and call him a sissy. The school, as Cronbach points out, also stresses that all right-thinking citizens concern themselves with social problems, government policies, and world affairs. Typically, the father of a lower-class youngster takes either a dim or indifferent view of all such preoccupations.

The most illuminating study ever made of the role of social class in our public schools unquestionably is that of Hollingshead in Elmtown. He spent the better part of two years mingling with that town's school children, teachers, and parents. He found the high-school youths had a good understanding of the class system, and quoted an elder citizen as saying: "These high school kids know what is what, and who is who; we don't fool them any."[5]

Hollingshead notes that the governing structure of the town's school system was class-oriented. To become a member of the board of education, he found, there are some informal ground rules. The only people considered for the board were those who owned property, were Republican, were Protestant, and were approved by Rotary. The board reflected, he found, the interests of the big property owners, who wanted to keep taxes down and were convinced that all youngsters of the lower class and many in the working class would not benefit from a high-school education. Hollingshead found many cases where teachers had catered to the town's more prominent families and cited that of one elderly woman teacher who was adored by the two upper classes and detested and distrusted by many in the three lower classes. They felt she graded with one eye on Society. The head of Elmtown's most socially prominent family praised this teacher because "she teaches every child in a different way; she knows each one's background and treats it accordingly." (Other studies have found that virtually all public-school teachers are of "middle-class" origin.)

In the student council, too, the children from the better families were found in double their strength in the student body.

The course of study a student chose in high school was considered a good indicator of status. Students told Hollingshead you couldn't "rate" if you took the commercial course, and were somewhat handicapped if you took the general course. The great bulk of the students of the two lower classes took those courses; the two top classes greatly favored the college-preparatory course. One girl said that youngsters in college-preparatory courses of study set themselves up as automatically better than everyone else and pretty much ran the place.

W. Lloyd Warner's group found much the same situation in Yankee City and noted that even "the percentage of each class who took the Latin course declines with lower position in the class hierarchy."[6]

To return to Elmtown, Hollingshead also found that youngsters from the top classes seldom miss a high-school dance or athletic event while most of the two lower-class youngsters said they attended few or none of them.

Bevode McCall relates that in Lansing, Michigan, football stars from the working class said they could get dates with "anybody" during the football season but not in between seasons. McCall has concluded that rejection by popular girls in the dating competition inspires many of the boys from the lower half of the economic scale to quit school. Class differences start becoming marked when interest in the other sex begins, because dating in the teens is the major basis of popularity. McCall states that youngsters from the lower classes "get excluded and drop out. It's not just intelligence."

Cronbach makes much the same point. Differences of intelligence between the youngsters from the lower classes and those from what he calls the middle classes are perceptible on an *average* but only slightly so. The higher-level youngsters show slightly more intellectual readiness for reading, perhaps because of environmental advantages they have had. He adds that the differences are unimportant because individually many in the lower classes are brighter than many in the middle range. This fact shows up in a study of vocabulary at the fourteen-year level. Youngsters at the working-class level (upper-lower) showed a range in word knowledge of from 18,000 to 60,000 words; youngsters in the semi-upper or upper middle class showed a range of from 35,000 to 57,000 words. While the poorest students were in the working class, so were the brightest.[7]

Of America's 39,000,000 school-age youngsters, about three quarters of a million (or 2 per cent) go to private schools rather than public or parochial schools. The private or "independent" schools that are near the family home are called "day schools" and cost about $650 a year on the average; those to which the youngster is sent away are known as "boarding schools" and cost about $2,000 a year. The exclusive private school offers a student social polish, somewhat more individual attention than in a public school, discipline, and an education that is sometimes superior but very often inferior to that available free of charge at a good public school.

The United States sociologist who has looked most searchingly at the private school is E. Digby Baltzell. He is himself a graduate of St. Paul's, one of the most elite of New England's Episcopal boarding schools.

Baltzell states that the private schools—along with the Ivy League universities—"serve the sociological function of differentiating the upper class in America from the rest of the population." They acculturate "the members of the younger generation, especially those not quite to the manor born, into an upper class style of life."[8] As American cities have expanded over the decades, it has become harder and harder in metropolitan areas for a wealthy family to establish eliteness on the basis of family lineage (as it can still be done in smaller cities where everybody knows who is really who). One result of this is the growing importance of going to a proper private school. Baltzell makes the point that the fashionable schools have become in a sense family surrogates or substitutes dedicated to training a national upper class. The private school is coming to loom larger than the family coat of arms in determining whether a young person is qualified to be accepted in the real upper circles.

What kind of families feel impelled to pay the extra $2,000 a year to send their growing youngster away from the family hearth at a relatively tender age to boarding school? Baltzell found that a majority of the young lads at St. Paul's in a recent year were descendants of alumni. We might refine the situation somewhat. While boarding-school youngsters come from all sorts of homes—including a few humble ones, for seasoning —the vast majority of students who are accepted appear to fall into one of these six categories:

1. Descendants of wealthy alumni.

2. Descendants of once-prosperous alumni who have come into difficult times. These youngsters, known to "have the stuff in them," frequently receive favored treatment when scholarships are awarded. Baltzell gained the impression that most of the scholarships awarded at such familistic schools as Groton and St. Paul's go to boys from "impecunious upper-class families."

3. Offspring of the new rich, too successful to be ignored. These youngsters need to be given a proper background so they can be a credit to the upper class.

4. Maladjusted or emotionally threatened youngsters from upper or semi-upper homes whose parents are separated, quarreling, or frequently away from home.

5. Exceptionally promising youngsters from moderate-income families who live in districts served by public schools that are poorly staffed or that draw most of their students from the two lower classes.

6. Children of ambitious semi-upper-class families seeking to improve their status or put it on a permanent basis.

The American-Canadian team of social scientists studying the suburban town they called Crestwood Heights interviewed a forthright mother who appeared to fall in the last category. She planned to send her daughter to a certain private school, she said, even though she felt the teaching standards were "much higher" at the local public schools. The best system, she had concluded, was to let your children get a "good academic grounding" in the public schools and then "finish at a private school and get the social graces." She planned to send her daughter, later, to private school "not because I think it is better for her but because I think it is socially necessary."[9]

Interestingly, the really rich—the families who count their

dollar wealth in the tens of millions—favor public schools for their children, perhaps to keep in touch with reality. *Fortune* magazine found in a survey of the super-multimillionaires that 41 per cent of the very rich used public schools for their children while 36 per cent used private ones. (The rest used both.)

There appear also to be regional variations in the likelihood of families sending children to private schools. Prospering families in the Northeast who wish to indicate their good breeding tend to think that a private-school education for their children is almost mandatory. (They typically explain the move, however, on the grounds that local public schools are inadequate for their child.) On the other hand, virtually all the upper-income families of the North Shore above Chicago send their children to the very fine local public schools. The wealthy families in Palm Springs, California, likewise virtually all send their children to the local public schools.

There are about three thousand private schools in America. Each city has its fashionable day schools for the early ages. Baltzell found in his investigation that the following sixteen leading Protestant boarding schools for young men "set the pace and bore the brunt" of criticism received by private schools for their so-called "snobbish" and "un-democratic" values, at least as of the focus period of his study:[10]

NEW ENGLAND—EPISCOPAL
St. Paul's
St. Mark's
Groton
St. George's
Kent

NEW ENGLAND—NON-DENOMINATIONAL
Exeter
Andover
Taft
Hotchkiss
Choate
Middlesex
Deerfield

MIDDLE AND SOUTHERN STATES
Lawrenceville
Hill
Episcopal High School
Woodbury Forest

Another school that probably should be included in the list of leading boarding schools is Milton Academy.

The five Episcopal schools plus Middlesex are considered most fashionable in most circles. They are sometimes jovially referred to as "St. Grottlesex." They tend to be paternalistic and their staffs supervise most of the details of the lads' lives. In contrast, Baltzell points out, the two oldest and richest schools, Exeter and Andover, are least exclusive socially, and stress self-reliance. Interestingly, Exeter graduates tend in overwhelming number to go to Harvard University while more graduates of Andover go to Yale.

The Hatches, in their study of newspaper accounts of leading society weddings in New York, found that the private schools most frequently listed for the groom, in descending order, were: St. Paul's, Groton, Hotchkiss, Andover, Taft, Pomfret, Exeter.

As for the girls, those who hope to move into proper social circles must by any means necessary become accepted at a school acceptable to local society. Typically, party lists planned by proper parents for their youngsters are drawn from, or checked against, school-enrollment lists. And most of the schools, aware of their role in screening future socialites, demand students whose fathers have commanding business positions, have membership in proper clubs, and have proper addresses. In the East, among the schools carrying the greatest social authority are these ten: The Masters in Dobbs Ferry, New York; St. Timothy's in Stevenson, Maryland; Ethel Walker in Simsbury, Connecticut; Westover in Middlebury, Connecticut; Miss Porter's in Farmington, Connecticut; Foxcroft in Middleburg, Virginia; Abbot Academy in Andover, Massachusetts; Chatham Hall in Chatham, Virginia; Baldwin in Bryn Mawr, Pennsylvania; the Madeira School, outside Washington, D.C.

Attendance at a proper private school is virtually mandatory for the girl who hopes to make a real debut. Of twenty-nine girls presented to society by the elite Las Madrinas in Los Angeles in 1958, twenty-seven were from private schools. And of the twenty-seven in private schools, eighteen were from Marlborough, the school deemed there to have the most social prestige.

At the private schools—for males or females—the students are taught how to dance and dress and talk and comport themselves. On the school rolls and announcements, a boy is not Rudy Sandringham as he might be listed in a public school. He is Rudolph Culbrith Sandringham III. Arrangements are frequently made by the school staff to see that heterosexual contacts are of the impeccable type. The entire student body of a proper boys' school may be invited to the dance or play of a girls' school.

Non-proper outsiders often have the notion that students who go away to fashionable private schools live there in pampered luxury. That is hardly the case. The emphasis typically is on the simple, austere life. Girls often are required to wear some sort of graceless uniform, or at least a jacket. The investigators of Crestwood Heights suggest this is to remind the girls that they are serving a sort of cocoon-like apprenticeship before they burst forth as butterflies of femininity to challenge their mothers. At the schools, much is made of the "democratic" atmosphere. Everybody is equal in this segregated or hothouse-type democracy. The ostentation and status striving and snubbing that might be encountered at a public school are frowned upon. Worldly possessions such as a car or radio frequently are banned. You can't tell a millionaire's son from a billionaire's. The students may even be required to sleep on hard mattresses.

The American boarding schools are modeled after the English "public" schools such as Eton, which for long trained the British ruling class. Baltzell suggests, however, that perhaps the American schools have imitated the British schools only superficially, at the polish level. The British schools have produced polished gentlemen but they have also produced great statesmen, men who paid the debt of special privilege by public service. Precious few of the products of American private schools have become great statesmen or jurists. Rare exceptions: Franklin D. Roosevelt and Dean Acheson. Less than 1 per cent of the graduates even enter public service at all. Tens of thousands, on the other hand, have drifted, as if beckoned by destiny, into brokerage, banking, corporate law, and executive offices, preferably on Wall Street.

Many prep-school students tend, when they go on to college, to be uninspired students despite the cramming they have got in the prep schools. Unmotivated to study, they have been content with the gentleman's C. (Also, many have been so intensively supervised at prep school that they haven't learned the self-discipline and self-starting required to excel at a college where they are on their own.) This has created a problem for the Ivy League colleges, which have traditionally favored the qualified sons of alumni, who mostly attend prep schools. This favoritism is probably reasonable since, being private institutions, they are to a large extent dependent upon gifts of wealthy alumni. In recent years, with the great rise in collegiate admission standards resulting from the growing demand for college facilities, the Ivy League colleges have taken more and more of the bright, success-oriented "hustlers" from the nation's public high schools. In 1958, Princeton finally became a predominantly public-school-educated institution. The public-high-school graduates tend to do better scholastically than the private-school graduates. One explanation given is that private-school graduates, not motivated to strive, frequently do not live up to the promise of their college-board examinations.

This lack of striving by many prep-school products poses a dilemma for Princeton officials. The editor of Princeton's *Alumni Weekly* points out that it would be "imprudent" of Princeton, in view of its dependence upon gifts from alumni, to "isolate itself from the upper classes" by admitting too many non-U high-school graduates. He urged a harder search of the prep schools for better scholars.

Whether you are a public-school boy or a preppie, there are clear advantages to going to an Ivy League college (rather than to just any university). Baltzell puts the advantage in overwhelming terms for people who aspire to the upper class. He says: "It is more advantageous, socially, and economically, to have graduated from Harvard, Yale or Princeton with a low academic standing than to have been a Phi Beta Kappa at some less fashionable institution."[11]

Ernest Havemann and Patricia Salter West put the advantage of going to one of these Big Three in dollar terms. In their study of 10,000 graduates of American colleges, they found that graduates of these three colleges (then averaging $7,365 a year) were earning $1,200 more a year than graduates of other Ivy League schools, $2,000 more than the graduates of seventeen technical colleges, $2,000 more than graduates of the Big Ten, and $3,000 more than graduates of "all other Midwest colleges."[12] (The fact that the Princeton-Yale-Harvard men were frequently the sons of wealthy businessmen to start with presumably helps account for their enviable income position.) Havemann and West also noted that, whatever the university, the students who are supported in college by their parents tend to end up with higher-paying jobs than the poorer boys who have to work their way through college.

W. Lloyd Warner and James C. Abegglen, in their study of the origins of successful business executives, found that the five schools most frequently listed were all Ivy League, in this order: Yale, Harvard, Princeton, Cornell, University of Pennsylvania. All thirty-six of the Yale men included in one phase of the study were sons of business or professional men. Not one was the son of a laboring man.

In just about any Eastern city, the elite large corporate law firms will show a number of Ivy League diplomas on the wall. At the highest-prestige law firm in Northeast City, 60 per cent of the partners were either Yale or Harvard men. The partiality for Ivy League men shows up in some odd ways. Herbert Kubly recalls his astonishment when he went abroad to serve as a Fulbright professor. Sixteen Fulbright professors were on board his ship. One of their objectives, while in Italy, was to present a strong case for American democracy. Kubly recalls: "Our first lesson in democracy came quickly, even before we left New York. When we embarked we discovered" that someone in Washington "had booked professors from Harvard and Yale into first-class cabins and those of us not in the Ivy League into second-class cabins."[13]

The Ivy League schools, it should be pointed out in fairness, produce more per 1000 graduates who become listed in *Who's Who* than any other group of colleges. However, as a group, they are outranked by several individual small Eastern colleges (Amherst, Wesleyan, Swarthmore, Hamilton, and Williams) and are pressed hard by several distinguished but less publicized non-Eastern colleges (Oberlin, De Pauw, Carleton, Reed, Knox, Wooster, Lawrence, Park, and Occidental).

Whatever school a poor boy chooses, his chances of getting ahead in a gratifying way will depend to some extent on the career for which he is studying. West has pointed out that a professional career (such as that of a scientist) offers much more opportunity to the poor-but-talented boy than a business career in a corporation. In business, she says, "there is a greater chance that your 'background' may defeat you." In some of the professions, in contrast, good college grades are far more likely to be decisive.

Even in the professions, however, there has been a sharply growing separation of the poor from the well-off as far as specific professions are concerned. West states that the students who must work their way through college now increasingly go into the lower-paid professions such as the arts, education, and the ministry; whereas the students who are family-financed during college increasingly tend to go into the more lucrative professions such as medicine, dentistry, and the law. C. Wright Mills of Columbia University suggests that some medical schools have been encouraging this trend, at least as far as medicine is concerned, by favoring applicants from well-off families and lengthening the period of training (especially for specialists) to the point where the specialists tend to be selected from the old, established families.[14]

Clubs and fraternities play a role in helping sons and daughters of the elite to develop their sense of unity among themselves and apartness from the general run of students. These clubs are valued at some of the Ivy League schools because of the influx of public-school graduates onto the campuses. Mills points this up vividly when he describes how young men are sized up in proper adult circles:

"Harvard or Yale or Princeton is not enough. It is the really exclusive prep school that counts, for that determines which of the two Harvards one attends." The clubs and cliques at college are made up of people who went to the proper private schools. "One's friends at Harvard," Mills explains, "are friends made at prep school. That is why in the upper social classes it does not mean much merely to have a degree from an Ivy League college. That is assumed; the point is not Harvard, but which Harvard? By Harvard one means Porcellian, Fly or A.D.; by Yale one means Zeta Psi or Fence or Delta Kappa Epsilon; by Princeton, Cottage, Tiger, Cap & Gown or Ivy. It is the prestige of the properly certified secondary education followed by a proper club in a proper Ivy League college that is the standard admission ticket to the world of urban clubs and parties in any major city in the nation."[15]

It might be noted that merely winning a degree from Yale, Princeton, or Harvard does not entitle one to join the local Yale, Princeton, or Harvard club in his city. One must be proposed, seconded, and approved.

At Harvard, the "right" Harvard (as Mills would put it) consists of only 15 per cent of the student body. The rest of the students are free to develop the Harvard ideal of an intellectual elite regardless of background. (For this, Harvard has earned, and justly deserves, a world-wide reputation.) The elite 15 per cent are typically sifted out at the sophomore level by the Hasty Pudding Club. Then, in the final years, if one survives the sifting, one may be invited to one of the dozen "final" clubs such as Porcellian.

Princeton has the appearance of a more democratic arrangement in its eating clubs. After a revolt of the sophomore class in 1949–50, it was agreed that every Princeton sophomore would receive an invitation to one of the seventeen eating clubs. What could be more democratic? Furthermore, every club began taking Jewish students into membership. Status lines, however, have reappeared. I have found Princeton students able to list with impressive unanimity the status ranking of the clubs, from the highest down to the seventeenth. Ivy, Cottage, Cap & Gown, and Colonial were the first four, and Prospect was Number 17.

In 1958, a group of twenty-three sophomores—fifteen of them Jewish—charged that they were being "railroaded" into Prospect, the lowest-status club, by the other sixteen clubs. One student, who had proven himself to be one of America's brightest lads by winning a National Merit Scholarship, listed seven reasons why he was not good club material. He was:

_____Short of stature.

_____Non-athletic.

_____A scholarship student.

_____An intellectual by repute.

_____A Jew.

_____A graduate of a public high school.

_____A son of a non-wealthy family.

At many universities including the great universities—with students coming from a wide range on the social scale—the fraternities play an important role in helping the more elite in background to protect their social rank. Certain types of "undesirable" students are often barred by national policy of fraternities at campuses having local chapters. Sometimes the exclusionary national policies are written, but more often these days they are unwritten or softly written since *some* college administrations have been cracking down on fraternities with too blatantly restrictive clauses such as those specifying that only students of "Aryan blood" are acceptable. Today, if there is any written restrictive policy, it is likely to be couched under such carefully chosen words as "socially acceptable."

Exclusiveness of fraternities and sororities is frequently based on family background, social poise, and the "right" racial characteristics and religious background.

Alfred McClung Lee, who conducted a study of prejudice on the American campus, tells of finding one sorority at the University of Missouri with a Greek-letter name that excluded students of Greek background, just because they were Greek. Greek is fine for the name of a fraternity or sorority; but when a modern Greek name is on a person, it sounds foreign, and so undesirable.[16]

In general, the mood of most students is toward less arbitrary exclusion of groups because of race or religion. It is the alumni dominating the national fraternity councils and their paid officers who mainly are fighting to keep exclusionary policies. A comparative study at Princeton of attitudes in 1932 and 1950 disclosed that the later-day students are much less willing to characterize by stereotype description people who happened to belong to any of ten ethnic groups.

There have been a number of moves in recent years to judge possible fraternity members solely on the basis of personal worth rather than by such gross categorical basis as ethnic background. One of the fastest-growing fraternities in America, Tau Kappa Epsilon, has never had a written or unwritten exclusionist clause and its chapters are committed to strive to choose members on the basis of personal worth and character. And all rushing at Amherst College has recently been on a specified democratic basis. All students achieving a certain level of scholarship are assured of a bid, and selection is supposed to be based primarily on the student's personal worth and interests.

But institutions focusing on personal worth and character (and not spurning people by categories) still tend to be exceptional. The national officers of a number of Greek-letter fraternities have resisted the idea of removing all restrictive policies, and have stubbornly opposed in most cases the idea of allowing each local chapter to set its own admission standards. Some have recoiled in horror at such a preposterous notion.

Banta's Greek Exchange in October, 1958, quoted at length a Washington, D.C., judge who is also an officer of the Interfraternity Research and Advisory Council on the dangerous potentialities of such notions. He said the thought of allowing each chapter of a national fraternity to choose freely its own members "gives me the cold shivers." The judge discussed also the agitation to remove clauses of "your constitution which restrict the selection of any new member by reason of race, color or creed." He pointed out that such action—while up to each fraternity to decide—would not necessarily silence such critics as college administrators. The administrators, he pointed out, are then likely to challenge the fraternity to "prove" its nondiscriminatory practices "by initiating into membership one of the formerly prohibited students."

He blamed much of the national fraternities' troubles on pseudo-crusaders (including fraternity men) trying to change the "national social fabric" by establishing some sort of Brotherhood of Man in the world. The idea of such a brotherhood, he said, belongs to the areas of work, education, worship, and talents. "I do not believe," he stated, "that the Brotherhood of Man was intended to apply to social privileges. . . ."

The situations I have pointed to in this chapter suggest, I believe, that our educational system is still a far-from-perfect incubator of democracy. If democracy is to be a reality in our nation, it should start in our schools. Further, I think we should all bear in mind that the meanness of class distinctions is more painfully felt during school years than during any other period of people's lives.

gauging social position

DURING THE PAST DECADE, SEVERAL SOCIOLOGISTS HAVE EN-
deavored to devise an index that could readily be used to
assign a class status to each individual being interviewed or
appraised, for comparative purposes. Such an index requires
the use of objective specifications.

The W. Lloyd Warner group devised one of the first
indexes to receive serious attention. It has been widely used
and several modifications have been made to meet specific
situations. Bevode McCall modified it somewhat in making
a study of Chicago inhabitants. August B. Hollingshead in
recent years has been using an index based on three factors:
occupation, education, and area of residence. Each is assigned
a weight. In 1955, Joseph A. Kahl and James A. Davis reviewed the various indexes then in use to measure socio-
economic status and concluded that the best measurable
predictors of status in descending order were: occupation,
education, source of income, dwelling area, house type, and
amount of income.

As McCall points out, the specific occupation, house type,
address, or income are not what determine status. They are
simply descriptive facts of life. The status arises from the
evaluations many people have in the backs of their heads
as to the social worth of such things—address, diploma, etc.—
as status symbols. Sociologists have built their indexes on what
they have learned from interviews are important indicators in
the minds of those people who automatically assign status to

people on the basis of such symbolic factors. This appears to include the great majority of the populace.

The minority of people who are relatively indifferent to status symbols still may have an anthropologist's curiosity about how the system of status assignment works.

We have seen during the course of this book that a host of factors carry weight with the status conscious. The six that sociologists have found most readily measurable on scales—occupation, education, income source, dwelling area, house type, and amount of income—work best when applied to a specific community. When any application is attempted on a national scale, they become at best crude indicators. This is particularly true of the last three. Conditions vary from town to town and the size-of-income factor is complicated, as we have noted, by a variety of anomalies.

What follows is an indication of the kind of scales the sociologists use to estimate the social position an individual holds in his community. I will list four scales. (I've eliminated from the six listed above the final one on size of income and have combined the two home factors, #4 and #5.) The "occupation" and "source of income" scales I'll cite are modifications of scales used by Bevode McCall in Chicago.

Since some of the seven-point scales are believed to be more accurate indicators of status than others, those are assigned more weight. The status score on each scale would be multiplied by the weight assigned to that scale. These are weights that might well be used: the "occupation" score would be multiplied by 5; the "education" score would be multiplied by 4; the "source of income" score would be multiplied by 3; and the "kind of home" score would be multiplied by 2. Thus, if on the "occupation" scale the subject's status level is 4, that would be multiplied by 5 for a score of 20 for that scale. The lower the score, the higher the status.

OCCUPATION

Status Level

1.   Major executives of large firms or successful licensed professionals with advanced degrees.

2. Major executives of small firms; middle management executives of large firms; moderately thriving licensed professionals; faculty members of the better colleges; editors, critics, commentators, and other opinion molders.

3. Minor-responsibility business jobs; white-collar supervisors; professionals without licensing protection; high-school teachers.

4. Supervisors of manual workers; skilled white-collar workers; technicians; high-responsibility blue-collar employees.

5. Salaried manual workers; semi-skilled white-collar workers; semi-professionalized service workers.

6. Semi-skilled manual workers; white-collar machine attendants.

7. Casual laborers, domestic servants.

EDUCATION

Status Level

1. Professional- or graduate-school attainment.
2. Graduate of a four-year college.
3. Graduate of a two-year college or at least one and one half years of college (but without a degree).
4. High-school graduate plus "trade school" or "business school" education or attendance for a year or less at a regular college.
5. High-school graduate.
6. Attended high school but did not graduate.
7. No more than eight grades of schooling.

SOURCE OF INCOME

Status Level

1. Most of income from inherited wealth.
2. Most of annual income from investments and savings gained by earner.

3.   Most of income from profits of business or fees from practice of profession.

4.   Most of income from salary of job or commissions on sales.

5.   Most of income from hourly wages from job or piecework.

6.   Most of income from private assistance (friends, relatives, etc.) plus part-time work.

7.   Most of income from public relief or non-respectable sources such as bootlegging.

KIND OF HOME

Status Level

1.   Own two homes, both with fashionable addresses.

2.   Fine, large, well-kept home in "nicest" part of town; or live in high-status apartment building with doorman and tastefully decorated foyer.

3.   A good, roomy house in one of the better sections of town or countryside; or live in a modern, well-kept apartment building.

4.   A small, modern development house costing less than $15,000; or a plain, non-fashionable larger one in a nice but non-fashionable neighborhood; or live in an adequate but rather plain apartment building.

5.   A double house or row house or an old walk-up apartment building where cooking odors and garbage are likely to be noticed in the hallways.

6.   A small, plain, run-down house or apartment, badly in need of paint or redecoration, in one of poorer sections of town.

7.   A dilapidated house or apartment in the poorest section of town.

The total score—when the weighted scores for each scale are added—can range anywhere from 14 to 98. For most people, a score of 25 or under would indicate they are members of the real upper class. A score of from 26 to 43 would typically indicate a semi-upper status. Those scoring between 44 and 61 would probably fall in the limited-success class. A score of from 62 to 79 indicates a working-class status. A score of 80 or more means the person would probably be considered to have a real-lower-class status.

PART THREE

strains
of status

the price of status striving

*"My brother is very proud of his superiority, and
he has great contempt for carpenters and mechanics
and such people [who] work with their hands. . . .
There is a carpenter who lives downstairs in our
house and though he is poor . . . he always looks
happy, never anxious and sick with worry the way
my brother does."*—R. PRAWER JHABVALA,
from the story, "The Interview."

←‑o‑►‑•‑←‑o‑►‑•‑←‑o‑►‑•‑←‑o‑►‑•‑←‑o‑►‑•‑←‑o‑►‑•‑←‑o‑►

THE HAUGHTY, ANXIETY-RIDDEN BROTHER IN "THE INTER-
view" is a "lettered man" doing clerical work in India. He
wears clean, white clothes, sits on a chair in an office, speaks
English. The lowly carpenter goes barefoot and speaks no
English, but he laughs and sings and even dances. Mrs.
Jhabvala's narrator says enviously of him: "I don't think he
gets weary of his work, and he doesn't look like a man who
is afraid of his superior officers."[1]

In America, we encounter similar contrasts. One night, recently, a taxi driver in New York began grumbling to me, his
passenger, about what a "lousy" business "hacking" is. He
yearned to get a job "selling" or something, but continued,
"Who in hell will take a hackie?" Previously, he indicated, he
had held a variety of petty white-collar jobs, including being

a photographer's assistant and a part-time "ballroom" dancing instructor. His name, I noted, indicated he was an Italian-American. He said that as a hackie he was lucky to average $75 a week, which he considered a pittance. I mentioned that I had heard that a nearby industrial plant paid workmen more than $100, and inquired if he had thought of trying that.

He recoiled in horror and almost swung us off the road. I had insulted him. He said he wouldn't consider such work. Why?

"You get your hands dirty. I don't like to get my hands dirty."

"What does your father do?"

(Shame in voice.) "Oh, he's just a laboring man. A stone mason."

"I hear masons are making good money these days."

"Yeah. He's got it fine now, if you can take that sort of thing. Makes $150 a week, easy. Has short days, long vacations. Even has an assistant. Still, I wouldn't want any part of it. He puts on dirty clothes." At this, the hackie made a face.

The strainers of America can be seen on many streets: people who have accepted the American Dream of limitless opportunities, but are having personal difficulty in making much headway toward achieving the dream. Inhabitants of some of our homogeneous suburban developments are often caught up in a particularly dangerous kind of straining in their consumption patterns. William H. Whyte, Jr., in his study of young management men, relates that many in their early days with a company move into a development alongside lower-level white-collar workers. The two families, at this stage in life, have approximately the same incomes, which is what brought them temporarily together on the same street. They are vastly different, however, in potential earning power. The executive trainee's family can, with some safety, live in a style of life beyond its present means, because it knows that, unless the breadwinner is notably incompetent, a series of automatic raises lie ahead. The white-collar family next door, making the same income but with few likely raises ahead, often strains to keep pace with the high-living neighbor to its grief. Whyte points out: "It is particularly hard for wives to grasp the fact [of the different prospects], and husbands who are in a fairly static job are under constant pressure from them to keep up."[2]

Many people, on the other hand, do resist the temptation to strain in emulative consumption. Working-class men who manage to set up their own small enterprise and prosper often continue to live pretty much in the workingman's style of life and in the same neighborhood. Engineers, also, tend to live contentedly, and relatively frugally, within their means. Anyone who lives among people who have a little less money than he does has a better chance of achieving contentment and avoiding strain.

In general, however, Americans outside the blue-collar group are strivers. A substantial number have difficulty adjusting to swift upward mobility; an even larger number have difficulty adjusting to the frustration of little or no mobility; and quite a few have difficulty adjusting to the assumed humiliation of downward mobility. Americans have difficulty accepting the fact, but a stairway can be tumbled down, as well as climbed up. This is especially true for those who have brief moments of glory, high esteem, or high prosperity, such as beautiful actresses, oil wildcatters, advertising account executives, television comedians, and star athletes. A sociological study was made of the careers of ninety-five championship-caliber boxers after their days of glory. Each had earned at least $100,000 in the ring. Most had their origins in the lower classes. Here is how they were found to be occupied:[3]

18 were unskilled workers, most commonly in steel mills.
 2 were wrestlers.
26 worked in, "fronted for," or owned taverns.
 2 were janitors.
 3 were bookies.
 3 were taxi drivers.
11 were entertainers of some sort.

3 were newsstand tenders.

2 were liquor salesmen.

2 worked in or owned gas stations.

1 was a custom tailor.

3 worked at race tracks.

1 was in "business."

18 were trainers or trainer-managers.

A large number, as the tabulation would indicate, under-went sharp declines in status, and they very frequently suffered prolonged emotional upsets.

Many socially declining or downward-mobile people turn to alcohol or drugs for support. Some become promiscuous. They often become known as troublemakers, with chips on their shoulders. Even their best friends become perplexed as to how to approach them without being snarled at. Wives find them disagreeable as mates. Such declining males are gloom-ridden, and those becoming seriously disturbed emotionally tend to develop sadistic-masochistic (destructive or self-destructive) attitudes. Two studies agree that the downward-mobile people who are referred to psychiatrists are among the most difficult of all types to aid. They rebuff the psychiatrists as well as everybody else.

The people who succeed in moving up the class scale in a conspicuous way must typically pay a price, too. As we have indicated, they feel impelled to take on new habits, new modes of living, new attitudes and beliefs, new addresses, new affiliations, new friends—and discard old ones. The resolute striver is a lonely man making his way on a slippery slope.

Often the upward striver is resented and rejected by the group he is leaving. Sociological studies in the Army have re-vealed that, when an individual begins "bucking for a promo-tion," he alienates himself—at least at the enlisted level—from his own group. His own group, in fact, may begin making "sucking and kissing noises" when the striver is sighted.

An effort to climb that fails can put the person involved into a particularly precarious position. Some time ago, a boy from an aspiring, moderately well-to-do Fairfield County,

Connecticut, family "went away" from the local high school to Choate, a high-prestige boarding school. In a few months he was back at the public high school. He had flunked out of Choate. Many of his old public-school classmates seemed gratified by his humiliation. More interesting, the lad, in scrambling to be re-accepted by his old public-school acquaintances, became loudly and almost continuously contemptuous of the whole private-school setup.

If an upward striver does succeed, however, and goes on to become a conspicuous success, his old associates left behind forget their old resentment and brag fondly of having known him when.

The person who succeeds dramatically in moving up the class scale tends to be, to begin with, relatively rootless. He or she has become isolated from the way of life that the average young person has with his neighborhood. W. Lloyd Warner, in his study of Yankee City, Jonesville, and of America's big-business leaders, was struck in each instance by the role that neighborhood ties play in hindering upward mobility. He was impressed by the odd fact that among the relatively few big-business leaders of lower-level family origin—sons of laborers, white-collar workers, farmers—a large proportion were of immigrant backgrounds. Their rootlessness, he concluded, gave them an advantage. They were, to begin with, disengaged from their backgrounds to an extreme degree. Warner comments:

"Consider the man born in a small community, the home of his family for generations. . . . His relations in space and through time form a pattern of commitments, engagements and obligations binding him to the physical and social space to which he is born."[4]

Warner concludes that, for mobility to occur, the many emotional and social obligations and engagements holding a man to his place must be broken. William Foote Whyte reached much the same conclusion after studying the college boy—who moves upward—and the corner boy—who does not—in Cornerville. Both are anxious to get ahead. "The difference between them," Whyte decided, "is that the college boy either does not tie himself to a group of close friends, or else is willing to sacrifice his friendship with those who do not advance as fast as he does. The corner boy is tied to his group by a network of reciprocal obligations from which he is either unwilling or unable to break away."[5]

The restless, migratory habits of many Americans, then, appear to be an asset for those aspiring to move upward. The moving van, in the words of Louis Kronenberger, is "a symbol of more than our restlessness; it is the most conclusive evidence possible of our progress."[6] Executing an end run by moving to a strange community has its advantages. A study of migration from Kentucky showed that sons who left their home communities tended to show more of a balance in favor of upward mobility than the sons who stayed home. The man who manages to make a spectacular advance within his own community must face across the class lines the past he has left behind. To some this is embarrassing. The investigators at Yankee City noted in fascination the numerous maneuvers attributed to Phillip Starr, a man of local lower-class origin who had succeeded within a lifetime in pushing all the way to the upper class. His family resolutely tried to prove its gentility. For one thing, Mr. Starr sought to make his parents seem upper class, too, by disinterring their remains in the city's lower-class cemetery and reburying them in the city's upper-class cemetery. Locally, the Starrs were classified as "new shoe money." They had purchased one of the finest old houses in the most select street and spent a small fortune furnishing it with authentic period pieces. Still, members of older families fussed that everything was "too perfect" and "overdone." The house was painted so often outside that neighbors claimed it shined too much. Mrs. Starr's parties were considered "too elaborate" and "done for effect." And the neighbors joked that the Starr limousine was so large that if the Starrs lost their money they could put a stove in the car and camp out in it for a winter.

A person who becomes adept at isolating himself from his past, and taking on the coloration of what he hopes is the future, may unwittingly take a manipulative attitude toward individuals around him. He can be charming, and yet he may seem to lack warmth. Such a person is wary of emotional involvement, and may even reach the point where, as Warner puts it, he "arouses a feeling of unpleasantness in others." Willis Wayde, the hard-driving upward-mobile hero of John P. Marquand's novel, *Sincerely, Willis Wayde,* is a great believer in putting on an impressive front and of being sincere. He complains, however, that it is sometimes hard to figure how to be sincere.

Among women, at least, there is further evidence indicating that the upward-mobile career woman is often driven by attitudes generated by humiliating childhood experiences. A study of mobile vs. non-mobile career women in Montgomery, Alabama, showed that the upward-mobile ones had at one time been rejected by their community. Some of these, as children, had also been neglected by parents who obviously favored a sister or brother.

Upward mobility also can put a severe strain on a marriage if the wife is less skilled than the husband in taking on new habits, attitudes, and friendships. Marriage is, as one sociologist put it, "a mutual mobility bet." Leland Gordon, economist of Denison University, cites the classic kind of situation where one partner is the loser: "When a bright young clerk in a chain store moves into a position as manager of a branch store, it is imperative that he join the country club set. But sometimes his salesgirl wife has not grown up with him. As he moves up and out, she is left behind. Many become alcoholics." Children, too, often find living with a rapidly upward-mobile couple a strain. They tend to feel isolated and insecure; and many compensate by becoming chronic talkers.

Both upward- and downward-mobile persons tend to be more prejudiced in their attitudes toward Jews and Negroes than people who are not in motion, socially.[7] Perhaps it is because they are insecure in their own status.

The tension, insecurity, and rootlessness characterizing many zealous upward strivers make them prone to certain emotional disorders. The mobility appears to increase mental strain. Hollingshead and his associates at Yale found that, when the social mobility of mental patients was compared with that of a control group of non-patients, the psycho-neurotics and schizophrenics both showed clearly a record of more upward mobility than the normal control group. Psychiatrist Jurgen Ruesch of the University of California has concluded that the upward mobile turn up in "unusually large numbers" among patients suffering psychosomatic ailments. Apparently they find themselves in new situations beyond their emotional depths, and the strain reveals itself in bodily ailments.

Hollingshead makes a distinction between "climbers" (who achieve at least some success in their aspirations) and "strainers" (who achieve little success despite their very considerable efforts). The climbers, he finds, often encounter their first serious trouble when they try to crash the highest social level, and are rejected as upstarts. They typically react with depression, severe anxiety, and, occasionally, suicide attempts. In contrast, the strainers are dreamers and schemers rushing from one pursuit to another. (James Thurber's *The Secret Life of Walter Mitty*, Hollingshead finds, is a quite accurate fictional portrayal of the typical strainer.) Hollingshead has found that many psychoneurotics and psychotics in the Class III or limited-success class were haunted by occupational frustration that they blamed on education. In one sample, more than 90 per cent of the psychoneurotics in his Class III felt handicapped by the amount of education they had received. Many, also, had aspirations that were far above their accomplishments. The growing barrier, based on education, between people of the limited-success class and those in the semi-upper class evidently has been making wrecks of some of the lower-level people without college education who still believe in the American Dream of unlimited opportunities.

Membership in each social class tends to impose its own kind of strain on people in it. There seems to be general agreement that the most severe strain (or the least capacity to withstand strain) is in the bottom class. People of that category have twice as many psychiatric breakdowns as they should have if mental illness were distributed evenly over the population. A team of sociologists and psychiatrists at Yale University, headed by August B. Hollingshead and Frederick C. Redlich, made an exhaustive study of the relationship between mental illness and social class.[8] These investigators found that a person in the bottom class (Class V) was eleven times as likely to suffer from schizophrenia as a member of the top class (Class I).[9] Schizophrenia, it should be added, follows to a large extent the general pattern of distribution of mental breakdown over the classes. (By this I mean it is not by its nature peculiar to the lowest class.) Some types of mental disorder do show some tendency to favor a certain class. The manic-depressives are three times as prevalent, proportionately, among the two upper classes as among people in the bottom Class V. Jurgen Ruesch has noticed a preponderance of psychosomatic reactions (ulcers, hypertension, allergies) in people of the lower-middle (or limited-success) class. He attributes this to a lack of expressive facilities, because of their drive to conformity and their excessive repression. And Joseph A. Kahl points out: "If the symbolic middle-class neurosis is obsessive compulsivity, complicated by ulcers, the upper-class illness is ennui, complicated by alcohol."[10] And, speaking of alcohol, earlier investigators have noted that among nationality groups the Irish have led, by several lengths, all others in alcoholism.

What is more startling, perhaps, is the discrimination shown against persons of the lower classes by psychiatrists, both in private practice and at the free or low-cost clinics. This discrimination, as we will note later, arises in large part from the inability of upper-class psychiatrists to communicate with lower-class patients; so that the patients are not regarded as good prospects for extended individual treatment.

The Yale team found that, even at the out-patient clinic where cost is no factor, "the higher an individual's social class position, the more likely he was to be accepted for treatment, to be treated by highly trained personnel, and to be treated intensively over a long period."[11] (Students treated the lower classes, residents-in-training tended to be assigned to middle-class patients; and the senior staff members took the higher-class patients.) It was found that these clinics spend eight times as much money treating a Class II patient as they do treating a Class V patient. There is a tendency to give individual psychotherapy to the higher classes, and administer shock treatment, drugs, organic therapy, etc., to the lower-class patients.

Hollingshead and Redlich report that this finding of discrimination "came as a 'bolt out of the blue' for the men who determined the policies of this clinic. It was certainly not planned. A similar situation is found in the public mental hospitals, where, also without regard to the ability of the patients' families to pay, the acute schizophrenics in Class III are more likely to get psychotherapy than Class IV and V patients in the same disease group who entered the hospital at approximately the same time."[12] The Class IV or V schizophrenic, they added, may receive one or two series of organic treatments in a public hospital. If these do not succeed, "the patient drifts to the back wards where, in stultifying isolation, he regresses even more into a world of his own."

19

the special status problems of jews

"Do you know the Levinsons? We like them very much. They are charming, but Jewish, so you can't mix everyone with them."—A HOSTESS who was organizing a party in Northeast City.

←o→•←o→•←o→•←o→•←o→•←o→•←o→

ONE OF THE PERSISTENT PUZZLES OF AMERICAN LIFE IS THE tendency in thousands of communities to erect barriers against Jews. Jewish people are singled out more than any other white ethnic category for such fence building.

The Cornell study of social discrimination in 248 United States communities found, for example, that in the majority of middle-sized cities Jews were discriminated against in all three of the tests of social acceptability used by the investigators. Those tests were admission to the country or city club, the exclusive residential area, and the Junior League. In only one out of fifty middle-sized cities were Jews accepted in all three categories.[1]

Why is it that, in 49 out of 50 middle-sized cities, the Jew is considered as not meeting all three tests of social acceptance? In the average city, the higher-level Jews meet all the existing eligibility standards in terms of business or professional success and education. If the Jew meets all the eligibility requirements, why isn't he accepted? Why do the barriers persist against him all across the American landscape, in both business and social life? Is the exclusiveness of elite non-Jews related to their own status-seeking activities?

This persistent treatment of the Jews in America as a group apart has become a question of mounting economic urgency. With the great growth of bigness in business organization, the Jew is seeing his world of opportunity shrinking. In the past, the Jews have survived by being able, in many cases, to prosper in their own enterprises. This assured them that they would not be at the mercy of a prejudiced Gentile employer.

Now, however, many Jews face the economic necessity of working within the hierarchy of the large corporations. The individual entrepreneur, at the producing level at least, is becoming more and more the lonely exception. Bigness is the mode of the era. And it is the rare large corporation that considers Jews on their qualifications alone in filling all its ranks. Some corporations shun Jews almost entirely. This is particularly true in insurance, banking, automobile making, utilities, oil, steel, heavy industry. Others profess hospitality to Jews; but then it often turns out that Jews are really welcomed only in the "inside" jobs requiring high intellectual capacity such as research, creativity, actuarial skill, etc. The "outside" jobs, calling for contact with clients or the public or with stockholders, are primarily reserved for Gentiles.

Another problem facing the Jew in the corporation is the five-o'clock shadow. Jew and Gentile may work amiably together all day in the corporate hierarchy, but, come five o'clock, the Gentile may go off to one of the city's elite clubs, and the Jew cannot follow. Or the Jew may have his own firm and see his biggest rival go into the town's elite club at five o'clock. And the elite social club, as we have noted, is becoming more and more the place where important business decisions often tend to jell. You will recall that, in Chapter 13, Mr. Thompson, one of Northeast City's biggest bankers, said, "An active banker belongs to every damned club in town. It is part of the game." The elite clubs, by excluding Jews, thus in effect severely handicap any Jews trying to play the "game."

For these and other reasons, many thoughtful Jews are trying to understand just what it is that causes the barriers to be erected against them.

It is hoped that what follows may offer both Jews and Gentiles some illumination on this curious aspect of our community life.

While I was in Northeast City talking with people who were identified as the "real powers" of the community, my primary, announced purpose was to study the elite structure of their city. I went into this quite thoroughly with each of them; and they were most co-operative and informative. I also had a second, unannounced purpose, and that was to draw them out, spontaneously and confidentially, on the subject of Jews. In this I was looking for insights that might explain why the lines were drawn against Jews at many points in the city's social and business life, especially at the elite or upper-class level. I was curious to know, in the face of the frequently stated great respect for Jews, why few Jewish names appeared among the officers of most of the banks, utilities and large industrial firms. (Mostly, the leading Jews were merchants, lawyers, or textile-plant operators.) Also, why were there either no Jewish names or few Jewish names listed as members of the elite men's club (Pioneer's), the elite women's club (Martha Washington), and the three leading country clubs? And why was it, I wondered, that Jews and non-Jews worked wholeheartedly together on civic fund-raising projects, but went their separate ways socially? (All names of clubs and individuals cited in Northeast City, I should add, have been altered and are fictitious.)

I did not ask any of these questions directly and bluntly. That would have endangered the free flow of communication. Instead, I sought to lead my informants—after they had become relaxed by talking about the city's elite clubs, churches, etc.—into a general discussion of the role of Jews in American life and in the city's life. Subsequently I guided them into the desired areas. I made it clear I was simply trying to unravel a situation that reappears in city after city, and was not peculiar to Northeast City, which is a representative middle-sized United States metropolis. And I sought to create a permissive atmosphere by expressing keen interest in whatever they said about Jews. In a few cases I experimentally raised arguments against their viewpoints. This, invariably, drove them into a more cautious, proper tone. Typically, they became quite voluble on the subject of Jews. The only one who was ill at ease throughout was a man on the membership committee of the most elite country club (Gentry). (Since conducting these interviews, which took place in November and December, 1957, I have conducted similar but less intensive probings with a score of upper-class individuals in Fairfield County, Connecticut, and the later findings have illuminated but not modified the impressions I gained in Northeast City. Altogether, I have sounded out forty-five upper-class non-Jews, confidentially and with seeming casualness, on the subject of Jews.)

I suppose I should declare at this point that I am a Gentile. That puts me in what Jerome Weidman calls "the enemy camp." On the other hand—to declare my biases as far as I know them—I have had the conviction, based on my personal encounters with Jews as neighbors and colleagues, that it is a pity more non-Jews don't get to know Jews as friends.

The elite informants in Northeast City were certainly not as hostile to Jews in their conversations as you would assume from all the barriers that have been put up against Jews in their city. In fact, several seemed a little ashamed of the barriers as hardly worthy of as civilized a community as they liked to think Northeast City is. An industrial president, Mr. Ross, said, "The Jews I know are very able people, very strong people." A leading banker, Mr. Thompson, said, "Jews have a delightful family life." And various informants spoke of individual Jewish leaders as being "a wonderful man" or "an awfully nice man." Some Jewish families have local roots going back more than a century. An official of the city's largest corporation said, "You don't find people nowadays at lunch cussing the Jews." Mr. Wallace, a realtor who, I was told, had a reputation some years ago of being hostile to Jews, apparently had changed or else my informant was misinformed. At any rate, Mr. Wallace told me, "I've had far better business treatment, in selling real estate, from Jews than from Gentiles. I've taken my worst gyppings from Gentiles."

In the social life of Northeast City, at least at the upper level, there is virtually no intermingling between Gentile and Jew. When I asked Mrs. Smyth, a First Family socialite, about the degree to which Jewish families take part in the city's club life, she said:

"They have their own lovely club." With that, she gave me a broad wink.

The only city club where there is much intermingling is the Downtown Club. And, as I've noted, several of my informants repeatedly made the point that it was a "businessman's club." The more restrictive Pioneer's Club, in contrast, was considered a "social" or "community" club. Even at the Downtown Club, I was told by two informants, the Jewish membership has been "under control." A former official (Gentile) of the club revealed how this "control" came about during his term of office. He was explaining to me that Jews constituted 7 per cent of the population of Northeast City, and related why he knew. He said the club had been receiving quite a few applications from Jews and Italians. At that point, he said, about 15 per cent of the club's membership was Jewish. (A large number of the downtown merchants are Jewish.) If all the applicants were accepted, the proportion of Jews would have risen to 20 per cent (still far short of their representation in downtown business enterprises). It was at this point, he said, "that we hit upon the idea" of finding the percentage of Jews in the total population of Northeast City (and also of the Italians) "so that the Jews and Italians would not overrun the place."

This man, in commenting on one quite elite club's exclusion of Jews, said: "That is more of a tradition than anything else. The club is just as well off without them. . . ." A great many of the city's civic organizations hold dinners and meetings at this particular elite and exclusionary club. In these organizations and civic drives, Jews often play an active, and occasionally a leading, part; and so they come, often unhappily, to this Gentile club to attend the functions. The city's leading fund raiser, commenting on this awkward situation, said: "I don't know how to justify the fact that Jews are excluded from this particular club. We are in everything together except socially. I'd hate to have to get up in front of anybody and try to explain it."

One well-known sociological force at work in causing many Gentiles to isolate Jews undoubtedly is that of status striving through exclusiveness. As the early sociologist, Max Weber, put it: "Status honor always rests upon distance and exclusiveness." To be exclusive, you must build fences to exclude those you like to think are not as elite as yourself. You can do this on personal worth, but it is much easier to exclude whole categories of people, such as Jews. A sales executive in Northeast City, while describing one local club in unadmiring terms, said: "Everybody can join that club, and I mean everybody."

Another sociological factor at work in Northeast City and elsewhere is status protection in the face of threat. Entrenched old guarders need a mechanism to put challengers in their place. Jews, being perhaps the most enterprising of all American ethnic groups, are commonly viewed as most challenging.

The influential Gentiles I consulted in Northeast City offered a great variety of explanations for the local social and business barriers. Some of the explanations, undoubtedly, are rationalizations. They have been developed to explain a situation that violates the American Creed and so is embarrassing.

Several of the explanations that turned up appear to represent fairly widespread "pictures in the mind," to use Walter Lippmann's phrase, which non-Jews have of Jews. All such pictures tend to become exaggerated over-generalizations. In some cases, traits attributed by my informants to Jews were inherently contradictory.

And in some cases the traits cited undoubtedly represented the non-Jew's own inner need for a scapegoat or whipping boy rather than objective fact. Psychologist P. H. Mussen studied the personalities and before-and-after prejudices of one hundred white boys who spent a month at a camp that

Negro boys also attended. It was found that the youngsters who had few aggressive needs and were well adjusted to their home, to their parents, and to their camp underwent a notable drop in their prejudices toward Negroes as a result of this first-hand contact. On the other hand, boys who showed strong needs for aggressiveness and dominance and who felt anxious or hostile toward their parents underwent some increase in prejudice toward Negroes during the month at the camp.

Even if the "pictures in the mind" about Jews found among the influential Gentiles of Northeast City are rationalizations or distorted stereotypes, they do indicate a state of mind in a typical city that both Jews and non-Jews of good will must seek to modify if the barriers are to be reduced. It is for that reason that I feel they should be brought into the open and inspected. It should be remembered that they represent only the derogatory aspect of my informants' attitude toward Jews, the explanations they mustered in order to account for undemocratic barriers.

In shifting through the explanations offered for the barriers, these ten contentions stand out. I will list them in the order of frequency with which they were raised.

1. *The alleged "clannishness" of Jewish people.*

This assumed clannishness, of course, where it exists, is quite probably the Jews' response to discrimination. Anyone who is being discriminated against feels better if he is among others in the same boat. No one likes to face discrimination alone. At any rate, ten Gentile informants in Northeast City cited this clannishness as an explanation for the fact that there was little social intermingling with Jews.

Mr. Wallace, the realtor, said: "Jews are the most clannish, integrated people there are. They've always been segregated so they stick together now." Two informants cited a situation at a local high school to support this point. It seems that school authorities became concerned because fraternities and sororities were developing along religious lines, and formally banned them. The Gentile sororities and fraternities, according to my informants, were disbanded, but the Jewish ones have continued underground with strong support from Jewish parents, who reportedly do not want their children seriously dating Gentiles.

For whatever reason, Jews in many communities do not seem to socialize much outside their own group. John P. Dean found, in his study of Jewish socializing in Elmira, New York, that Jewish couples who were in social cliques overwhelmingly were in all-Jewish cliques.[1] While I was in Northeast City, a Jewish couple invited me out to a Saturday-night supper. There were twelve other people there. It was a delightful group. Since the problem of Jewish apartness was very much on my mind then, I could not escape noticing the fact that all twelve people present were Jewish. You do not encounter this kind of 100 per cent grouping together of Gentile and Jew in many other communities, including my own in Fairfield County, Connecticut. In my neighborhood, Jew and Gentile alike seem to think in terms of individual interest, and give no thought to religious homogeneity in preparing invitation lists.

This alleged clannishness of Jewish people, to the minds of my Gentile informants, not only helps explain the apartness that exists, but is a factor in convincing them that the apartness should continue as long as Jews lead their own social life. In Northeast City, they felt the assumed clannishness posed an inundation threat to any Gentile club that lowered its barriers. Mr. Ross, an industrialist, said: "When they clan up within a club it is not good."

There is no good evidence that modern Jews are any more clannish than Gentiles. Studies among children, in fact, indicate that Gentile children are more clannish than Jewish children.[2] More to the point, perhaps, is the discovery that the same people who accuse the Jews of being standoffish also accuse them of trying to be too eager to integrate with non-Jews. One group of investigators devised a scale of traits sometimes credited to Jews. On one scale were traits indicating "seclusiveness." On the other scale were traits indicating "intrusiveness." To a very large extent (correlation of .74) people who accused Jews of being intrusive also accused them of being seclusive.³ The same people who agreed emphatically that Jews tend to resist the American way of life agreed with the paired statement that Jews go too far in trying to hide their Jewishness by changing their names and taking on Gentile manners and customs. In other paired statements, people agreed both with the statement that Jews keep apart in their social life and that they try too hard to gain social recognition from non-Jews. Some Gentiles argue that these traits are not necessarily mutually exclusive. In general, however, it seems reasonable to conclude that there is a vast amount of irrationality in the Gentile attitudes. Many Jews feel, with good reason, that they are damned if they do and damned if they don't.

Whatever the precise situation is in this area, beclouded with irrationality, it seems clear that any easing of the barriers would be aided by a reduction of the self-segregating tendencies of both groups.

Historian Max Lerner feels that the cohesiveness of Jews may have intensified during the thirties and forties as an instinctive response to news of Hitler's persecution of the Jews, and of the trials of Jewish people abroad in building their new Israeli state. He states that the "emphasis within the American Jewish group shifted away from assimilation toward a sometimes overmilitant assertion of their uniqueness and separateness as a historical community."⁴ Apparently, however, the trend has now been reversed. The American Jewish Committee made a study of a community called "Riverton." This reveals that younger Jews are twice as eager to participate socially in their general community as older Jews.⁵

2. *The alleged assertiveness of Jewish people.*

This sometimes came up, from Northeast City informants, in back-handed references such as: "He's not aggressive like some Jews." A highly admired Jewish lawyer was referred to as being "aggressive, but not in a way that bothers." Among the elite Gentile informants, nine made some comment that assumed that assertiveness was a Jewish trait.

Mr. Potter, one of the city's leading bankers, said: "I know the feeling of one or two clubs. The fear is that some might be the pushy type." Mrs. Fox, a socialite, said of one local Jew: "He is not as grabby as most Jews." Her college-age daughter had been dating a Jewish boy whom she liked very much, and she said that the Jews she knew personally "are just as nice as you could wish." Later she made this remark: "Gentiles can be just as grabby—but don't have the reputation."

This image of assertiveness, psychologists find, is the kind of stereotyped nurtured by a great deal of selective remembering and selective forgetting. A non-Jew will remember the assertive Jew and not think of the modest, self-effacing Jew in terms of Jewishness. Similarly, he may encounter brashness in dozens of Gentiles without thinking of brashness as being a Gentile trait.

3. *Jewish people are seen as different.*

This feeling, frequently expressed, probably reflects the "consciousness of kind" factor at work. Many people apparently can't rise above their primitive birds-of-a-feather flocking impulse. Mr. Green, partner in one of the city's most elite law firms, said many of the city's leading Jews didn't seem to catch the Northeast City "spirit." He wasn't able to explain what that "spirit" was, with any clarity.

Partly, the sensing of differentness in Jewish people probably has a religious basis. Partly, it may spring from the physiognomy of some Jews. One bank president in Northeast City, Mr. Williams, talked at length about facial differences, real or imaginary, he had perceived in German Jews as distinguished from East European Jews. He mentioned a prominent, widely respected Jewish lawyer in town and said, as if in wonderment, "To look at him you wouldn't know he was Jewish." And, partly, the sensing of differentness may spring from the fact that traditionally Jews have been city people and are identified in people's minds with the cosmopolitanism of the city. (They were long excluded from owning land.) Harvard psychologist Gordon W. Allport suggests that people who felt hostile toward cities may unwittingly have transferred their hostility to Jews.[6] In some small American towns where there isn't a single Jewish resident, anti-Semitism has been found to run high.

4. *Jewish people are "smart."*

Six of the prominent Northeast City Gentiles made references to this in one form or another; and it is difficult to assess how much of this is admiration and how much of it is envy or apprehension.

Mr. Potter, the banker, said of Jews: "They are so damned much smarter than the rest of us. They have intelligence. They go for education. They do everything so well."

I mentioned this allegation of brightness to a Jewish acquaintance. I assumed he would be flattered by this allegation. Instead, he went to his library to produce some charts proving that Jews aren't any brighter than anybody else. The facts seem to be that any difference between Jewish intelligence and the United States average is slight, and could be accounted for by the fact that few Jews are in the lower or working class and the fact that Jews have long cherished scholarship and intellectual attainment.

5. *Some Jewish people behave in ways that bother some Gentiles.*

The reverse also, of course, is true.

Mr. Potter, the banker, in talking of the exclusionary policies of clubs, said: "Anyone would want Joe Goldstein in the club. He is soft-spoken. The fact is, however, that a percentage of Jewish people are considered to be noisy. They don't have the good fortune I have of having a weak voice." And another banker, Mr. Williams—who has no Jews in his organization—said: "Certain traits stick out. They have a certain manner of speech, they are argumentative and wave their arms."

There may be a differentness between Gentile and Jew in temperament that has some basis in fact, as generalizations go. The Jewish home builder in Chicago, in talking of his Jewish homeowners, described them as "explosive" and eager for new experiences. He attributed this to the pressures under which they live. A sociologist in Chicago, in talking of Jews, said they tend to be more "volatile" than Gentiles. The wife of a playwright mentioned that predominantly Jewish audiences tend to be more excitable than Gentile audiences. She attributed this to the fact that many "are geared so high."

6. *Jewish people tend to be individualists.*

This was usually cited by Northeast Gentiles to explain why Jews were not found among the executives of the major corporations in town. Individualism is a trait traditionally cherished in America; but in the modern era of corporate "team playing" we are seeing a conflict between ideal and practicality. Mr. Smith, head of a machinery company, said he used to have a Jewish sales director, but that he had not worked out well. He explained: "He suffered a lack of teamability—you've got to have that these days." And an executive of one of the city's largest corporations said, in accounting for the dearth of Jewish people in its management ranks: "My personal impression is that Jewish people by inclination and by training like to run their own businesses. A lot of this is in their upbringing." And Mr. Kelly, a top executive, said: "Jews don't care to work for the big organization. They want to establish their own business. We have very few applications from Jews." (Knowing his hostility, if I were a Jew I certainly wouldn't apply!)

7. *In business, Jewish people are bold and impatient.*

Mr. Whitcomb, head of one of the city's larger corporations and a civic leader, said: "The bright Jewish fellow isn't temperamentally inclined to take the long haul of working twenty-five years to get to the top of a company. Sidney Klein and I were good friends. [Sidney Klein was for long the city's most successful Jew.] Sid worked in a cigar store as a lad. He couldn't see it when I went to work for Consolidated Corporation. He said he would rather get in a small company and get there faster. He would chide me about my $2 raises, while he was already making big money. The Jews know you can make it faster in a small company." And Mr. Johnson, a banker, asserted that commercial banking doesn't really appeal to Jews because they are interested in "something a little more speculative. Their viewpoint is: If you see a good chance to make a good profit, go after it even if it is a long chance." In short, this is the old-fashioned American spirit of risk-taking so insistently glorified in public statements by our Gentile industrial statesmen, who cautiously manage their own corporations by committee, with the counsel of survey makers and Univac machines.

8. *Some Gentiles feel Jewish businessmen are impersonal and not "fair-minded."*

Several Northeast City businessmen said they would feel uneasy if they got in a jam and had to deal with Jews. One asked: "If this plant got into trouble, would Jews back us up as much as non-Jews if they saw a loss coming up?"

This attitude of the Gentiles would appear to be merely an illustration of "consciousness of kind" again at work. If a person gets into a jam, he feels he will receive a better break from his "own kind" of person, who should feel a group loyalty to be nice to him. Jews presumably feel the same way. (Very often, it should be added, the treatment one gets, in a showdown, from his "own kind" leaves him wishing he had left his fate to an objective outsider.)

9. *Many Jewish businessmen are felt to be money-minded.*

When I reviewed the notes of my interviews on the Jewish situation in Northeast City, I was struck by the frequent use the Gentile informants made of the words "money" or "dollars" in talking of Jews. This was so common that I suspect the word "money" has become imbedded in the Gentile's image of Jews. Other earlier investigators have come upon this same "money" image. A business leader, who was briefing me on the leading citizens of Northeast City, described eighteen or twenty in detail. Virtually all were obviously men of wealth. But only when he mentioned a Jewish man did he use the word "money." He said of this Jewish businessman: "He is very successful—made a lot of money." Mrs. Smyth, the socialite, said of Jews: "They have money."

Here again we appear to be in the misty area of stereotype and projection. According to a study by Dorothy T. Spoerl, Jewish students being tested showed no more preoccupation with "economic value" than did Protestant or Catholic students.[7] Another study showed that the same people who deplored the money-mindedness of Jews were the ones who agreed overwhelmingly with the questionnaire statement that "financial success is an important measure of the man" and that "every child should learn the value of money early." As for the widespread image of Jews as "international bankers" and "Wall Street brokers," this amuses even the Wall Street folks. The truth is that there are relatively few Jews in either category.

10. *The wives of Gentile and Jew often create the barrier.* Mr. Ross, the industrialist, felt that Gentile wives are often more likely to be "petty and narrow" about Jews than their husbands. He said the wives are more concerned "about social status, and more apt to become intense about the Jew." And Mr. Kyle, the contractor, said, in trying to explain why most of his clubs excluded Jews: "In choosing new members for a club, you scrutinize not only the man but his wife. A man may be fine, but his wife may not get along with other women. Women are more isolated. And there is bound to be some jealousy on the part of our women if the Jewish women have mink coats and our women do not."

In many communities, there is far more self-segregation of both Gentiles and Jews at the wife level than at the husband level. And, significantly, it is the wife, rather than the husband, who makes most of the social arrangements for a family. Dean found, in his study of Elmira, New York, Jews, that the women were much more likely to be self-segregating than their husbands. He found that while only 12 per cent of the Jewish men confined their community activities to purely Jewish organizations, 48 per cent of the wives did. Whatever the reason for this greater isolation, it would indicate that the wives have fewer personal, friendly contacts with Gentiles than their husbands do.

The foregoing seems to represent the broad outlines of the barrier in Gentile outlook separating the higher-status Gentile and Jew in a representative American city. Much of it, as indicated, is evidently just a picture in the minds of

Gentiles produced by lack of personal contact with real-life Jewish people that might correct the distortions.

The Northeast City businessman who seemed to have had the most first-hand contact with Jewish people was Mr. Wallace, the realtor. And he made what was perhaps the most accurate summary of the situation. He said: "Jews are just like everybody else—good, bad, and stinking." Perhaps I should add that I talked with three leading Jewish businessmen in Northeast City. What particularly impressed me, in view of what I had been hearing, was that all three men were the complete reverse of the stereotypes. They appeared to be restrained, responsible, soft-spoken, fair-minded, patient, subdued in their tastes, and very proud of their city. They acknowledged the barriers. In fact, they seemed philosophically —almost good-humoredly—resigned to them as handicaps that had to be accepted. Still more interesting, they spoke with warm respect of several of the Gentile leaders who had, when pressed to account for the barriers, uttered derogatory stereotype comments about Jewish people.

The kind of Gentile attitudes I have cited, whatever their substance, seem to represent the state of mind that must be modified before any effort to produce substantially more intermingling between Gentiles and Jews will be really successful. This state of mind seems to stand as a challenge to both Gentiles and Jews of good will.

The Gentile informants, I should stress, were far from unanimous in their support of the barriers or in being critical of Jewish people. Several, during the long and frank talks, never once uttered a remark that could be construed as critical of Jewish people. They seemed to feel the barriers were archaic hangovers.

I estimate that 60 per cent of my Gentile informants of Northeast City were at heart persons of good will. It was the older informants who were inclined to be *least* interested in reducing the business and social barriers against Jews. The 60 per cent who might reasonably be classified as persons of good will seemed uneasy about their local situation, and expressed a wish that it be different.

Mr. Ross, the young industrialist, said he favored "a good representation" of Jews in the community's clubs. He said: "It irritates me when Jews are eliminated." Mr. Johnson, the banker, mentioned approvingly the fact that the local yacht club had begun taking in a few Jewish members. He related that, before this policy change, "they wanted me to serve on the board, but they had a fast rule against Jewish people. I said to them, 'Look, I can't do it. Your rules are not compatible with my philosophy.'" Later, the rule was changed, and Mr. Johnson is now on the board. Mr. Johnson was perhaps the Jews' warmest friend among the Northeast City business leaders I consulted. When he was asked what was required to reduce the barriers, he replied: "A peaceful climate. I believe that people are naturally gregarious and interested in knowing their fellow man better. They want to associate, but don't want to be forced. It would be fine to live without arbitrary barriers between Christian and Jew, if they can blend in gradually and very naturally. What interrupts this blending is the forced situation. When mixing is forced, you only have hard feelings and defiant announcements that 'Our club will never have Jews.' But when the pressure is off, club members having good Jewish friends—who are willing to be accepted as individuals—can win backing."

It is my impression that the most important step to be taken in any community to reduce business and social barriers between Gentile and Jew is to develop a broader base of informal, friendly intermingling. Successful Jews who would like to belong to elite clubs now dominated by exclusionary Gentiles should examine their own socializing habits for self-segregating tendencies. They can't expect to be comfortable in a club with Gentiles if they haven't gotten to know these people first, through informal home entertaining and friendly intermingling in community affairs. And the latter typically don't require invitation. The same applies to Gentiles who would like to see a reduction of barriers.

It was a woman in Northeast City, the socialite Mrs. Carlson, who seemed to offer the best insight on how to reduce barriers. A lovely, gracious young mother, she is a former national officer of the Junior League. When I asked her what the Junior League practice was on barring Jewish women, she said: "Some clubs do, and some don't. I found that the local policy is usually determined by the local pattern of socializing. Jewish members will be found in those towns where the young Jewish and Gentile women travel back and forth a good deal in each other's homes, where they have gone to school together, have many things in common, and actually know each other as friends. This genuine basis of friendship seems to be the most important factor."

In the few cases I encountered where Gentile informants in Northeast City were sponsoring Jewish individuals for membership in their clubs, there was already established a genuine basis of friendship. They had come to have a high regard for each other as a result of working together on community or business projects and had entertained each other's families often in their homes. Personal friendship appears to be a more powerful motive than any abstract sense of justice in getting barriers removed.

And friendship can take root only where there is informal intermingling. Gentile families might well think back over their entertaining of the past year. If they have a number of Jewish acquaintances and did not include any of them in their home entertaining, it is quite probably not an accident. They have probably been accepting, wittingly or unwittingly, their Jewish neighbors as a segregated group.

Jewish families, too, might well scrutinize their home entertaining of the past year. They have perhaps confined themselves entirely to other Jewish families because they did not wish to take the risk of creating embarrassment by inviting someone who is possibly hostile to Jews. Such an apprehension is becoming more and more unrealistic. The barriers that persist today persist more out of habit than hostility. There has been a notable drop in hostility in the past decade. An official of the American Jewish Committee made the point, in a recent chat, that the protective shells Jewish people have acquired in the past are today much thicker than necessary.

He pointed out that in a number of American communities, large and small, Jews and Gentiles have established excellent relations. A half dozen that he cited in particular are these: Wilkes-Barre, Pennsylvania; Cincinnati, Ohio; Portland, Oregon; San Francisco, California; Norfolk, Virginia; St. Paul, Minnesota; Seattle, Washington.

In any community, the prevailing climate of segregation or intermingling is largely the total of what individual families are doing in their socializing.

trends

nine pressures toward a more rigid society

"The workers' 'stairway to the stars' in Jonesville and America is no longer an open highway. Climbing step by step to bigger and better jobs for most workers and their sons is a story of the past."
—W. LLOYD WARNER, University of Chicago.

◆—o—►·◄—o—►·◄—o—►·◄—o—►·◄—o—►·◄—o—►·◄—o—►

AMERICAN IDEOLOGY HAS STRONGLY SUPPORTED THE NOTION that the United States is unique in the world as a place where a poor boy can start at the bottom and become a great captain of industry. Furthermore, according to the prevailing ideology, these opportunities for modern poor boys have been growing.

Both assumptions deserve scrutiny.

Certainly it is true that opportunities for upward mobility for the lower classes are greater in the United States than in most of Latin America, where class lines and class distinctions are still quite firmly drawn. Italy, too, to cite another example, offers relatively much fewer opportunities to the upward striver than the United States.

Highly industrialized Western nations, however, are a different matter. Sociologists, such as Seymour M. Lipset of the University of California, who have made comparisons between the United States and other industrialized nations in regard to mobility, find the situations have recently been quite similar. When the occupations of sons are compared with their fathers' in the various countries, the amount of upward shifting (measured on the arguable basis of shifts from manual to non-manual occupations) is approximately the same in the United States, Western Germany, France, and Sweden. Studies at Harvard have found that the upward mobility in the Soviet Union has recently been about the same as in the United States.

As for the second, more crucial proposition—that the opportunities for the boy of the lower classes are growing—a great body of evidence adds up to the conclusion: not proven. It is true that such a boy who is bright enough and fortunate enough to get a college education has a good chance for upward mobility, although not as good a chance as a boy with the same education from a well-to-do family. However, for the boy who goes to work for a company without the benefit of the college education, the prospects for upward progress are distinctly less promising than those that a boy in the same situation faced a generation ago. And it should be added that the opportunities for the poor boy in America have always been fewer than the history books have implied.

Let us look for a moment at a few of the studies bearing on this question of whether we are moving toward a more open or more rigid society. First, what is the situation with the population as a whole?

Richard Centers found in a nationwide sampling several years ago that sons are more likely to be in the same occupational class as their fathers than in any other class. He found that 71 per cent of them were at a level "relatively similar" to their fathers'.[1] More recently, Sociologist Bernard Barber has asserted that most mobility "in both the past and present has been mobility of relatively small degree."[2]

What about the big fortune builders? Sociologist C. Wright Mills made a study of the 275 richest men in America since the Civil War. He found that, in the 1900 generation, 39 per cent came from lower-class families. By 1950, the "top-rich" coming from such families had shrunk to 9 per cent.[3] My own investigation in 1958 of new multimillionaires who had built fortunes of at least $10,000,000 within the past twenty years without the benefits of inheritance bears out this finding. I found, by crisscrossing the United States, several dozen individuals who met these rather exacting specifications of being modern self-made multimillionaires. Most were bold, old-style entrepreneurs in building, insurance, moneylending, drilling, entertaining, farming, company raiding or rejuvenating, shipping, or innovating new products. They took their profits in capital-gains form. Even by confining my search to relatively "self-made" men, however, I found only one of genuine lower-class origin. That was William Blakley, the mysterious Dallas rancher, driller, insurance man, aviation tycoon, and former senator. His family worked as ranch hands in the early days of Oklahoma.

And what about our more successful salaried business executives? The most imposing study in this field is the examination of the lives of 8,300 executives made by W. Lloyd Warner and James C. Abegglen.[4]

They found that our current big-business leaders were recruited from the families of big-business executives eight times as often as would be expected under random placement. Family for family, they found that a big-business executive's family is forty-five times as likely to produce a future big-business executive as the family of a semi-skilled laborer.

To look at it in another way, two thirds of all our current big-business executives come from business or professional homes. (There are, however, interesting variations by business groups. Among our current stock and bond brokers, the proportion rises to three quarters; and among our railway and transportation executives, it drops to about two fifths. In the latter two groups, nearly a quarter of all executives come from laboring backgrounds.)

When a comparison is made between this generation's executives and those of 1928, there is a slight gain in executives with laboring backgrounds. This gain disappears, however, when you look at just those men who become *heads* of their companies. Here, Warner and Abegglen report, "the proportion of sons of big business and professional men . . .

has increased somewhat." The sons of laborers are found more often at the second-level business positions such as secretary, treasurer, and controller. That is where their slight gain noted in the past generation has been made.

Furthermore, Warner and Abegglen found that, even among the laboring sons who became executives, half were college graduates. They conclude that the Horatio Alger type of hero, the two-fisted laborer rough but brilliant, who works up the line from production through supervision to management, has been "almost entirely superseded" and is so rare as to be unique. The younger the group of executives being studied, the less likely you are to encounter such modern-day up-from-the-bottom successes.

The Warner and Abegglen figures show that there are more boys from the lower classes in executive positions at large corporations than at small corporations. My findings in Northeast City show the same paradox. The explanation, of course, is that top positions in small corporations are more likely to be inherited or attained through nepotism. Big corporations are too big to inherit. Another interesting discovery by Warner and Abegglen is that boys of non-elite origin have a harder time breaking into old, established firms than into new firms in rapidly expanding fields. (Supermarket selling and television production would be two examples.) In new fields, they found that only 44 per cent of the executives were college graduates. (Among executives as a whole, 87 per cent had some college training, 57 per cent actually graduated.) My findings among the new super-multimillionaires (who almost all made their money by pioneering new firms or new fields) are even more striking. Only one in four was a college graduate.

Fortune magazine made a study of nine hundred top-management executives that produced a similar picture of declining opportunity for the sons of workingmen. It found that less than 8 per cent came from workers' families. Nearly two thirds were the sons of businessmen. Furthermore, when the study was confined to present-day executives who were still under fifty years of age, only 2½ per cent came from workers' families. That would indicate a rather startling drop in opportunity has been occurring recently. (Sons of farmers showed a drop, too.)

Why do the sons of businessmen seem to have such a commanding lead? Partly it is being supported at the good schools, where one meets future business associates. Partly it is money and having the inside track. Partly it is having influential family friends. Partly it is knowing, and being able to afford, the accustomed style of life. And partly, of course, they absorb some of their fathers' know-how. But it goes further than the cynical "he who has gets." The business or professional man's son comes from a home where ideas and books—or at least book learning—are usually respected, and where there is an expectation that he will get a higher education and "make something of himself."

Viewing our mobility situation as a whole, several pressures are working for more fluidity, more openness. Working against these, however, are a number of pressures pushing us insistently toward more rigidness in our social structure. In this pushball contest, as I see it, the ball is slowly moving toward the end of the field labeled "rigid society." I shall devote more attention to the forces for rigidity not only because they seem to be more dominant at present, but because they represent a challenge to our traditional ideology.

First, briefly, what are the pressures toward a more open class system? Here are six forces that have been encouraging a large upward current of strivers from the lower ranks of our society. The first three are definitely diminishing in effectiveness.

1. *The opportunities present in the opening up and settling of new communities.* A frontier town was an ideal place for any person of talent, whatever his origins, to prove his worth. Today, we are still building new communities, but they are mostly mass-produced, mass-merchandised ones at the fringes of our cities. Many builders operating on a modest scale ten or fifteen years ago have become multi-million-dollar operators, thanks in large part to the easy availability of United States government credit for home builders. Many of the

nation's most spectacular modern success stories are in the building field.

2. *The differential birth rate.* For years the upper-class families weren't producing enough babies to fill their own ranks. The fecund mothers were in the blue-collar classes. Since World War II, however, the top three classes have been making considerable progress toward reproducing themselves.

3. *The surge of immigrants constantly coming in at the bottom of our society.* For many decades each new contingent helped press upward on the status scale those immigrants who had come a generation earlier. Today, most of the immigration is highly selective: skilled technicians, professionals, etc. The raw, unskilled immigrants coming in at the bottom in the old sense are mostly Puerto Rican—and they, of course, are not immigrants at all, but rather fellow citizens.

4. *The billions of dollars being spent by advertisers to persuade Americans to "upgrade" themselves through consumption.* Advertisers are our most ardent crusaders for more upward striving at the material level. I shall survey in more detail the mixed blessings of their dedication to upwardness in the next chapter.

5. *The growing availability of a college education to all classes.* There has been a great increase in all levels of educational accomplishment. In the thirties, most American adults had not attended high school. Today, 6 out of 10 have either a high-school or college education, and 1 in 14 now over the age of twenty has a college degree.

This factor, however, to some degree is illusory. College boys from well-to-do homes have a big edge in the business corporation over poor boys who had to work their way through school. And, as I've indicated, the well-to-do boy has an edge over the poor boy in the more lucrative professions. In fact, the poor boy is often discouraged from even starting preparation for a medical career. A study of 333 physicians in four cities concludes: "The most conspicuous tendency in these data is that of a declining amount of self-financing in recent decades. This appears to indicate that the 'democratization' of the medical profession in recent times has not been achieved," at least by self-financing. It notes that "a medical degree is becoming increasingly costly in terms of the candidate's time, so that self-financing by students is increasingly discouraged."[5]

6. *Technological progress.* This is perhaps the most massive factor favoring upward mobility. As noted in earlier chapters, this has opened up many new opportunities at the white-collar and technical level. The demand for technicians to manage complex machines and aid the professionals has risen more sensationally than that for any other type of personnel. There has also been a tremendous expansion in the industries that service products, such as TV repair and auto repair.

Some of the gains in the number of white-collar people, it should be added, also are illusory, since a very large proportion of the new white-collar jobs has been for women clerical workers; and there is further a question how much real progress is involved when a man quits a blue-collared factory job to become a white-collared store clerk. At any rate, the growing man-hour productivity in America has produced a rising living standard that has convinced millions of families that they are better off and getting somewhere.

Now let us turn to the pressures toward a more rigid society. I will cite nine such pressures. The first six are on-the-job factors: they affect millions of Americans at their everyday work.

1. *The elimination of steppingstone jobs in office and factory.* Automation is wiping out a broad band of jobs that used to be steppingstones. These jobs call for progressively more skill and talent. The old-fashioned kind of company was organized in such a way that a worker at the bottom could become a skilled worker, then a foreman, and then a manager by gradual steps. Today, most factory jobs lead nowhere.

A most vivid and frightening explanation of just what is happening appeared in a publication issued by *Changing Times,* which is read primarily by businessmen. Its 1958 *Success Book,* edited for people choosing a career, tried to picture the world they would find a decade hence. It predicted: "The people of tomorrow's mechanized factory will fall into two layers. On the lower level will be the semi-skilled workers who run the machines. On the upper level will be the trained and educated engineers, researchers and managers who will design and purchase the machines, and sell the product. Going from one level to the other will mean quite a jump."

To illustrate, it described many of the marvelous automated machines in office work that will send telegrams to warehouses, write invoices, make address plates, enter bookkeeping data, order inventory replacements, send out bills. Then it explained: "Once upon a time a clerk could work his way up to assistant bookkeeper, then to bookkeeper and finally perhaps to treasurer. But, under the new system, the clerk will be most anyone who can push buttons and feed tape. He won't really ever learn anything about bookkeeping. Neither will the repairman that keeps the machines running."

2. *The trend to require specialized pre-job schooling.* In the case just cited, the man who gets to be bookkeeper and then treasurer is the bright graduate of a business school who comes into the company by what is called lateral entry. He doesn't start at the bottom.

Today, the trend is to recruit from the colleges, technical and business schools rather than from the working personnel. At the Mill in Jonesville, Warner found that every person in a managerial job, with one exception, had been brought in, specially trained, from "outside." In short, managers and technicians are drawn from quite a different population, just as are officers in the military services. Today, you don't move up from enlisted to officer ranks either in military or corporate life just by being a good soldier. You go away to school. And the kind of school you go to pretty well fixes the ceiling on your future potentialities. The man who spends two years after high school learning to be an engineering technician has very little chance of ever being considered—by the big corporation—anything but the aide he is, unless he manages later to get further schooling.

One woman, investigating the careers of business executives, reported admiringly, but with notable inaccuracy: "A young man from a comparatively poor family, provided that he is able to make his way through college, can start *at the bottom* in a large corporation and eventually work his way to the top." The italics are mine. By "bottom" she means starting as a second lieutenant, not as a private. Warner and Abegglen spell this out quite bluntly in reporting on the growing use of management-training programs. They have become the primary source of candidates for management positions. In many cases, these programs are closed off to men from the factory and office. The training programs are usually limited to college graduates. And often the acceptable colleges themselves are specified.

The American Management Association made a study of the lives of 325 company presidents. A report on its study advised anyone hoping to become a president first of all to go to college. It suggested Princeton, "if you can make it," but added that in any case you should go somewhere.

Even at the lower laboring level, the requirement of pre-job training is becoming a serious ceiling. To become a skilled worker in the automobile industry, for example, you must graduate from high school, and then go into apprentice training. It is almost impossible for an assembly-line man of several years' experience to become a skilled workman. To qualify for apprentice training, you usually have to be no older than twenty-one. This trend to the pre-schooled specialist is not unique to America.

In the summer of 1958, the Dutch captain of a great transatlantic liner began reminiscing to me about how he went to sea as a boy of fifteen, and over the years worked his way up to his present eminence. I asked him if a boy today could do the same, and work up to becoming a captain. He looked startled, and said:

"Oh, no! You have to go to school if you want to be an officer."

"Then you mean that the crew must always be crew, unless they go away to school?" I asked.

"Yes . . . ," he replied, I thought rather sadly.

3. *The fragmentation of skills.* The efficiency engineers,

with their time and motion studies, have gone wild in breaking down jobs scientifically to their simplest motion components. By such narrowing of jobs, they enable management to hire lower-skilled—and, of course, lower-paid—people, and to spend less money training them. The mechanical engineers have likewise gone wild designing machines that can be operated by a simpleton. In the offices, many white-collar jobs are being depressed as more and more jobs require primarily finger dexterity. A federal manpower commission has observed that some large-office managers look for the unambitious, not-too-bright girls. Girls are often preferred who have perhaps ten years' total schooling, and who will be content to remain fluttering their fingers over their machines until marriage and/or pregnancy takes them away.

The Yankee City investigators found that in that city's shoe factories the introduction of mechanization had smashed the skill hierarchy by which youngsters gradually learned to become journeymen, and then proud and respected master craftsmen. The investigators couldn't find a single job now requiring more than medium skill. The vast majority of jobs could only be classified as low-skilled.

Throughout American offices and factories, the semi-skilled operatives are coming more and more to dominate the scene numerically. In pre-fabricated housing factories, jobs once done by skilled craftsmen are now done by semi-skilled machine operators, who may feed a machine that makes twenty-two simultaneous cuts.

Sociologist Ely Chinoy, who worked at a plant among 6,000 automobile workers, reported that only 1 in 20 was rated as a skilled craftsman. And, in other automobile plants, even the skilled men are angry about what is happening to their skill. Toolmakers have complained that many of the automobile companies keep a skilled man on just one machine, and this, in a sense, makes a second-class mechanic of him. They point out that machinists who work in the independent job shops receive broad experience in handling a number of machines.

One corporate executive who has faced up to the social

implications of this fragmentation of jobs is James C. Worthy, vice-president of Sears, Roebuck & Co. He has been pleading for a reversal of the trend.[6] Over-functionalization, as he terms it, is destroying the meaning of the job for the individual employee, and is boring the employee to the point where the only thing he likes about it is the pay envelope. Worthy reports that studies conducted at Sears show that, where jobs are broken down too finely, low output and low morale result. In contrast, he has found, those jobs requiring sustained effort and the performance of more complete sets of tasks (e.g., salesmen, supervisors, master mechanics) have workers with the highest levels of enthusiasm for their jobs.

4. *The growth in bureaucracy.* We have already commented on the relentless growth to bigness in our institutions. (And I am not speaking of just our industrial corporations.) Such big institutions appear to require a well-recognized hierarchy of authority in order to operate efficiently. Sociologist Peter M. Blau, who has specialized in studying bureaucracies, finds that they have four basic traits in common: impersonality, a system of rules, a hierarchy of authority, and specialization.

All add up to a threat to democracy when the bureaucracies are multiplied across the landscape. The impersonality—imposed by necessity—leaves people in the lower ranks feeling isolated and unattached. The system of rules often breeds contempt or resentment toward the organization. The hierarchy of authority, which, as we have seen, seems to require its visible symbols of status, leaves those of low status and power feeling intensely unequal, and inclined to have little interest, initiative, and loyalty. And specialization tends to set up a tight pattern of stratification.

James Worthy, of Sears, also is among those pointing to the perils of over-specialization of function. Although he feels it can be avoided with forethought, the trend has been toward specializing not only individual jobs but the functions of entire departments. The management engineers bring together vast numbers of employees performing the same specialized function, and make a department of them. Often, he charges, functions are separated out of their context; and an elaborate administrative hierarchy and system of controls is necessary to supervise the units and pull them together. Such elaborate, complex organizations, he finds, require a driver-type leader, whose subordinate managers tend to go by the rule, and have no taste or capacity for self-reliance or initiative in running their departments.

5. *The growing isolation of rank-and-file employees from management.* In older days, when our institutions were smaller, workers often developed warm friendships (or at least intense personal relationships) with their immediate superiors, and often chatted helpfully with the owner-manager. Today, the top management, at most, is likely to show up for the day-before-Christmas handshake. Otherwise, in many offices, shops, and factories, the "higher ups" are never seen. Often they are in other parts of the city, or in other cities. Workers in shipyards, one investigator found, have direct contact with people from the front office so rarely that the occasion is notable. In such rare situations, it was noted, the worker may drop his eyes or remove his hat, but after the front-office officials have passed, the worker is likely to thumb his nose or make other gestures of contempt. (Even off the job, the only contact working-class people have with white-collar types is with their merchants.)

Management, for its part, appears, in many instances, to be developing an attitude of condescending lordliness toward its labor force. In 1958, the *Harvard Business Review* carried a most provocative discussion entitled, "Is Management Creating a Class Society?" Its author, Benjamin Selekman, noted that corporate executives are fond of talking about their concern for human relations, and about the social and moral responsibilities that business statesmen (such as themselves) bear. Then he added: "But their statements and actions, on the basis of economic and political views, sharply contradict the moral philosophy they profess in speeches and articles." Selekman noted that businessmen give labor little or no credit for increasing the nation's productivity, and regard labor as a cost to be reduced as far and rapidly as possible. He concludes: "What should concern us is . . . a division in industry creating an elite which looks down on those who do the daily work."

6. *The role of big unions in freezing men and women to their jobs, and discouraging initiative.* Perhaps what we have here is another form of bureaucratization that is an inevitable response to the growth of big corporations. At any rate, the unions are growing in importance as a fixing factor. Whether intended or not, unions are creating for workers a static social order of their own. They are developing a system of fixed "estates" in life reminiscent of medieval guilds. In return for offering the workers security, recognition, and dignity, the workers surrender freedom to arrange their own affairs except as they can influence a union's decisions. Initiative beyond the call of duty becomes pointless because, at least in the automobile industry, whatever promotions to any slightly better-paying jobs are available are decided on the basis of impersonal seniority rules. Chinoy found, in his automobile-industry study, that before union rules came into force an enterprising worker could find ways, informally, to learn enough as a helper to get himself classified as a skilled worker. That possibility was virtually eliminated when the union began insisting that men work only within their job classification.

Sociologists Seymour M. Lipset and Joan Gordon, in a study of mobility, upward or downward, of trade-union members of the San Francisco Bay area, produced findings that seem to have a bearing on the above. They found that working people who were either upwardly or downwardly mobile were less likely to belong to unions than workers who had not moved from the status of their fathers. And if the mobile workers did belong to unions, they were unlikely to be active members. Their second finding concerned workers who aspired to jobs that represented a change from their present jobs. Non-union workers were much more likely to be optimistic that they could achieve their goal than union members.

The result of all these pressures toward rigidity in the work lives of most people in the three supporting classes in America is a diminishing upward mobility, and a slackening of ambition. And these three classes, it should be added, constitute the great bulk of the United States population.

Look, for a moment, at what is happening to the working class, which consists mostly of solid, conscientious people who would like to believe in the American Dream. While these people's material position has improved, their social position has deteriorated. A hard-working semi-skilled operative learns, after twenty-five years on the job, that the seventeen-year-old kid next to him, who just quit high school to go to work, is making, within a few pennies, the same hourly wage he is. The thousands of men around him, in fact, are all making very close to the same money he is.

And the repetitious arm movement he makes hour after hour is excruciatingly boring. His father, he recalls, was poor, but a craftsman who was proud of the barrels he made. Here the machine has all the brains, all the reasons for pride. Perhaps the rules also forbid him to talk to workers nearby, or to get a drink of water except at the break period.

Even if the plant is a marvel of engineering and the bosses are as nice as they can be, the operative is still bored. A study at a meat-packing plant, celebrated in management circles for its solicitude for the worker, showed that the workers, while grateful for the effort, were just as bored and uninspired as assembly-line automobile workers have been found to be.

This average worker also typically has little aspiration. And it is not because he is lazy. He is just realistic. Chinoy found that only 5 of the 62 automobile workers he interviewed at length had any real hope of ever becoming foremen, and these five were all relatively young. In Jonesville, a leading minister asked this challenging question of a member of the Warner investigating group: "Where in this town can a man start to work, and be able to work himself up to a really good job? There isn't any future for anyone who is working at the Mill . . . they never advance into top positions. . . . It is this kind of thing, I think, which is turning us into a class society."[7]

The foremen, too—who are the top sergeants of industry—are typically without aspiration. They realize they have gone as far as they can. C. Wright Mills reports that only 1 foreman in 5 believes he will ever get above the foreman level. The technicians, engineering aides, etc.—although considered by workers to be an elite—know there is a ceiling of realistic aspiration for them. Joseph A. Kahl points out that the modern corporation is very much like government civil service. In both, he says, a person chooses the basic level within which he will work by the type and extent of his education. After that, progress tends to be routinized and is dictated by what is possible within bureaucratic competition.

There are three main levels, or areas, of competition in the corporation, and the overwhelming majority of the personnel begin and end their careers at the same level. Those levels are:

> The managers and planners.
> The technical aides and functionaries.
> The workers.

To return, briefly, to the problems of the workers at the bottom, they are learning a great deal these days about frustration. Warner and Abegglen, who in general seemed friendly enough to the 8,300 executives they studied, made this point: "Management should remember that many workers are aggressively hostile because they have lost hope for tomorrow."[8]

Many of the workers on assembly lines, various studies have shown, have learned to daydream. In fact, they show more desire to "own my own business"—or otherwise somehow become "independent"—than white-collar people do. They dream of having their own turkey farm or gas stations—or anything that offers escape. Chinoy, in talking with his sixty-two automobile workers at length, found seventeen seriously scheming to make a break. When he checked back four years later, only three of them had successfully moved into another field. One was a policeman; one had his own tool-and-die shop; the third was attending a local college.

I kept thinking of this evidence of frustration and boredom in rank-and-file American industrial workers recently while living temporarily in the Spanish fishing village of San Feliu de Guixols. Each morning I rose at dawn to watch the herring fishermen as they returned from their all-night struggles out on the blacked-out sea. Nine barefoot men manned each of the tiny boats. As they beached their boat, each man seemed to have a responsibility. Invariably they seemed to be in a quietly jovial mood. They joked and laughed as they stretched. One basket of fish was always reserved for the men; and one man would divide the fish into nine equal piles. As the men headed for home, they would gather up their pile of fish in a little sack they carried for that purpose; and in twos and threes they would stride down the village street. Their chests were out and their heads were high. They were pictures of men who felt pride and satisfaction in their way of life.

All of these pressures toward rigidity apparently are having their effects on the aspirations of our young people. Survey after survey shows a sharp trend away from aspirations to be an adventurous entrepreneur or intellectual pioneer or a social nonconformist. William Zabel, while president of the Princeton debating society in 1958, observed, "Anything you do out of the ordinary brings ridicule." The aggressive ambition, long assumed to be peculiarly American, just doesn't show up on any substantial scale in the surveys any more. Scholastic Magazines, in a study of high-school youths, found that 50 per cent more wanted to work for a "large company" than wanted to have their own company. A study made by psychologists at Harvard University and Colby College of attitudes of youths around the world (ten nations) found that Mexicans and Egyptians, for example, showed a great deal more drive and enthusiasm to make themselves and their nations great than Americans. In fact, the main preoccupation of American youths—presumed leaders of tomorrow—was to qualify for a "rich, full life." They typically spelled it out in material terms such as hi-fi sets, outdoor barbecues, and furnishings for their homes. The old saying that "Every boy can grow up to be President" would strike many of the young Americans in the survey as pretty corny.

In addition to the six economic pressures toward rigidity just cited, there are three other principal pressures toward a more rigid society. Since I have already mentioned them in previous chapters, I will just touch on them lightly here.

First is the growing tendency for people to confine their socializing to their own socio-economic layer. As Warner pointed out in connection with Jonesville, the lodge no longer offers the means of meeting the important men of the community on a friendly basis. Among ethnics, A. B. Hollingshead found in New Haven a growing tendency for the compartmentalization of the ethnics to "become more rigid with the passage of time." And E. Digby Baltzell discovered, in his study of the upper class in Philadelphia, that somewhat of a "caste situation" seemed to be developing. Specifically, he pointed out that a comparison of older and younger generations of the upper class revealed that the younger members were much more likely to have the proper religious affiliation (Episcopal), to go to the proper private schools, to belong to the most exclusive clubs, and to live in the most fashionable neighborhoods.

Second is the growing tendency of politicians to treat ethnic and economic groups as blocs, and to base their campaigns on assembling a winning combination of blocs.

And finally we have the rather frightening, headlong trend toward social stratification by residential area. The proliferation of homogeneous developments has accentuated this trend. A developer outside Philadelphia has 1,200 split-level houses. The price of the houses runs between $18,000 and $20,000. He told me he had some executives, attorneys, and doctors, but that most of his buyers were "engineers of the same educational level" from nearby Radio Corporation of America plants. His buyers, he said, have a salary range of $7,500 to $10,000. And he added: "Most have two children."

The "Interurbia Study"—conducted by the J. Walter Thompson advertising agency, Yale social scientists, and *Fortune* magazine—found that the wave of the future is more residential stratification. (The Interurbia studied was the built-up band of humanity stretching from Boston to Washington.) The report of the study predicted that we would see more fragmentation in living conditions. It foresaw a series of communities, each catering to not only a specific income group but to groups of specific ages, tastes, and habits.

All in all, we are in the process of becoming a many-layered society.

Status is crystallizing. The boundaries between the various layers are becoming more rigid.

For those frozen into the lower layers, frustration is a commonly felt emotion. They still have their vote. If the frustration mounts, and we simultaneously go through an economic setback, we may well get a movement for the nationalization of industry. Such nationalization had frequently developed in countries where the dominant groups refused to work to soften rigid class differentiations that existed.

The opportunities for any notable upward mobility for people in our three supporting classes boil down, in the vast majority of cases, to these three:

1. You can marry off an attractive daughter to a higher-status male. That's still being done occasionally.

2. You can try to see that your children get a college education. That doesn't guarantee anything, but does at least qualify them for consideration for semi-upper-type jobs and friends (see Chapter 24).

3. You can create the feeling that you are getting somewhere by stepping up your consumption of material goods. This is made possible, for most people, by the general rise in buying power. We will see what is being done to encourage people to take this route—success, status, and fulfillment through self-indulgence—in the following chapter.

exploiting the "upgrading urge"

"So we see this increasing social unrest, all caused by the false impression of American life cooked up by a bunch of eggheaded art directors. . . . It's a Madison Avenue version of Russian roulette with all barrels loaded, and somebody's gonna get hurt."—CLARE BARNES, JR., Consultant Art Director, in *Art in Advertising.*

←◦→•←◦→•←◦→•←◦→•←◦→•←◦→•←◦→•←◦→

THE ROLE OF ADVERTISING MEN IN THE EMERGING CLASS picture is both curious and portentous. For solid business reasons, they are ardent champions of an open-class society.

Advertisers have approximately eleven billion dollars at their disposal to spend each year on persuasive messages that, they hope, will influence our consuming behavior. In the past few years, they have been busily trying to discover the facts of class and status, and to apply their findings in shaping their sales appeals.

Some of their effort and study is directed toward making sales appeals more realistic in terms of the tastes and habits of the members of the particular socio-economic class they are trying to woo as their most likely customers (i.e., if it is beer you're selling, don't use a drawing-room setting. If it is swimming pools, don't use loud colors). Such realism would seem wholly commendable. If the average American family *must* be

subjected to 1,518 sales messages a day—that's the estimate—
let them be reasonable, realistic messages.

A great many advertisers, however, are not content with
merely being realistic about class. They want to put some
sizzle into their messages by stirring up our status consciousness. In fact, they sometimes playfully call themselves "merchants of discontent." They talk profoundly of the "upgrading
urge" of people, and search for appeals that will tap that urge.

Many of the products they are trying to sell have, in the
past, been confined to a "quality market." The products have
been the luxuries of the upper classes. The game is to make
them the necessities of all classes. This is done by dangling
the products before non-upper-class people as status symbols
of a higher class. By striving to buy the product—say, wall-to-
wall carpeting on installment—the consumer is made to feel
he is upgrading himself socially. Or the limited-success-class
housewife can achieve that feeling by paying a few cents more
each day for the brand of cigarette that is puffed so elegantly
by the genuine Park Avenue matron in the cigarette advertisement.

Much of this exploiting of the "upgrading urge" is aimed
at the workingman. As we have noted in the last chapter, the
modern factory operative has very little opportunity to upgrade himself in his productive role in life. The advertisers,
however, are continuously inviting him to upgrade himself, or
herself, at least in his own mind, by adopting the consuming
patterns of people in the higher classes.

Ely Chinoy, after studying the automobile workers, makes
the point that these people have "anonymous jobs and standardized wage rates." The only visible way left for them to
advance in the world, he says, is by acquiring material possessions. And he adds: "With their wants constantly stimulated
by high-powered advertising, they measure their success by
what they are able to buy." A new car standing in front of
one's home is seen as a symbol of advancement. New living-
room furniture, a washing machine, and television are seen as
further confirmation that one is "getting ahead."

The blue-collar people are adored by the mass merchandisers because, first of all, there are so many of them. And second, they are by nature free spenders and now have more money—and more installment credit—than they are accustomed to handling. In the past their needs have been quite simple, in keeping with low incomes. White-collar workers, in contrast, have less loose money, because of the requirements of their way of life. They are trying to live like the semi-upper-class people, often on working-class incomes.

Selling a higher-class level of living to blue-collar workers, however, is not as easy as it might seem. The snag, of course, is that our way of life simply doesn't offer the workingman a fighting chance to move up to a higher-prestige class. Most of them are resigned to being working folks all their lives, and are not inclined to emulate the upper classes. They know what is what. As the Social Research, Inc., study of Wage Town wives puts it: "They have no burning desire to get above their class." They'll buy television because it is a gadget geared to their taste, but they need prodding and "educating" to desire many of the traditionally higher-class products the mass merchandisers desire to move in such vast numbers, such as the electric rotating spits or gourmet foods. Advertisers are being admonished by the marketing experts that these people need to have their desires steered into new directions. At the least they can be induced to want to upgrade themselves by learning to want more wondrous, more expensive, or more sophisticated products.

Advertisers also are being advised of the exciting possibilities offered by the children of blue-collar families who have managed to take up white-collar roles in life. The Institute for Motivational Research suggests to advertisers that they should "welcome" such people into their new status positions, by seeing that they get well launched with the proper status symbols. It has found, from its researches, that the changes required to take up the new role are far from "painless." There is often considerable uncertainty and self-doubt. The Institute suggests this is the "fertile moment" to develop new brand loyalties by helping the newcomer feel comfortable with his new collar. This can be done, it says, by helping him know the ins and outs of the proper trappings. "The typical 'white-collar' products," it says, "such as fashionable clothing, fashionable home interior products of all kinds, golfing equipment, more sophisticated foods must make this type of person feel that he belongs."

Not only are advertisers ardent champions of upward mobility (or the illusion of it), but they are ardently in favor of more education for everybody, and are in favor of more motherhood. Again, they have some sound, solid reasons for their idealism. A study of consumer expenditures by Alfred Politz Research, Inc., revealed that a household whose bread-winner has had *some* college education spends two thirds more than the family whose head never went beyond grade school. (Higher income presumably is the primary explanation.) The same study revealed the fact—exciting to marketers—that families with children spend $300 to $500 more a year than families without children.

Advertisers also are enthusiastic champions of the Negro's right to consume the good things of American life. Negroes—as they have acquired skills and buying power—have become a $15,000,000,000 market. (The average Negro family reportedly buys twice as much liquor as the average white family.) Also, Negroes are particularly responsive to advertising appeals stressing status because we have forced them to be so preoccupied with status. Their publications take pride in reporting Negro millionaires who ride in Cadillacs; and the publications make the point that "no self-respecting Negro would smoke a cheap cigarette."[1] Another factor that makes Negroes excellent prospects for such products as television is that they are often barred from many places where other Americans enjoy pleasurable pursuits (such as restaurants and country clubs). They must take their pleasures where they can. And they have been repulsed so much that they often seem to need a specific "invitation" from marketers and merchandisers to buy a product, or go to a store, before they feel at ease in doing so.

The prize darlings of the advertisers, however, are the families who move about a great deal. The Interurbia study, already cited, found that people who move frequently undergo a tremendous "upgrading urge." With each move a family makes, it tries to get a better house and more of the "extras." These families often leave rented city apartments with only a modest assortment of worldly goods and become people of property with a hunger for hard goods (such as cars, appliances, etc.). If they move into an area where quite a number of the neighbors have clothes driers, they feel they must have one, too, and quickly.

Other studies of new suburbias have disclosed that the residents are ripe for any goods sold to them as keys to social acceptance. And studies of people who have achieved a toe-hold in the white-collar group reveal that these people like to be told that they now "deserve" the finer, more solid material things in life, and that for them buying the "right" thing has become a "birthright." When people borrow money to achieve all this birthright, they should be assured that by going into debt they are "on their way up."

A home developer in Baltimore who has completed a half-dozen vast tracts is able to sell 20 per cent of his houses at each opening to owners in the older tracts. The average upgrade in price is between $5,000 and $10,000.

Sales strategies for harnessing the "upgrading urge" have probably been most exhaustively studied—and assiduously employed—in the marketing of automobiles. The automobile makers have spent small fortunes exploring the status meaning of their product. They have noticed that people who live in developments tend to leave their long, bright cars parked out on the street in front of the house, instead of putting them in the garage. It was concluded that such people seek, through the car, a status enhancement which they may not be able to get from a home that looks too much like every other house in the block.

The would-be sociologists, writing sales copy for automobile manufacturers, began bearing down on status-enhancement themes more heavily than ever in the late fifties. With 50,000,-000 cars on the road, the challenge was to make car owners by the millions desire to turn in the models they presently owned. The cars became still longer and more expensive-looking. The status meanings of this were brought insistently to the public's attention.

Plymouth quoted a happy family, standing before their long-long car, as disclosing proudly, "We're not wealthy . . . we just look it!" Dodge, in one of its radio commercials, depicted an admiring man exclaiming excitedly to a Dodge owner: "Boy, you must be rich to own a car as big as this!" And, in another commercial, a wife was angry because her husband was making her wade a long distance through six inches of snow to reach the country-club door. He explained that he didn't want to drive up to the door in their "little car," and that they couldn't afford a big car. She retorted that they could, if they bought a new swept-wing Dodge.

Other automobile manufacturers used phrases with double meanings to convey delicately the possibility of enhancing social status through purchase of their car. Ford depicted an actress pointing to the Ford's enormous tail lights, and explained that they "let the people behind you know you are ahead of them!" Edsel, in picturing across two pages of color a family driving up to a $60,000 or $70,000 house, stated: "They'll know you've *arrived* when you drive up in an Edsel." (The italics are Edsel's, not mine.)

The Edsel people, in their image-building before introducing their car, studied the social status of each brand of car on the market, and decided that their car should be seen as the car for the young executive on his way up, a semi-upper trainee. The validity of their approach could not be put immediately to a fair test, because a temporary slump developed in the automobile market just as the car was being introduced.

Writer E. B. White of *The New Yorker* noted that there were still some people in America who see a motorcar primarily as a mode of transportation, but that you would never gather that from a study of sales messages. He wrote: "From reading the auto ads you would think that the primary function of the motorcar in America was to carry its owner first into a higher social stratum, then into an exquisite delirium of high adventure."

That these advertising campaigns, which promised higher status and exquisite delirium, had achieved no little success is seen in the fact that Americans in the late fifties were spending more of their total income on the family chariot than they were in financing the homestead, which housed the family and its car or cars. Home builders, at their 1958 convention, cited this as a deplorable situation demanding correction.

Over the years, the automobile makers succeeded in building up a status hierarchy for automobiles that was well understood by the public. And it was well understood—motivational studies showed—that one could enhance his own status if he was able in his car buying to move up the hierarchical ladder: from Ford, Chevrolet, or Plymouth; up to Pontiac, Dodge, Mercury, Studebaker, etc.; perhaps to Buick, Oldsmobile, Chrysler, etc.; then up to Imperial, Lincoln, or Cadillac.

Cadillac was at the top of the ladder, or to switch metaphors in mid-sentence, the end of the rainbow. At John P. Marquand's "Happy Knoll" country club, a committeeman seeking to recruit a new member boasted that "Happy Knoll" had eight members who owned Cadillacs, while the rival club only had two members with Cadillacs, "the newest three years old."

As American motorcars kept getting longer in the late fifties, several governors and city officials begged the automobile industry to ease traffic problems by shortening the cars. (Some cities were being forced to rip parking meters by the roots from concrete curbings and plant them farther apart so that elongated vehicles could squeeze in.)

New York's Mayor Robert Wagner was one such official appealing for smaller, shorter cars. To set an example, he said that "no new Cadillacs are being ordered" by his city for its high dignitaries. It turned out that forty-nine officials were riding to work in chauffeur-driven Cadillacs. Soon after the mayor's appeal, however, it was disclosed that his own City Controller Lawrence Gerosa had ordered, at city expense, a new $6,392 Cadillac for himself. Gerosa defended the seeming defiance of the mayor by saying: "The top officials of the city, for the dignity of their offices, should have Cadillacs."

(And, he said, it would "embarrass" other top officials if he didn't have one.)

As the Cadillac became the ultimate symbol of success, complications from a prestige standpoint developed. The car was also sought out by those now-prosperous people with deprived origins who had come up the hard way. Some people might find difficulty in buying a fine house in an exclusive area because of the hidden barriers; but they could, if they had the money, or credit, buy the finest in prestige-laden limousines. Pierre Martineau, perhaps the nation's leading authority on the symbolic meaning of automobiles, makes the point that, as Cadillac developed vivid meanings as a success symbol for many newly self-made men, some upper-class people of older wealth—who were already well recognized as successful people —turned to cars that were less emphatically indicators of success. (Others in the marketing field subsequently noted the same point.) In my county, one young wife who is an heiress of one fortune, and who married into another, drives a rather beat-up four-year-old Ford station wagon. She can afford to show conspicuous reserve. So even the Cadillac makers were not without their image problems.

Other blurrings developed in the status meanings of automobiles. The makers of lower-priced lines, under pressure to find new buyers, had introduced longer, fatter, more expensive, more powerful, and more luxuriously designed models that competed directly with their traditional superiors in status such as the Pontiac, Dodge, and Mercury. As *Time* magazine has pointed out, the Chevrolet grew two feet in two decades, to become bigger than the Oldsmobile of ten years earlier and more powerful than the Cadillac of five years earlier. Meanwhile, Buick, not content with being the chic, sleek car for doctors and upward-mobile semi-upper-class people, began competing downward for new recruits. It stressed how low priced some of its models were, and underscored this broadening of its image by sponsoring boxing matches on television.

As a result of all this recruiting, both upward and downward, the status gap between different makes of motorcars shrank, and the Detroit-made motorcars in their various multi-

hued, elongated forms began seeming less significantly different than they used to. Consequently, some of the makes began
losing a little of their effectiveness as status symbols. The way
was open for many of the nation's taste makers to show their
distaste for the trend toward homogenization in Detroit by
becoming enthusiasts of the small—and often expensive—foreign car. In Hollywood, the higher-level status strivers began
trying to buy Dual-Ghia convertibles, after Frank Sinatra and
Eddie Fisher led the way. Price: about $8,000. One big ap-
peal was that only one hundred a year were supposed to be
made.

The typical buyer of foreign cars (even the low-cost, economy ones), it should be noted, was not the workingman but
rather the high-status executives, architects, or television directors. As these taste leaders turned in increasing numbers to
more compact cars—in their search for visibly distinctive status
symbols—the rank and file of automobile buyers, long accustomed to striving for even-bigger cars as symbols of higher
status, were confused as to which way to turn.

The automobile makers of Detroit began hedging in their
bets by casting dies for additional, more compact lines (which
would at least restore readily visual distinctiveness), but they
were still convinced from their surveying that the average
American wants a big, bright car.

The Institute for Motivational Research advised automobile
marketers in late 1958 that opportunity might lie in the direction of more elegance and exclusiveness. It proposed that
they should "consider lifting the ceilings on car prestige." The
Institute pointed to the increased amount of money that many
Americans had been making recently. Perhaps, it suggested,
Detroit should put out some really expensive, super-elegant
cars, "with touches of hand-crafting" that would put a crimp
in anyone's pocketbook. "Today," it pointed out, "there is not
much immediately attainable beyond the range of three fairly
high-priced makes that a really successful person can buy."
Presumably it meant Cadillac, Imperial, and Lincoln, which
are typically in the $5,000 to $10,000 range. Then it noted:
"When this is compared to the upper limits of buying a boat,

the contrast is apparent."[2] A tidy little 43-foot cabin cruiser priced at, say, $49,500 offers more of a challenge, I gather, to the seekers of really distinctive status symbols. Cadillac, eager to firm up its image as the highest-status car in the land, has already plunged into the $14,000-and-up class with its luxurious air-conditioned Eldorado Brougham, complete with perfume bottles, lipsticks, and drinking cups.

Marketers, then, are striving to promote upward mobility —at least at the consuming level—for solid, business reasons. Should this be considered a healthy or unhealthy factor? One hesitates to draw any decisive conclusions; but in either case the conclusions are depressing.

On the positive side, there is the fact that the marketers, by promoting status striving through the purchase of goods, are giving people the sense that they are getting ahead. This, at the lower levels, is largely a consumption gain. But should we deprive people who are stuck in their jobs of even this psychological satisfaction? If we can't give them a fair chance at making their livelihood in a creative way that offers them the opportunities to advance, should we take away from them —to return to the Roman parallel—their circuses?

On the other hand, what do we do to people when we constantly hold up to them success symbols of a higher class and invite them to strive for the symbols? Does this increase class consciousness in a way that could become dangerous in an economic turndown? And, in this constant conversion of luxuries into necessities, are we pushing people to the point where their expectations are so high—and they live so close to the brink of insolvency—that even a mild prolonged belt-tightening would leave them in an ugly mood? Further, by encouraging people constantly to pursue the emblems of success, and by causing them to equate possessions with status, what are we doing to their emotions and their sense of values? Economist Robert Lekachman has observed: "We can only guess at the tensions and anxieties generated."

Finally, aren't the advertisements giving Americans a dangerously distorted picture of how the average American lives?

Clare Barnes, Jr., consultant art director and author of the humorous best-seller, *White Collar Zoo*, has taken his fellow directors in the advertising business to task. In *Art and Advertising* (Summer, 1956), he issued a memorable blast. Advertising, he said, "has done more to cause the social unrest of the Twentieth Century than any other single factor." He granted that advertising has done wonders in raising the standard of living, but said that advertisers, in the way they had gone about creating a demand for their products, had concocted "a false and erroneous impression of the social scene today." At this point he invited his colleagues to skim through a few of their advertisements aimed at the masses to see how they picture the "average family." If the scene is outdoors, he said, "we see a house that cost eighty thousand dollars if it cost a nickel. The backyard, where the two beautiful ladies are talking over the fence about a new detergent, is filled with great old trees, beautifully landscaped gardens that extend back to what looks like a golf course for dad. Around in front of the house are several cars this average family owns, the station wagon, the new Cadillac, and a sports car for the kids. When the ads show the interior of the house it is obvious that another eighty thousand bucks has gone into the furnishings of this average American home. Wall-to-wall carpeting, flawlessly decorated, beautiful antiques or even more expensive contemporary furniture, air conditioning, every imaginable facility in the kitchen to give Mrs. Average more time for her many worthwhile activities."

And then he went on to describe the advertisements to sell toilet soap. These advertisements show a gorgeous model with a Hattie Carnegie gown in a setting of marble and mirrors. He said she plays the part of the "average dame." Barnes observed that the average man (or woman) seeing these glowingly distorted depictions of himself then looks at his own setup. Perhaps he is sitting in his union suit with egg on his face, and a 1932 refrigerator behind him. "He becomes understandably restless, to say the least," says Barnes. (There is no suggestion that the average man has to earn all these things.) Mr. Average Man, Barnes continued, "figures he is underprivileged, ill-housed, ill-clothed, ill-fed. He is ripe for any demagogue who comes along and says that air conditioning for every home is a necessity of life, an inalienable right of every citizen. A vote for this demagogue is a vote for free air conditioning for every citizen, regardless of race, creed or place of national origin. Eventually a law is passed, sure enough, and the Government provides air conditioning for the have-nots at the expense of the haves."

Mr. Barnes expresses apprehension that the whole thing is going to explode, and advertising is going to be blamed.

PART FIVE

implications for the future

should status lines
be maintained?

*"The folks on top probably like it better than those
on the bottom."*—CLIFTON FADIMAN, *The
New Yorker.*

◄—○—►·◄—○—►·◄—○—►·◄—○—►·◄—○—►·◄—○—►·◄—○—►

IN THE COURSE OF THIS BOOK I HAVE PROCEEDED ON THE
assumption that a more open society is preferable to a more
rigidly stratified one. That assumption, perhaps I should point
out, is not unassailable. There is much to be said for a clear-cut
hierarchy of status. Here, briefly, are some of the principal
arguments for a clearly stratified society.

1. *Stratification is necessary in order to get difficult tasks
performed.* A man who undergoes years of arduous training
necessary to become an accountant will be motivated to
undergo that training only if there is a reward at the end. One
reward, of course, is the satisfaction of being an accountant.
But most people require additional rewards—even the Soviets
are discovering—in the form of pay and prestige. On an island
in the lagoon of Venice, virtually all youngsters born there
assume they will go into the glass industry. When they are
twelve years old they are tested. The most gifted ones become
glass blowers and are trained for roles that have the highest
pay and prestige. The rest take over the various jobs of preparing and handling the glass, and have less pay and prestige.

This might be viewed as a natural order for an efficient

society. As the saying goes, carpenters need kings, and kings need carpenters.

2. *Many people tend to accept a status hierarchy—and their place in it—naturally.* One of the textile workers in Paterson, New Jersey, who was interviewed by sociologists seemed to recognize the naturalness of differentiation. He asked: "If there were no rich people, who would the poor people work for?"

As Russell Lynes has observed, "It may be sad to say it, but a great many people seem to want to know where they and other people belong, if only so they can move out of their niche into one they believe is better."

In some societies at least, status is cheerfully assumed. During the summer of 1958, I talked with a Venetian gondolier who obviously was very pleased with his $1,050 gondola. I inquired how one went about becoming a gondolier.

"It is simple," he said. "You are the son of a gondolier." This arrangement seemed wholly satisfactory to him and he said he had never seriously considered any other station in life.

Many people in the lower classes, further, seem to accept automatically as superior the judgment of their superiors. In the armed services, enlisted men who come up for courts-martial have the right to request that other enlisted men be on their trial panel. This privilege is not typically requested. Most enlisted men prefer to leave their fate up to officers.

Three sociologists of the University of Chicago have been conducting a fascinating study of the role of social status in jury deliberations.[1] Using actual jury panels in Chicago and St. Louis, they have arranged for several dozen juries to listen to recordings of two actual trials and then go into deliberation.

The assumption in a jury, of course, is that all members are equal. And all members must concur before a verdict is reached. In practice, the investigators found that higher-status jurors tend to dominate the proceedings. (This may be because they have had experience in taking charge of things and lower-status jurors haven't.) At any rate, a juror who was a proprietor was three and a half times as likely to be chosen by fellow jurors to be foreman as a common laborer. Interestingly, in at least a third of the cases, the first juror to speak up after they sat down was elected foreman.

Before they deliberated, each juror was asked privately what he thought the verdict would be. It turned out that the verdicts favored by proprietors on the jury were, more often than not, the ones finally agreed upon. After the deliberations, jurors were asked privately which jurors had, in their mind, contributed most to the decision. In general, those with higher social status were felt to have carried the most weight. Finally, jurors were asked what kind of people they would like to have on a jury—in terms of four occupational categories—if a member of their own family was on trial. The majority favored professionals and proprietors.

3. *Life is said to be more stable and serene in clearly stratified societies.* This viewpoint was most effectively articulated perhaps by anthropologist Ralph Linton after he had studied many of the world's primitive societies.[2] In this world, he said, you can have one of two kinds of status. You can have a status that you have "achieved" yourself through your efforts and talents; or you can have a status that society automatically "ascribes" to you. When people are going through a change of adjustment to their environment—as during our own frontier days—there is a great demand for the special gifts that can be provided best by people who achieve their status. Class lines crumble. If, however, your society is well adjusted to its environment, then there is little demand for people of unusual talent, and a society of ascribed status—where little attention is paid to seeking talent outside the born elite—is likely to produce more tranquillity. Linton said:

"Americans have been trained to attach such high values to individual initiative and achievement that they tend to look down upon societies which are rigidly organized and to pity the persons who live in them. However, the members of a society whose statuses are mainly prescribed are no less happy than ourselves and considerably more at peace."

For example, he explained: "Where there can be no rivalry in vital matters and no social climbing, snubbing becomes unnecessary and indeed meaningless. . . . Members of different classes can form friendships that are the stronger because their interests can never clash. . . . Membership in a rigidly organized society may deprive the individual of opportunity to exercise his particular gifts, but it gives him an emotional security which is almost unknown among ourselves."

An echo of this thinking appeared in the pages of the London *Observer* when it held a contest a few years ago for the "best defense" and the "best attack" on class distinctions. One reader rising to the defense wrote: "Stratification by class releases the individual from preoccupation with his own personal failures."

4. *A society that encourages status striving produces, in contrast, a good deal of bruising, disappointment, and ugly feelings.* If a society promotes the idea that success is associated with upward mobility, those who can't seem to get anywhere are likely to be afflicted with the feeling that they are personal failures, even though the actual situation may be pretty much beyond their control or capacity to change. Educators and ministers would seem to have a responsibility here to try to ease the damage; and some are doing it. Educational psychologist Lee J. Cronbach has asked his fellow educators this blunt question: "How much should the school urge children to be ambitious and mobile, in a society where most of them will find jobs calling for little skill?" And one of America's leading ministers, the Reverend Dr. Robert J. McCracken of New York's Riverside Church, has in sermons admonished his listeners to be realistic about ambition. It is an admirable quality, he said, but added that we are not all equal in native capacity. "Most of us," he said, "are modestly endowed and we shall not achieve effectiveness or happiness until we recognize it."

The person standing still in a culture that glorifies upward progress often suffers hurts. The greater menace to society, however, is the person moving downward. Any society that has a good deal of upward circulation is bound to have some downward circulation, too. We can't all stay at the high level our elders or we ourselves achieve. The person being declassed is, as previously indicated, almost invariably in an ugly mood.

He is seething with humiliation and apprehension. If society has not developed a mechanism for quickly and gently helping him find a new, more humble niche, then he becomes a bigot, a searcher for scapegoats, and an eager recruit for almost any demagogue who promises to set up a completely new social order.

5. *The culture found in a stratified society, some say, is more satisfying, interesting, and stimulating than that found in a homogenized society.* In such a stratified society you have levels of culture, and you have a long-trained elite dictating what is good and proper for each class. In modern America, where especially at the consuming level the masses have to a large extent become the dictators of taste, we have to endure the horrors of our roadside architecture and billboards; our endless TV gun-slinging; our raw, unkempt, blatantly commercialized cities; our mass merchandising of pornographic magazines; our faceless suburban slums-to-be; our ever-maudlin soap operas. Voices have been crying out for the restoration of some kind of elite that can set standards and make them stick. Ortega y Gasset was one of the first to deplore the revolt of the masses. Harvard's historian Arthur Schlesinger, Jr., has bemoaned what he calls the "conspiracy of blandness" coming over American life. In England, sociologist T. H. Pear has viewed somewhat uneasily the breaking down of class distinctions there. What is it doing, he asks, to the polish of social life, and the long-famed gentle manners of English folk? And he adds the wistful observation that he thinks of rank—as exemplified by royalty—as making England interesting and picturesque.

These, then, are five of the principal arguments that can be offered in favor of stratification. All run counter to the ideals of the prevailing American ideology. A society of ascribed status such as Linton described may offer a Hindu security and happiness in knowing his place, but it is hardly appropriate for mid-twentieth-century America since it shows little interest in the discovery of new talent. We confront in America a historical situation that cries out for a society of achieved status. We are badly maladjusted to our environment and are becoming more maladjusted every month. For example:

—We are in a state of precarious adjustment in our relations with other major societies (notably Russia's).

—We are still desperately trying to adjust to the growth of vast bureaucratic institutions.

—We are still trying to adjust to a way of life that calls for frequent uprooting of our people and moving to new addresses.

—We face the challenge of absorbing 100,000,000 additional persons in our populace within the next twenty to twenty-five years.

—We face the challenge of learning to live with a technological plant more awesome, prodigious, and frightening than anything the world has ever known.

For all these reasons, we need to draw upon all the talent and intelligence we can muster. We need to encourage by every means possible the discovery and advancement of people of unusual potential in our three supporting classes. In a rigidly stratified society, such people are not even considered.

The challenge to us is to recognize the realities of our current class situation. The main reality is our tendency toward greater rigidity in our stratification while pretending that precisely the opposite is occurring. We are consigning tens of millions of our people to fixed roles in life where aspiration is futile, and yet we keep telling them that those who have the stuff will rise to the top. We don't even allow them the satisfaction of feeling secure, dignified, and creative in their low status. And, socially, we look down upon them.

Because of this frustration and isolation imposed upon many members of the supporting classes, we have a frightful shattering of integrity. This shows up in the extraordinarily high psychoses rates we encounter as we approach the bottom of our social scale. And it shows up in the fantastically high delinquency and crime rates among the younger poor of America. In Spain, where class lines are better understood and accepted, you have vastly more poverty but relatively little accompanying juvenile delinquency.

Perhaps it also shows up in something medical investigators have noticed. As you get near the bottom of the social scale, there is an abrupt rise in a disorder called anomie—feeling isolated, loosely attached to the world, and convinced that things are tough all over.

Status distinctions would appear to be inevitable in a society as complicated as our own. The problem is not to try to wipe them out—which would be impossible—but to achieve a reasonably happy society within their framework. If we accept that context, much can be done to promote contentment, mutual respect, and life satisfaction.

There appear to be two principal approaches. One is to promote more understanding between people of the various class groupings in our society. The other is to make class distinctions less burdensome by making certain that people of real talent are discovered and encouraged to fulfill their potential regardless of their station in life. In the two final chapters, we shall explore these two possibilities.

23

problems in understanding

*"People who had become neighbors did not riot
against each other."*—A. M. LEE and N. D.
HUMPHREY, after analyzing the Detroit race
riot of 1943.

◄—○—►·◄—○—►·◄—○—►·◄—○—►·◄—○—►·◄—○—►·◄—○—►

WE HAVE SEEN IN EARLIER CHAPTERS THAT THE AVERAGE
American in his friendly associations is becoming more and
more limited as far as diversity is concerned. Usually he confines himself to people in his particular niche. He doesn't know
much about people on either side of him in the social grid who
seem different because they come from outside his world, and
may be of different ethnic origin. Furthermore, he doesn't
know much about people above or below him on the prestige
scale of social classes. His job, his neighborhood, and his
church—because of stratifying tendencies—have increased this
isolation.

Some would argue that associating only with your own kind
makes for a more pleasant life. Otto Butz quotes a Princeton
senior of upper-class origin—his father is a successful Midwestern businessman—who articulated this view: "Most people, true enough, I wouldn't invite for a drink to my country
club. But this is not a matter of disliking them or feeling
superior to them. We are simply different. Intimate social
contact would be pointless and probably boring on both
sides."[1]

Somehow the lad sounds insufferable. His blinders are on

for life. And he likes it. He is oblivious to the other 99½ per cent of the people of the United States who live outside his arid little niche. He will never know the exhilaration and fascination of having as friends such colorful and often wonderfully articulate folks as clam diggers, house movers, volunteer fire chiefs, antique salesmen, mental-hospital nurses, bill collectors, farmers, marriage brokers, zoo keepers, divorce lawyers, airline hostesses, rare-bird collectors, and house detectives. The proper young man from Princeton is not like the vice-president I know of a half-billion-dollar corporation who includes among his closest friends a ninth-grade schoolteacher and an amiable, talkative motorboat salesman. He finds them more diverting and relaxing than anyone else he has encountered in recent years. And our Princeton lad is not like the gray-haired corporation president in New York State who told me: "If I were a young fellow starting out, I would get to know all sorts of people and learn how they live and how to get them pulling for you. I don't mean just the big people of your own social level. Knock around with the 80 per cent or 90 per cent of our wonderful people whom we erroneously call the masses." He explained that the reason he had made a sideline of dabbling in local politics during most of his adult life was that it helped him keep in touch with reality, and with people's aspirations and needs. Keeping a hand in politics, he felt, was the most important thing he did during his long rise to the presidency of his corporation.

A lively and friendly curiosity about people around us who lead lives that are quite different from our own can add spice and enrichment to our own. Even if there is no particular desire to develop personal friendships, still an understanding of their way of life and their aspirations can make life for us all a great deal easier in our overcrowded nation of strangers that is developing.

We should begin by taking a hard look at our hundreds of one-layer development communities where the houses are all built to sell to a group with specific socio-economic and often ethnic characteristics. This new-style segregation conceived by builders is at the root of much of the growing cleavage between status groups. Not only is our neighborhood socializing at Plywood Estates development confined to people all-too-much like ourselves; but our children, in walking to school, see only homes pretty much like their own. And at the school, they learn to know only children pretty much like themselves. At the churches, stores, hospital, and "community" center, we see more of the same. It is all too tidy, too neatly packaged, too sanitary, and too juiceless.

Adjoining our Plywood Estates, but with a clear-cut dividing line, is another firm's slightly lower-priced development. It may specialize in Albanian-Americans earning $6,000 to $7,750. The appearance of thousands of Albanian-Americans across the boundary makes us search every Albanian's face, bearing, and behavior for telltale evidence that he is somehow different from us. And since these particular Albanians are living in a development well known to be lower-priced than our own, many of us—with only that flimsy basis—develop a picture in our heads of all Albanian-Americans as being distinctly different from us and somehow inferior to us. The appearance of so many Albanian-Americans in one spot magnifies in our mind the differentness of Albanians. If we need a scapegoat, they're it, and tensions rise. We become prejudiced about all Albanians. On the other hand, if an Albanian-American couple lived a few doors from us in an old-fashioned kind of community, we would know them personally as Joe and Ethel Zog, and judge them for their personal worth.

A number of sociological studies have established that genuine acquaintance (rather than simply sight acquaintance) lessens prejudice. This holds true whether the acquaintances are Albanians, Jews, Negroes, or Mohawk Indians. And it holds true with particular force if the people who seemed so different are from a status level in their own group that is equal or superior to our own status.

One comparative study of particular interest (since so many cities are arguing the issue of interracial public housing) was that made of the attitudes of white housewives living in integrated projects (New York City) and housewives living in segregated (all white) projects (Newark, New Jersey).[2] In one of the comparative tests, only 6 per cent of the segregated white wives in Newark indicated they thought of Negroes as being "sociable, friendly, cheerful," whereas 33 per cent of the white New York City wives living as neighbors of Negroes checked those traits. On the negative side, fully a third of the segregated white Newark wives (who rarely had any direct acquaintance with Negroes) thought of them as being "low class, noisy, rowdy, impulsive, primitive, drink a lot." Among the New York white wives who knew Negroes as neighbors, only 9 per cent checked those traits. A majority of the wives in the integrated New York project reported that their attitudes toward Negroes had become more favorable since living in the project. Only a few said their attitudes had become less favorable.

An Army study among soldiers produced a similar finding. It found that the more personal contact white infantrymen had had with Negro soldiers, the less evidence they showed of harboring any prejudice.

S. I. Hayakawa, the authority on attitude formation, makes the very important point that Negroes now bear a heavy responsibility in helping whites accept them naturally. The battle for equal rights, he says, is now moving from the courts to the field of personal relations. He states:

"The Negro, to a degree hitherto impossible, can set the tone of social and business intercourse by the clues he gives in his speech and behavior as to how he expects to be treated." If he acts obsequiously or nervously or self-consciously or over-assertively, the whites will respond accordingly. "If he acts naturally, they will, in 9 cases out of 10, act naturally too and be happy and relieved that meeting a Negro was not the ordeal they thought it was going to be."

Hayakawa went on to explain that "the secret of acting naturally [is to] forget as far as possible that one is Negro." The Negro who is a biochemist or a parent at a P.T.A. meeting should expect to be treated as just another biochemist or parent. "But if you are a biochemist or a parent and expect to be treated as a Negro, people are going to treat you as a

Negro, whatever that means to them." Acting naturally, of course, as he points out, is easier said than done.

It is being discovered that people are more willing to accept (with a minimum of protest) a situation that puts them with a previously excluded group if individuals or institutions they respect lead the way. Significantly, on college campuses, it has been the fraternities with the highest prestige that have led the way to integrating minority-group members. (Perhaps the leadership of the socially secure makes it safe for lower-status fraternities to do the same.) The Laurelhurst Beach Club of Seattle, for more than a decade, had accepted virtually no new Jewish members. For ten months every year, Jewish and non-Jewish children of the neighborhood played together; but during the two summer months every year, the non-Jewish children went to the club and the Jewish children could not follow. Several of the most respected citizens of the community, including a law-school dean and a minister, led the way for an anti-discrimination amendment. Later, at a mass meeting, more than five hundred members voiced unanimous support for the change.

In several situations studied, the in-group had vigorously objected when the proposal to eliminate barriers against minorities (on the job, in dormitories, or in housing projects) was first proposed. But when authorities moved firmly and told them they could like it or get out, they accepted the change as something that was beyond their control, and soon were turning their attention to other matters. This firm approach is particularly likely to be successful (and to be secretly welcomed) if the people in the in-group have been a bit conscience-stricken at finding themselves in an anti-democratic stance.

An interesting experiment in promoting understanding between people who seem on the surface different is the Panel of Americans. At twenty-five American colleges and universities, teams or panels consisting typically of five students go about the countryside talking about themselves and inviting searching, blunt questions. Typically, a panel will consist of students of these five group identifications: Catholic, Puerto Rican,

Jew, Negro, and white Protestant. They go into high schools and junior high schools, into union halls, churches, P.T.A. meetings, etc. Each member tells what it means to be a member of his or her group. The New York University panel, for example, went to Peekskill, New York, where there had been a great deal of hostility between different groups, and appeared before junior-high-school students in the afternoon. That evening, the panel was to appear before the P.T.A. So many pupils insisted their parents attend that the session drew the largest crowd in the organization's history. Weeks later, reports came back to the P.T.A. that the effects of the meeting were being noted even in supermarkets where more neighborly chatting was observed between housewives of different ethnic and racial groups.

Another place where we should begin taking a hard look is at the tight hierarchical stratification of superiors-subordinates in the large company. At what point does bureaucratic growth become seriously anti-democratic? What can be safely done in the big company—where Peter M. Blau reported finding "profound feelings of inequality and apathy" in the lower echelons—to restore more democracy and more understanding? A few experiences perhaps will be instructive:

—At a large insurance company, a study was made of twenty-four clerical sections to find what kind of leadership produced the best results in output.[3] There has long been an assumption, Blau points out, that the lenient, democratic-type leader in a company is less effective than the disciplinarian who rides herd on subordinates. He is presumed to be a victim of the weakness of indulgence in order to prove what a good fellow he (or she) is.

The insurance study produced clear evidence to the contrary. It was found that the section chiefs who closely supervised the work of their clerks and gave detailed instructions were less successful in meeting production goals than the section chiefs who gave their clerks freedom to do the work in the best way they felt it could be done.

—The United States Steel Company stumbled upon an important key to improved employee understanding and efficiency when it sought to find ways to cut financial and man-hour losses due to accidents. In the past, its officials had used the authoritarian approach of posting instructions on the bulletin board. Violators of the instructions were sent home for a day. Still, accidents persisted. There seemed to be a point below which the accident rate could not be cut. The company's leadership decided upon a new "psychological" approach. It began calling in the employees in groups of three or four and asking for their suggestions on how their particular operation could be made safer. These sessions are held in clean conference rooms. Thousands of them have been held. Coffee is served. At a plant near Pittsburgh, I listened as a group of four workmen analyzed step by step their job, in which a team of eight men lift one-thousand-pound rails and take them to a designated spot. It was an exciting experience. These workmen argued about who should give the signal to lift, how they should place their feet, and so on. A gray-haired man named Charlie got up and gave a demonstration of the theories he had developed over the years. For the first time these men were seeing that their job, physical as it is, was important; that their advice was important; and that they could help improve the safety and efficiency of their own operation.

This new approach to safety—called "Operations Attitude" —was first introduced in the Chicago plant that had the highest accident rate of any of the company's main plants: 2.29 accidents per million man-hours. Within two years, that rate had been cut to the sensationally low .66, the best in the company's entire history.

More impressive, the company began getting some pleasantly unexpected dividends. Wherever employees were consulted about their job, morale generally rose, and so did production.

—The experience of West Germany's industry indicates that more and more bureaucratization need not necessarily be the wave of the future for the United States. Until recent years, Germany's industries were notoriously bureaucratized and cartelized. Today, West German industry is swinging back toward greater emphasis on the individual. Team research is being spurned in favor of individual research. Large industries deliberately are decentralizing and giving plant managers more authority and more responsibility for profit and loss. Meanwhile, Germany has been seeing a growth in middle-sized companies. In the chemical field, the great bulk of the companies are now medium sized. Only three are big in the prewar sense. While this democratization has been going on, West Germany has been astonishing the world with its economic progress.

Still another area where large improvements can be made in understanding is between our upper-class professional people and the people of the lower classes they are supposed to serve. (We will discuss educators in the next chapter.) As we have noted, there is often a grievous lack of communication or insight that diminishes the professionals' effectiveness.

Consider the matter of sex. The marriage manuals, written by "authorities" from the upper classes, are enormously preoccupied with elaborate pre-union techniques of foreplay. For couples of lower educational levels, such recommended techniques actually diminish the likelihood that the woman will find satisfaction from the experience. Furthermore, such techniques so earnestly pontificated are viewed by these couples as so much intellectual eroticism and dillydallying. The upper-level doctor who brusquely requests the lower-level patient to strip for a physical examination also is revealing his lack of understanding of the mores of people in the lower classes, who typically are deeply embarrassed by such requests.

The sex laws of the nation, too, are unrealistic in terms of the mores of the great majority of the people. These laws are written by lawyers and lawmakers typically from the upper levels of our society. The Institute for Sex Research estimates that 95 per cent of the total male population could at some time be prosecuted as a sex-law violator of one sort or another.

And psychiatrists, for all their erudition, have a great deal to learn about the public they are supposed to serve, according to the findings of the Yale group of sociologists and psychiatrists (see Chapter 18). These psychiatrists expressed annoyance and revulsion at the behavior of lower classes that they encountered during therapy. They were shocked by the sex mores of the lower classes and they were disgusted at wives from the lower classes who accepted beatings from their husbands as a natural and reasonable part of life.

And there were communication failures that annoyed the psychiatrists. One psychiatrist related: "I had to repeat, repeat, repeat." Another said: "She was a poor, unhappy, miserable woman—we were worlds apart."[4]

A part of the problem is that the people in the two lower classes tend to be dubious that anything worth while can be accomplished by a head doctor. They prefer to think of ailments as having a physical basis. For example, they account for the mental illness of relatives as being due to such things as "bad blood," a "bump on the head," and "too much booze."[5]

August B. Hollingshead and Frederick C. Redlich, speaking for the Yale team, advise psychiatrists to examine their professional biases. They feel much must be done to improve communication between psychiatrist and lower-class patient. And psychiatrists, they conclude, should undertake to school themselves on the social structure within which they operate, and the life values of people of the various classes.

All of us might lead more effective lives, and quite probably more serene ones, if we sought to understand our whole society and not just our particular niche in it.

widening the gates to opportunity

"For the American youth who really wishes to succeed, a college degree has become a basic requirement. Unlike in previous decades, however, the degree is no longer so much a help in competing for a good job as it is a requirement to enter the race."—ARNOLD GREEN, Pennsylvania State University.

←→•←→•←→•←→•←→•←→•←→

WHILE RELAXING AT A COFFEE HOUSE IN BUFFALO NEAR THE campus of a local college (State University of New York) in late 1958, I heard an all-too-typical story of the changing opportunity picture in mid-century America. My informant was a waiter (named Joe) who was a tall, thoughtful, personable, husky, articulate young man with a crew cut. Joe was working to keep himself in college and he explained to me, under questioning, why he was still only a freshman at the age of twenty-two. He had believed in the American Dream, and lost four years as a result.

Joe has six brothers and sisters; and his father is a financially strapped Civil Service clerk. When Joe graduated from a local high school with good grades, he decided it would be too much of a burden on his family to try to go to college. Besides, he had a girl and he wanted a car and spending money. So he went to work for a large manufacturing corporation in the area. He began on the assembly line. Soon convinced that there was no possibility of progress there, he switched to being a crane operator, and later became a stock-room clerk. He worked hard, and everyone seemed satisfied with his work. But he felt he wasn't getting any place. Joe related:

"I had just taken it for granted that I could qualify for better jobs, but I was bumping my head against a very low ceiling. Even in the cafeteria there was a wall between where I could eat and where the office force ate. I was labeled 'plant.'"

Every few months Joe went to the personnel office to ask about getting on the "office" force. The people there at first seemed surprised by his appearance before them. They took out his file card, which showed he had a high-school education, and said they couldn't think of anything he might qualify for at the moment. Later they seemed to treat him as a nuisance. Joe continued:

"It took me a long time to realize just what the situation was. In twenty years I would still be in the stock room or operating a machine. So," said Joe with a sigh, "I'm trying college. It is hard to get the hang of studying after four years, but I'm doing all right." He is studying abnormal psychology. A university professor who knows Joe's background spoke of him in admiring terms.

Not all corporations require a diploma to "enter the race" —to use Arnold Green's phrase—but the trend is strongly in that direction. A number of studies agree that more than three quarters of the higher executives of our larger companies now have had some college education. And one study found that, during the quarter century from 1928 to 1952, there was a 78 per cent rise in the number of top executives who were college graduates.

Joseph A. Kahl quotes an executive who states that, while only half of the executives of his own age group are college men, about 90 per cent of the men "starting out now" are "college." Raymond W. Mack of Northwestern University reports that, out of one hundred promising management men who had been sent by their company to that campus for an eight-week training or broadening course in the liberal arts, only four had never been to college before. And those four were all in the older, over-forty, category.

The large corporations looking for management trainees appear to be more insistent on confining their search to college men than the smaller companies, which often are more old-fashioned and have to scratch harder to find qualified men willing to take a chance on a smaller company. Our aloof Princeton senior quoted by Otto Butz in the previous chapter made a point of this. He said, "I am now confidently looking forward to entering the world of big business." The lad said he had just "had myself interviewed" by more than a dozen different companies. He reports: "I found that as I talked with the representatives of the smaller and more conservative and provincial companies I inevitably detected a feeling on the part of the interviewer of resentment . . . toward me. When, on the other hand, I was being looked over by the really large and dynamic enterprises, the situation was exactly the opposite . . . both of us would immediately feel a sense of easy rapport. The reason for this, as I quickly realized, was of course that the progressive corporations with the truly big potential are the ones which staff their top executive levels with my kind of person."[1]

Each year, more than six hundred large companies send recruiters to college campuses in search of possible management material. What has convinced many large companies that they should confine their management-training programs to college men? There is little question, of course, why this is happening when they are looking for men with skills in law, chemistry, engineering, etc. Many eventually become executive material. But what about the non-professional college men who go into the large companies in such large numbers?

One explanation, of course, is the growing complexity of management and production problems. College-trained experts in business methods are said to be needed. But if that is so, why do so many college-trained executives preside in fields far removed from their course of study? Sociologist Melville Dalton found that 62 per cent of the college-educated executives he studied "were engaged in duties not related to their formal training." He cited examples: "The industrial relations department was headed by officers with degrees in aeronautical and chemical engineering, a divisions superintendent had specialized in medicine, a superintendent had majored in law."[2]

Another explanation offered is that in these complex times corporations need "brains." That, too, has a large element of truth. But what kind of brains? Patricia Salter West reported, after studying 10,000 college graduates, that "academic ability, or whatever ability is measured by college marks, makes very little difference to success in business."[3]

The executive cited a moment ago who said that 90 per cent of the men starting now were "college" offered an explanation that hardly sheds light on the situation. He said that top management had learned over the years that the college man is a "dollars and cents" asset because he is a better risk for "promotion." And then he added: "The mortality is not as high. Providing they have a well-rounded and balanced personality. That's the essential thing, of course. You've got to have a well-balanced man who gets along with people, which is the first essential."[4]

So there you have it.

Certainly, college adds *something* in the way of know-how or viewpoint or social poise that enhances a businessman's chance of progressing in the corporation. At the same time, however, we should not overlook two technical, informal factors that undoubtedly have a great deal to do with the trend toward making the executive suite a college club.

One is the growing use of the blueprint approach to the selection of personnel, with the growth of thousands of vast business institutions. In any bureaucracy, we noted earlier, impersonality is a pervading feature. It is easier for a personnel department to draw up its job specifications and then "go by the book." Its officials impersonally build their organization tables and, for each level, assign minimum qualifications. Typically, the minimums become higher in terms of schooling with each step up the hierarchy. It's neater that way.

The other informal factor is the growing "professionalization" of business executives. The growth of business schools and management-consulting firms has perhaps helped this trend along. At any rate, we are seeing an effort by the executives themselves to protect their in-group by limiting the number of possible challengers and at the same time enhance its prestige by confining it pretty much to a diploma elite.

Patricia Salter West quotes "a big corporation executive" as saying he realizes fully that a college education is no magic way to make "a silk purse out of a sow's ear." But then he adds: "Still, we always pick our junior management from the colleges just on the statistical probabilities; we have a little better chance of getting a good man out of a bunch of college kids. I know it's unfair to a lot of good men who never get considered, but it's worked out to be good economics for us. Too, deciding in advance to pick a college boy gives you a good way to eliminate a lot of candidates right off the bat."

Whatever the reasons, this fascination with the diploma as a badge of eligibility apparently is becoming a permanent feature of life at the well-established corporation. In a good many other areas, this fascination is also becoming a permanent feature. While in Buffalo, I learned that an obscure little college nearby whose name would not be recognized by one American in a hundred now requires any beginning instructors it hires to have a doctor's degree. It has been stated that the late Albert Einstein would have been unable to teach science at a United States high school because he never took any education courses.

In many areas, the kind of education we have largely determines the status we will have throughout our adult life. Although this has its oppressive implications, at least it should be noted that education is a more humane and enlightened measure for stratifying society than ancestry or family wealth. The educational have-nots in our adult world at least have the hope that their children can succeed through education, where they did not. August B. Hollingshead noted that some of the parents in the lower classes of Elmtown had a "blind, almost pathetic faith" that education would enable their children to gain something from life that was denied to them. And Eleanor Roosevelt has observed with her usual eloquence: "What sustains us as a nation . . . [is] the feeling that if you are poor . . . you still see visions of your children having the opportunities that you missed."

If education is to be the main key to a higher-status way of life, then the availability of education to all of high native ability becomes crucial. If the channels of access to higher education become clogged at the lower levels, then we will indeed have a rigid society, and a potentially inflammatory situation.

As sociologist Richard Centers put it after sampling national attitudes: "If non-reward should become more universally the citizen's lot than it is now, we can only expect disillusion and radicalism to become more prevalent."[5]

As I see it, the situation, then, is this. If the American Dream is to have reality—and if we are to have available the talent of our most capable young people for the challenging years ahead—it seems imperative that we clear and broaden the channels of access to higher education for those qualified.

As things stand today—despite the clamor for more scientists—a vast amount of brain power is going to waste. And most of the wastage is in the three supporting classes. Look for a moment at a few of the evidences of wastage.

—The Army found during World War II that 5,000 soldiers who scored in its very highest mental group had never gone beyond eighth grade.

—A study of a large graduating class of a New York City high school revealed that half the youngsters with I.Q.'s of more than 135—or near the genius level—did not go on to college.

—Sociologist Joseph A. Kahl reports that two thirds of the American youngsters who would appear to be good college material—those with I.Q.'s of 117 or higher—never graduate from college.

All estimates appear to agree that the number of bright

high-school seniors who do not go on to college each year runs into the hundreds of thousands.

Furthermore, class position seems to have a good deal to do with the failure to go to college. A study of 1,000 Milwaukee high-school graduates who were all rated as "college material" showed that, while nearly 100 per cent of those from upper-income families had gone on to college, the percentage dropped to around 25 per cent for lower-income families. Similarly, a study at Harvard revealed that, among the boys judged to be the brightest, the expectation of going on to college was far greater among those from homes of executives, doctors, and lawyers. In fact, the expectation at that level was three times as great as it was among sons of semi-skilled workingmen. Sociologist Elbridge Sibley—after studying school records in Pennsylvania—has concluded that a decision to go on to college is influenced far more by the father's occupation than it is by the son's I.Q.

One reason for this unquestionably is the cost of going to college. Higher education, the key to higher status, must be bought with money. And as social psychologist Herbert H. Hyman points out, money is "the very commodity which the lower classes lack."

The cost of going to college has doubled since 1940 and is expected to double again by 1970. America's colleges typically are desperately short of funds. They can't pay faculty members anywhere near the salaries their skills command in private industry. And college enrollments are expected to double in the coming decade. As a result of these pressures, Columbia University's Eli Ginzberg points out, a trend is under way in which "more and more of the costs of a college education are assessed against the student."[6] The social danger here, he agrees, is that "if tuition is raised to cover cost, without a simultaneous increase in the number of scholarships and loans, parental income rather than personal ability will determine who gets an advanced education and who does not."

Currently, the average American student must pay between $1,600 and $1,700 to stay a year in college. The costs vary, of course, according to the type of college. Here, very roughly,

is what I have found one may expect in the way of total cost
per year at five types of college today:

State university	$1,300
Private coeducational school	$1,800
Institute of technology	$2,050
Private men's college	$2,175
Private women's college	$2,425

These prices, of course, include the cost of food and lodg-
ing, and assume the student is going to "go away" to school.
A boy (or girl) is going to eat at least $400 worth of food in
nine months whether he is at home or school. (Costs are
substantially less if he or she lives within commuting distance
of the college to be attended.) The colleges have been developing a number of ingenious schemes for helping students—
and their parents—finance college educations. The ways open,
aside from the parents' bank accounts, include installment
paying, learn-while-you-work plans, loans, scholarships,
summer jobs. It can be demonstrated quite convincingly that
money is no absolute barrier for the bright and enterprising
student. Still, the trend is away from self-help. While most
students today earn some of their college expenses, they earn
a smaller percentage of the total cost than they did in former
years. Patricia Salter West reports that, in the group of several
thousand college graduates she helped study, it was discovered
that the percentage who had earned *most* of their expense
money dropped from 49 per cent to 31 per cent when graduates over fifty years of age were compared with those under
fifty. Apparently, "working my way through college" is becoming more and more a figure of speech.

Another serious handicap of the bright youngster from the
lower classes is his (or her) lack of motivation. He could
often find a way to get to college if he had a burning desire,
but he hasn't learned to aspire to a college education or to
dream in large terms. This factor of low motivation has been,
until recently at least, widely overlooked by educators.

The common lack of motivation encountered at the lower
levels has developed for several reasons. A youngster from

the lower classes, first of all, may be rather sour on the educational process as a result of being snubbed at the dating age by youngsters from the upper classes. Hollingshead quotes the truant officer in Elmtown as saying that he didn't blame the youngsters from the lower classes for becoming disgusted and quitting. He said: "When these kids get into high school, especially the girls, it's mighty hard on them. Some girls have better clothes than others, they have more money. . . . These [the poor] kids get snooted, and you can't blame them for feeling the way they do."[7]

Furthermore, the most tempting goal in life for many in the lower levels, because of the environment of defeatism they live in, is to get by and live it up. Money for the moment becomes the goal. With money they can buy a car and have more fun with the girls and free themselves from dependency on their parents. They haven't been encouraged to think further than that. Quitting school to get a job promises the money they desire.

While Joseph A. Kahl was working with the Harvard Laboratory of Social Relations, he and his colleagues sought to explore this matter of low motivation with youngsters in the Boston area. They chose twenty-four boys for intensive study. Each boy was interviewed at considerable length, and so was his father. All twenty-four of the boys were from the supporting, or "common-man," classes. Their fathers were blue-collar workmen or petty white-collar job holders. The crucial point is this: all the boys were college material with I.Q.'s that put them in the top fifth of the population, yet only half of them planned to go to college; half did not.[8]

The investigators found that, in general, the boys who did not plan to go to college, and their parents, too, had an attitude toward life different from that of the college-oriented boys and their parents. Sons reflected parents, Kahl relates, to a remarkable degree in their values about life. Families that were not college-oriented lived by a philosophy of "getting by." They were resigned to life and felt that college—when they thought about it at all—was beyond their grasp. Families that were college-minded were geared to "getting ahead," and the fathers typically felt they had been frustrated in life by lack of education. Of the twelve boys who had no plans to go to college, eleven came from families where the "getting by" philosophy was dominant. They had been conditioned by their families not to expect much from life. They were bored with school, and felt that running around with their gang of friends was the most important thing they could do. And they tended to look upon the boys taking the college-preparatory course as stupid and sissified, as "fruits" who carried books home at night. On the other hand, the boys who yearned to go to college viewed the non-strivers as being "irresponsible" and not knowing "what was good for them."

Katherine Archibald, in her study of shipyard workers, tells of one keen-minded worker who hadn't shared his father's "get ahead" aspirations. He had quit school at fifteen. "My dad kind of wanted me to finish high school and then go on to college," he recalled sadly, "but when I saw all the other fellows with their girl friends and their cars and lots of money I couldn't wait any longer so I got a job." Typically, such young men can start out making what seems to them like excellent pay. It is almost as much as their semi-skilled fathers are making after working several decades. What they come to realize, after it is too late, is that they will be making the same pay, except for possible across-the-board raises in the "scale," twenty years hence. And then they may have a wife and several children to support.

Those two factors then—the high cost of college and the low motivation toward college caused by an environment of resignation, ostracism, and hedonism—help account for the "wastage" of a very large percentage of our brighter young people. Some of the youngsters, those who feel they have been priced out of the college picture, feel badly frustrated. For the others, the resigned hedonists, the frustration typically comes later.

If the American Dream is to have meaning to the majority of our young people, they must be encouraged to do their best. And they must be convinced that, if they do their best, they will be considered on their merits.

How can they be encouraged to do their best, and be assured that if they do they will be considered? These are questions that deserve the most earnest attention of our business leaders, our government leaders, and our educational leaders. Each of these groups has a heavy responsibility if we are to achieve the goal of a genuine circulation of talent. Consider first the implied responsibility of the nation's business leaders.

Every large business institution would seem to have a responsibility to recruit at least some of its management personnel from its own family of employees. A number of companies are meeting this responsibility and have been recruiting some of their management trainees from the ranks of foremen and clerical workers.

Those corporate executives who feel their upper ranks should consist primarily of college men would seem to have a responsibility to offer college scholarships to talented youngsters in communities where they have plants. And with every scholarship, their company should offer a supplemental grant to the college accepting the youngster. Our hard-pressed colleges typically lose money on every youngster they educate. The loss must be made up by gifts or government grants. A substantial number of companies now offer scholarships, but only a very few offer with them supplemental grants to the colleges.

Finally, if our business enterprises are going to demand that their management men and women have college degrees, they would seem to have a responsibility to help ambitious, capable people already with the company to get that degree. A number of companies now are starting to accept this responsibility and opportunity. Many have been instituting job-training programs—sometimes confined to younger employees—to increase their supply of needed technical skills. And a growing number have been instituting programs to assist the ambitious employee to acquire either a two-year or four-year college degree. General Electric, for example, has an "engineering apprentice" program for promising high-school graduates who pass a qualifying three-and-a-half-hour test. A group of apprentices work together at rotating jobs at a GE plant, and spend nine hours a week, evenings and Saturdays, attending classes taught by university professors. At the end of four years, they have two years of college credit. Those who wish to continue will be given tuition aid for night study. The most promising can even get scholarships and leaves of absence to study full time.[9]

Quite a number of companies now have "tuition aid" programs for night study at local college campuses. Many of these specify, however, that the course of study must be clearly related to the employee's present job. Usually, the course must teach specific technical or professional skills badly needed by the company. A survey by the Commerce and Industry Association of New York revealed that, while 38 per cent of the 455 companies reporting contribute to the cost of their employees' off-the-job education, less than 3 per cent would help foot the bill for schooling in subjects not related to their job. This disqualifies the lad who would like to learn how to be president of the company, or of the United States.

To conclude the thought, the leaders of America's major enterprises seem to have a responsibility—if they persist in confining their management to college-trained men—to make certain that the colleges are available to any ambitious youngster of talent whatever his background. This would mean they must help the private colleges maintain high standards of scholarship while simultaneously maintaining reasonably low charges for promising applicants. And it would mean the companies must set aside far more money for scholarships and tuition payments than most of them have considered doing thus far.

Government leaders, state and national, also need to start thinking in larger terms about education. With the growing depletion of our natural resources, people are becoming our main resource. And here quantity is not enough. Adding another hundred million people to our population is going to create far more problems than it will solve.

Thought might well be given to exempting from taxation

money spent for higher education. The state governments should consider undertaking periodic state-wide testing programs to uncover their potential future leaders, so that the youngsters and their parents can be encouraged to harness the talent. Oklahoma, which has been anxious to attract new industries involving advanced technology, has done this with gratifying results (with tests provided by Science Research Associates). Furthermore, the state and federal governments, if the wasted talent of the supporting classes is to be utilized, must vastly expand their programs of aid to public institutions of higher learning and of individual subsidies or scholarships.

In this they might consider examples set by the nations of northwestern Europe. England, for example, is far ahead of us in spotting its brightest boys and encouraging them to get the best education available regardless of family finances. At the secondary level, sons of tradesmen and trade-union leaders and workingmen go to Eton in very considerable numbers virtually expense free. These bright boys of non-elite families from the state schools are called "guinea pigs" because a long-term experiment has been in progress to see what happens when U and non-U boys are mixed, with their origins kept secret as far as possible. At the college level, most of the students in England today, even at Oxford and Cambridge, have grants. The government grant is based on family income. The less the income, the more the grant. In West Germany and Denmark, similarly, the governments have made it quite easy for youngsters of proven talent to receive scholarships.

In America, government assistance seems especially urgent in aiding students in graduate school seeking to qualify as professionals. It is in the scientific professions requiring long and intensive training, particularly medicine, that the poor youngsters of talent are finding themselves most clearly frozen out.

One of the more hopeful developments, in terms of the government's role, is the growing interest the military services are showing in encouraging men of promise to study toward craft skills, technical proficiency, and college degrees while in the service. This came about because the services found that in their recruiting they could excite young men more with promises of education than they could with the "See The World" promise. At Otis Air Force Base on Cape Cod, in the course of one afternoon, I saw 150 men come into the "education center" of the base to see about furthering their education by taking college and other courses. One sergeant, who was making a career of the Air Force, came into the service with an eighth-grade education. He expected within two years to complete work for a bachelor's degree in business administration. The center has on its shelves the catalogues of virtually every American college. Many offer correspondence courses for servicemen. Whenever fifteen men at the base express interest in taking a subject, a course will be organized with texts and instructors. At the time I was there, courses in college algebra and European history were being offered. The instructors came down from Springfield College. At the same time, many men at the base were taking night and Saturday courses in nearby New Bedford and Falmouth. The Air Force was paying three fourths of the tuition, and provided transportation. Any man in the Air Force who gets within a semester of earning a college degree can apply for temporary leave at full pay while he completes his work for the degree. The only restriction, again, is that it has to be somehow related to his military assignment.

Our nation's educators, particularly at the public-school level, have perhaps the greatest responsibility in developing a greater circulation of talent. They are the arbiters of whether it is ever recognized and ignited in the first place.

Teachers, it would seem, should first of all examine their own subconscious biases. Bevode McCall reports that most teachers are unskilled in the nuances of social-class differences. And Hollingshead found in Elmtown that in both guidance and grading teachers showed a preference for the upper-level students. On the I.Q. tests, 30 per cent of the brightest students were in the working class or Class IV. That was not accurately reflected in the grades given. One reason the lower-level students don't produce up to their capacity, Hollingshead speculates, is that they come from a home environment of frustration, worry, or failure and haven't been trained to respond positively to competitive situations such as tests (as the upper-level youngsters have). They need guidance. Yet they are least likely to get it from the schools. The lower a child's social status, the fewer the chances were that the teacher would take an interest in him or her. This, perhaps, is because those youngsters in the lower classes do not invite help. If teachers had a better understanding of the psychology of the various classes, they would be more likely to identify, inspire, and guide the youngsters of talent in the two lower classes.

The bright youngsters must be recognized early; and sometimes this brightness is not too obvious. A Columbia University educator has pointed out that it is easy enough to identify the "able and ambitious" student but considerably more difficult to locate his potentially able but unambitious classmate. Youngsters at the lower levels have often had ambition frightened out of them. Or they have lived in such a state of mental isolation that, despite innate ability, they have few inner resources upon which to build. Years ago, C. C. North made a perceptive observation about this mental isolation of the low in status. He said that low status operates to "limit the source of information, to retard the development of efficiency in judgment and reasoning abilities, and to confine the attention to the most trivial interests in life."[10] That statement is a measure of the challenge to our nation's educators. A combination of aptitude testing and sympathetic attention to each youngster from the start should go a long way toward promoting the discovery of talent in our lower classes. This discovery and encouragement of talent among those of modest status seems to offer our best opportunity for keeping our social arteries open and forestalling the further development of sclerosis.

This book began as an exploration of the class behavior in the United States in this era of unparalleled material abundance. One of the most insistent themes that developed was that status seekers are altering our society by their preoccupation, in the midst of plenty, with acquiring evidences of status. The people of this country have become increasingly preoccupied with status primarily because of the impact on their lives of big housing developments, big advertisers, big trade-unions, and big corporate hierarchies. As a result, democracy is still more of an ideal than a reality.

The forces of the times seem to be conspiring to squeeze individuality and spontaneity from us. We compete for the same symbols of bigness and success. We are careful to conform to the kinds of behavior approved by our peers. We are wary of others who don't look like our kind of people. We tend to judge people by their labels. And all too often we judge people on the basis of the status symbols they display.

All this is hardly a credit to us as a people. We profess to be guided in our attitudes by the body of ideals set forth by our Founding Fathers. The Founding Fathers would wish us to be individualists, free thinkers, independents in mind and spirit. They would admire, I believe, a delightful elderly Negro woman I know who is widely beloved despite her strong preferences and dislikes in people. She runs a private enterprise that possibly nets her $2,000 a year and is, despite more-than-ordinary adversity, a supremely serene woman. A few weeks ago, she and I were discussing a family we both know. The family is probably worth $250,000. It has two fashionable homes, three cars, and full-time help. This elderly lady, however, has no use for them. She dismissed them scornfully as "common." She had judged them strictly on their personal qualities. And in her view they were found wanting. She found them shallow, crude, pleasure-minded people and felt they had botched the job of giving their children decent standards to live by.

I think we should all be happier, and live more stimulating lives, if, like her, we judged people not by the symbols they display and the labels they wear but rather by their individual worth.

And while becoming practicing individualists we should work to make opportunity a reality in our land of the free. Our people should be able to believe in this reality from personal and observable experience rather than by reading about it on billboards.

In this time of transcendent challenge and danger to our way of life, it seems clear that we can endure and prevail only if the vast majority of our people really believe in our system. They must be genuinely convinced that our system offers fairer rewards and opportunities for the fulfillment of human aspiration than any other.

reference notes

CHAPTER 1

1. August B. Hollingshead and Frederick C. Redlich, *Social Class and Mental Illness* (New York: John Wiley & Sons, Inc., 1958), p. 162.
2. Louis Kronenberger, *Company Manners* (New York: The Bobbs-Merrill Co., Inc., 1951), p. 189.

CHAPTER 2

1. William Foote Whyte, *Street Corner Society* (Chicago: The University of Chicago Press, 1943), pp. 261–63.
2. Alex Inkeles, "Social Stratification and Mobility in the Soviet Union 1940–50," *American Sociological Review*, Vol. 15 (August 1950), pp. 465–79.
3. Eva Rosenfeld, "Social Stratification in a 'Classless' Society," *American Sociological Review*, Vol. 16, No. 6 (December 1951).
4. "How to Make a Fortune—New Style," *Ladies' Home Journal*, January 1959.
5. Peter M. Blau, *Bureaucracy in Modern Society* (New York: Random House, 1956), p. 2.
6. C. Wright Mills, *White Collar* (New York: Oxford University Press, 1956), p. 63.
7. Mabel Newcomer, *The Big Business Executive* (New York: Columbia University Press, 1955), p. 61.

CHAPTER 3

1. T. H. Marshall, "Social Class, a Preliminary Analysis," *The Sociological Review*, Vol. 26 (1934), pp. 55–76.

2. Richard Centers, *The Psychology of Social Classes* (Princeton, New Jersey: Princeton University Press, 1949), p. 74.

3. August B. Hollingshead, *Elmtown's Youth* (New York: John Wiley & Sons, Inc., 1949), pp. 11–48.

4. Joseph A. Kahl, *The American Class Structure* (New York: Rinehart & Company, Inc.), p. 186.

5. Arnold Green, *Sociology* (New York: McGraw-Hill Book Co., 1956), p. 276.

6. C. Wright Mills, *op. cit.,* p. 204.

7. August B. Hollingshead, *op. cit.,* p. 70.

8. Joseph A. Kahl, *op. cit.,* p. 193.

9. *Ibid.,* p. 203.

CHAPTER 4

1. Max Shulman, *Rally Round the Flag, Boys!* (New York: Doubleday & Company, Inc., 1957), p. 3.

2. Milton M. Gordon, "A System of Social Class Analysis," *The Drew University Bulletin* (Madison, New Jersey), August 1951.

3. August B. Hollingshead, "Trends in Social Stratification: A Case Study," *American Sociological Review,* Vol. 17, No. 6 (December 1952).

4. Gregory P. Stone and William H. Form, "Instabilities in Status: The Problem of Hierarchy in the Community Study of Status Arrangements," *American Sociological Review,* Vol. 18, No. 2 (April 1953).

5. Cleveland Amory, *The Proper Bostonians* (New York: E. P. Dutton & Co., Inc., 1947), p. 14.

6. Kimball Young and Raymond W. Mack, *Sociology and Social Life* (New York: American Book Company, 1959), p. 194.

7. E. Franklin Frazier, *Black Bourgeoisie* (Glencoe, Illinois: The Free Press, 1957), p. 235.

8. Christopher Rand, series on Puerto Ricans in New York, "Reporter at Large," *The New Yorker,* Nov. 16, Nov. 30, Dec. 7, Dec. 14, and Dec. 21, 1957.

CHAPTER 6

1. *The New Consumer, Chicago Tribune* Research Division, *Chicago Tribune,* Chicago.

2. Ralph Bodek, *How and Why People Buy Homes* (Philadelphia: Municipal Publications, Inc., 1957).

3. David L. and Mary A. Hatch, "Criteria of Social Status as Derived from Marriage Announcements in *The New York Times,*" *American Sociological Review,* Vol. 12 (August 1947), pp. 396–403.

4. *The New York Times*, March 4, 1957 (Part of a series on "Society" of modern American cities).

5. *Where Shall We Live, A Report of the Commission on Race & Housing* (Berkeley, California: University of California Press, 1958).

6. *Wall Street Journal*, April 7, 1958, p. 1.

7. *Time*, February 24, 1958, p. 19.

8. David Boroff, *The New York Post*, April 20, 1958.

CHAPTER 7

1. Raymond W. Mack, "The Prestige System of an Air Force Base: Squadron Ranking and Morale," *American Sociological Review*, Vol. 19, No. 3 (June 1954).

2. "How Does Your Income Compare With Others?" *Collier's*, November 23, 1956.

3. Richard Carter, *The Doctor Business* (New York: Doubleday & Company, Inc., 1958), p. 85.

4. C. Wright Mills, *op. cit.*, p. 119.

5. Seymour E. Harris, "Who Gets Paid What," *Atlantic Monthly*, May 1958, pp. 35–38.

6. C. Wright Mills, "The Middle Classes in Middle-Sized Cities," from *Class, Status and Power*, edited by Reinhard Bendix and Seymour Martin Lipset (Glencoe, Illinois: The Free Press, 1953), p. 206.

7. Delbert C. Miller, "Industry and Community Power Structure," *American Sociological Review*, Vol. 23, No. 1 (February 1958), pp. 9–15.

8. John Gunther, *Inside Russia* (New York: Harper & Brothers, 1957).

9. Bevode C. McCall, Research Memorandum, Report #3 on the *Chicago Tribune Sample Census*, February 15, 1956.

CHAPTER 8

1. *Time*, "Executive Trappings," January 24, 1955, p. 80.

2. *Wall Street Journal*, "Status Symbols," October 29, 1957, p. 1.

3. *New York World-Telegram and Sun*, February 25, 1957, David Knickerbocker.

4. Melville Dalton, "Conflicts Between Staff and Line Managerial Officers," *American Sociological Review*, Vol. 15, No. 3 (June 1950).

5. *Ladies' Home Journal*, February 1958.

6. *Wall Street Journal*, November 13, 1957.

7. William Attwood, "The Position of the Jews in America Today," *Look*, November 29, 1955.

8. C. Wright Mills, *White Collar*, p. xvii.

9. A. H. Raskin, "The Moral Issue that Confronts Labor," *The New York Times Magazine*, March 31, 1957.

10. "Occupations of Federal White Collar Workers," June 1955, United States Civil Service Commission, Washington, D.C.

CHAPTER 9

1. *The New Consumer*, p. 25. (See also "Class Is Open for Discussion" by Pierre Martineau in *Motivation in Advertising* [New York: McGraw-Hill Book Co., 1957], pp. 163–72.)

2. Pierre Martineau, "The Store Personality," *Harvard Business Review*, January–February 1958.

3. *Ibid.*

4. Bernard Barber and Lyle S. Lobel, "Fashion in Women's Clothes and the American Social System," *Social Forces*, December 1952.

5. William Foote Whyte, *op. cit.*, pp. 106, 258.

CHAPTER 10

1. Thomas Griffith, *The Waist-High Culture* (New York: Harper & Brothers, 1959).

2. E. Digby Baltzell, *Philadelphia Gentlemen* (Glencoe, Illinois: The Free Press, 1958), pp. 50–55.

3. Katherine Archibald, "Status Orientations Among Shipyard Workers," from *Class, Status and Power*, p. 396.

4. Leonard Schatzman and Anselm Strauss, "Social Class and Modes of Communication," *American Journal of Sociology*, January 1955.

5. David Gottlieb, "The Neighborhood Tavern and the Cocktail Lounge," *American Journal of Sociology*, May 1957.

6. *The New York Times*, February 8, 1958.

7. Saxon Graham, "Class and Conservatism in the Adoption of Innovations," *Human Relations*, Vol. 9, No. 1 (1956), pp. 91–99.

CHAPTER 11

1. August B. Hollingshead, *Elmtown's Youth*, p. 239.

2. William Foote Whyte, "A Slum Sex Code," *American Journal of Sociology*, Vol. 49 (July 1943), p. 24.

3. A. C. Kinsey, W. B. Pomeroy, and C. E. Martin, *Sexual Behavior in the Human Male* (Philadelphia: W. B. Saunders Co.,

1948); same authors plus Paul H. Gebhard, *Sexual Behavior in the Human Female* (Philadelphia: W. B. Saunders Co., 1953); and report in *McCall's,* March 1958, on the findings of the Institute for Sex Research on pregnancy and abortions.

4. Robert F. Winch, *Mate Selection: A Study of Complementary Needs* (New York: Harper & Brothers, 1958).

5. Macfadden Publications research report, *The Invisible Wall* (New York: 1957).

6. Julius Roth and Robert F. Peck, "Social Class and Social Mobility Factors Related to Marital Adjustment," *American Sociological Review,* Vol. 16, No. 4 (August 1951).

7. Richard Centers, "Marital Selection and Occupational Strata," *American Journal of Sociology,* Vol. 54 (1949).

8. W. Lloyd Warner, *Democracy in Jonesville* (New York: Harper & Brothers, 1949), p. 75.

9. August B. Hollingshead, "Trends in Social Stratification."

10. R. J. R. Kennedy, "Single or Triple Melting Pot? Intermarriage Trends in New Haven, 1870–1940," *American Journal of Sociology,* Vol. 49 (1944), pp. 331–39.

CHAPTER 12

1. Bevode C. McCall, "Social Class Structure in a Small Southern Town" (doctoral dissertation, University of Chicago Library).

2. *Time,* January 13, 1958, p. 12.

3. Allison Davis, Burleigh B. and Mary R. Gardner, *Deep South* (Chicago: University of Chicago Press, 1941).

CHAPTER 13

1. Dixon Wecter, *The Saga of American Society* (New York: Charles Scribner's Sons, 1937).

2. E. Digby Baltzell, *op. cit.,* p. 337.

3. Max Lerner, *America as a Civilization* (New York: Simon and Schuster, Inc., 1957), p. 636.

4. W. Lloyd Warner, *op. cit.,* p. 138.

5. *Ibid.,* p. 119.

CHAPTER 14

1. August B. Hollingshead, *Elmtown's Youth,* p. 246.

2. David L. and Mary A. Hatch, *op. cit.*

3. Mabel Newcomer, *op. cit.,* pp. 47–48.

4. W. Lloyd Warner and Paul S. Lunt, *The Social Life of a*

Modern Community (New Haven: Yale University Press, 1941), p. 358.

5. *Information Service*, 27, Part II, May 15, 1948, Federal Council of Churches.

6. Liston Pope, "Religion and the Class Structure," *The Annals of the American Academy of Political and Social Science*, March 1948.

CHAPTER 15

1. Paul Lazarsfeld, "The People's Choice," from *American Social Patterns*, edited by William Peterson (New York: Doubleday & Company, Inc., 1956), p. 129.

2. Richard Centers, *The Psychology of Social Classes*, p. 66.

3. Paul Lazarsfeld, *op. cit.*, p. 123.

4. Samuel Lubell, *The Future of American Politics* (New York: Doubleday & Company, Inc., 1956).

5. Leo Egan, "Can Rockfeller Save the GOP in New York," *The Reporter*, October 30, 1958.

6. William H. Whyte, Jr., *The Organization Man* (New York: Simon and Schuster, Inc., 1956), p. 300.

7. Gerhard E. Lenski, "Social Participation and Status Crystallization," *American Sociological Review*, Vol. 21, No. 4 (August 1956).

CHAPTER 16

1. M. Macdonald, C. McGuire, and R. J. Havighurst, "Leisure Activities and the Socio-Economic Status of Children," *American Journal of Sociology*, Vol. 54 (1949), p. 505.

2. James West, "Learning the Class System in Plainville, U.S.A.," from *Readings in Social Psychology*, edited by Theodore M. Newcomb and Eugene L. Hartley (New York: Henry Holt and Co., Inc., 1947), pp. 475–77.

3. Arnold W. Green, "The Middle Class Male Child and Neurosis," *American Sociological Review*, February 1946.

4. Lee J. Cronbach, *Educational Psychology* (New York: Harcourt, Brace & Co., 1954). See section on class differences.

5. August B. Hollingshead, *Elmtown's Youth*, p. 148.

6. W. Lloyd Warner and Paul S. Lunt, *The Social Life of a Modern Community*, p. 363.

7. Mary Jean Schulman and Robert J. Havighurst, "Relations Between Ability and Social Status in a Midwestern Community,

IV, Size of Vocabulary," *Journal of Educational Psychology*, Vol. 38 (1947), p. 437.

8. E. Digby Baltzell, *op. cit.*, p. 293.

9. John R. Seeley, R. Alexander Sim, and Elizabeth W. Loosley, *Crestwood Heights* (New York: Basic Books, Inc., 1956), p. 307.

10. E. Digby Baltzell, *op. cit.*, p. 306.

11. *Ibid.*, p. 319.

12. Ernest Havemann and Patricia Salter West, *They Went to College* (New York: Harcourt, Brace & Co., 1952), especially Chapter 15.

13. Herbert Kubly, *An American in Italy* (New York: Simon and Schuster, Inc., 1955), p. 2.

14. C. Wright Mills, *White Collar*, p. 120.

15. C. Wright Mills, *The Power Elite* (New York: Oxford University Press, 1956), p. 67.

16. Alfred McClung Lee, *Fraternities Without Brotherhood* (Boston: Beacon Press, 1955), p. 15.

CHAPTER 18

1. R. Prawer Jhabvala, "The Interview," a short story, *The New Yorker*, July 27, 1957, pp. 25–29.

2. William H. Whyte, Jr., *op. cit.*, p. 307.

3. S. Kirson Weinberg and Henry Arond, "The Occupational Culture of the Boxer," *American Journal of Sociology*, Vol. 57 (March 1952), pp. 460–69.

4. W. Lloyd Warner and James C. Abegglen, *Big Business Leaders in America* (New York: Harper & Brothers, 1955), p. 193.

5. William Foote Whyte, *op. cit.*, p. 107.

6. Louis Kronenberger, *op. cit.*, p. 175.

7. Joseph Greenblum and Leonard I. Pearlin, "Vertical Mobility and Prejudice: A Socio-Psychological Analysis," from *Class Status and Power*, pp. 480–90.

8. August B. Hollingshead and Frederick C. Redlich, *Social Class and Mental Illness.*

9. August B. Hollingshead and Frederick C. Redlich, "Social Stratification and Psychiatric Disorders," *American Sociological Review*, Vol. 18, No. 2 (April 1953).

10. Joseph A. Kahl, *The American Class Structure*, p. 192.

11. Jerome K. Myers and Leslie Schaffer, "Social Stratification and Psychiatric Practice: A Study of an Out-Patient Clinic," *American Sociological Review*, Vol. 19, No. 3 (June 1954).

12. August B. Hollingshead and Frederick C. Redlich, *Social Class and Mental Illness*, p. 351.

CHAPTER 19

1. John P. Dean, "Patterns of Socialization and Association Between Jews and Non-Jews," *Jewish Social Studies*, Vol. VII, No. 3 (1955).
2. A. Harris and G. Watson, "Are Jewish or Gentile Children More Clannish?" *Journal of Social Psychology*, Vol. 24 (1946), pp. 71–76.
3. T. W. Adorno *et al.*, *The Authoritarian Personality* (New York: Harper & Brothers, 1950), pp. 66–75.
4. Max Lerner, *op. cit.*, p. 510.
5. John Slawson, "Social Discrimination," American Jewish Committee, New York City.
6. Gordon W. Allport, *The Nature of Prejudice* (Cambridge, Massachusetts: Addison-Wesley Publishing Co., Inc., 1954), pp. 250–51.
7. Dorothy T. Spoerl, "The Jewish Stereotype," *Yivo Annual of Jewish Social Science*, Vol. 7 (1952), p. 268.

CHAPTER 20

1. Richard Centers, "Occupational Mobility of Urban Occupational Strata," *American Sociological Review*, Vol. 13 (April 1948), pp. 197–203.
2. Bernard Barber, *Social Stratification* (New York: Harcourt, Brace & Co., 1957), p. 431.
3. C. Wright Mills, *The Power Elite*, p. 105.
4. W. Lloyd Warner and James C. Abegglen, *Big Business Leaders of America*.
5. Stuart Adams, "Trends in Occupational Origin of Physicians," *American Sociological Review*, August 1953.
6. James C. Worthy, "Organizational Structure and Employee Morale," *American Sociological Review*, Vol. 15, No. 2 (April 1950).
7. W. Lloyd Warner, *Democracy in Jonesville*. See section on "Mobility in the Factory for Managers and Workers."
8. W. Lloyd Warner and James C. Abegglen, *op. cit.*, p. 230.

CHAPTER 21

1. Max Lerner, *op. cit.*, p. 524.
2. *Printers' Ink*, November 21, 1958, p. 65.

CHAPTER 22

1. Fred L. Stodtbeck, Rita M. James, and Charles Hawkins, "Social Status in Jury Deliberations," *American Sociological Review*, Vol. 22, No. 6 (December 1957).

2. Ralph Linton, *The Study of Man* (New York: D. Appleton-Century Co., 1936). Especially Chapter 8, "Status and Role."

CHAPTER 23

1. Otto Butz, *The Unsilent Generation* (New York: Rinehart & Company, 1958).

2. Morton Deutsch and Mary Evans Collins, "Interracial Housing," from *American Social Patterns*, pp. 7–42.

3. Peter M. Blau, *op. cit.*, p. 70.

4. August B. Hollingshead and Frederick C. Redlich, *Social Class and Mental Illness*, p. 344.

5. *Ibid.*, p. 341.

CHAPTER 24

1. Otto Butz, *op. cit.*, quoting Princeton senior No. 2.

2. Melville Dalton, "Informal Factors in Career Achievement," *American Journal of Sociology*, Vol. 56 (March 1951), pp. 407–15.

3. Patricia Salter West, "Social Mobility Among College Graduates," from *Class Status and Power*, p. 474.

4. Joseph A. Kahl, *op. cit.*, p. 276.

5. Richard Centers, *Psychology of Social Classes*, p. 148.

6. Eli Ginzberg, *Human Resources: The Wealth of a Nation* (New York: Simon and Schuster, Inc., 1958), p. 144.

7. August B. Hollingshead, *Elmtown's Youth*, p. 346.

8. Joseph A. Kahl, *op. cit.*, p. 286.

9. *Popular Science*, September 1957, p. 115.

10. C. C. North, *Social Differentiation* (Chapel Hill, North Carolina: University of North Carolina Press, 1927), p. 247.

Index

index

ENJOY ENJOY!
"HARRY GOLDEN'S BEST BOOK"—N.Y. TIMES

M-5035 50c

Other novels by Harry Golden:
M—5011 "Only in America" 50¢
M—5021 "For 2¢ Plain" 50¢

If your bookseller does not have these titles, you may order them by sending retail price, plus 5¢ for postage and handling to: MAIL SERVICE DEPT., Pocket Books, Inc., 1 West 39th St., N. Y. 18. Enclose check or money order—Do not send cash.

PUBLISHED BY POCKET BOOKS, INC.

NOW YOU CAN HELP CHILDREN READ

with growing pleasure and greater understanding

A wonderful book has just been published which shows you how. It is called:

A PARENT'S GUIDE TO CHILDREN'S READING

The author is Nancy Larrick, past president of the International Reading Association. In writing the book she had the help of consultants from 18 civic, educational and youth organizations. The project is sponsored by the National Book Committee, Inc., a nonprofit group devoted to fostering the wiser and wider use of books. Pocket Books, Inc., is publishing the book in a paper-bound edition on a nonprofit basis as a public service.

A PARENT'S GUIDE TO CHILDREN'S READING is an authoritative, illustrated handbook. It contains annotated lists of available and recommended titles, classified by age groups, from thirteen years down. It tells "why" and "how" and "what." It will be of both immediate and continuing help to every teacher, librarian, camp counselor, P.T.A. member, etc.—but especially helpful to every parent.

Now you can get this friendly, informative guide for only 35¢ wherever books are sold. If you want lots of 25 or more, the publisher will give a discount of 20%. If your bookseller does not have it, you may order from this coupon: